Table of Contents

Introduction

Youth gang membership is a serious and persistent problem in the United States. One in three local law enforcement agencies report youth gang problems in their jurisdictions.[1] One in four high school freshmen report gangs in their schools.[2] Limited resources at the national, state, tribal and local levels make it more important than ever that we make full use of the best available evidence and clearly demonstrate the benefit of strategies to prevent gang-joining.

In acknowledgment of these realities, the Centers for Disease Control and Prevention (CDC) and the National Institute of Justice (NIJ) formed a partnership to publish this book. It is critical that those who make decisions about resources — as well as those who work directly with youth, like teachers and police officers, community services providers and emergency department physicians — understand what the research evidence shows about how to prevent kids from joining gangs.

The NIJ-CDC partnership drew on each agency's distinctive strengths: NIJ's commitment to enhancing justice and increasing public safety is matched by CDC's dedication to health promotion and prevention of violence, injury and disability. By combining perspectives, lessons and evidence from public safety *and* public health, NIJ and CDC provide new insights into the complex problems of gangs and gang membership.

Public health and public safety workers who respond to gang problems know that after-the-fact efforts are not enough. An emergency department doctor who treats gang-related gunshot wounds or a police officer who must tell a mother that her son has been killed in a drive-by shooting are likely to stress the need for prevention — and the complementary roles that public health and law enforcement must play — in stopping violence before it starts.

Given our shared commitment to informing policy and practice with the best available evidence of what works, CDC and NIJ brought together some of the nation's top public health and criminal justice researchers to present core principles for gang-membership prevention.

Why Are Principles So Important?

It would seem to go without saying that we should try to prevent kids from joining gangs. But why publish an entire book on principles rather than just a straightforward recipe for preventing gang-joining?

There are at least four reasons to focus on principles of prevention:

1. Much of what we know about preventing gang membership is drawn from research in other prevention fields, such as juvenile delinquency and violence prevention.

2. Joining a gang is a complex process that involves both individual volition and social influences; therefore, it is difficult to imagine that a single "recipe" for preventing gang membership would be effective for all at-risk youth across the array of social contexts.

3. Our focus on prevention principles better equips us to confront the specific public health and public safety issues linked to gang membership: interpersonal violence, truancy and school dropout, alcohol and substance abuse, and a host of related crime and health challenges.

4. By emphasizing principles, we seek to move the public discourse beyond an overly simplistic notion of gangs and gang problems — in an effort to cultivate an understanding of the complex array of social patterns and individual behaviors that are encountered under the rubric of "gangs."

The consequences of gangs — and the burden they place on the law enforcement and health systems in our communities — are significant. The simple truth, however, is that gang intervention and suppression activities and strategies for providing medical services to gang members and victims of gang violence, although critical, are not enough. We must implement early prevention strategies to keep youth from joining gangs in the first place. Indeed, we believe that, faced with current economic realities, prevention is the smartest, most economical approach to solving the gang problem and its cascading impact on individuals, families, neighborhoods and society at large.

Consider the impact of violence. In the U.S., homicide is the second leading cause of death among adolescents and young adults: it results in an average of 13 deaths every day among those ages 10-24.[3] However, the number of violent deaths tells only part of the story: More than 700,000 young people are treated in U.S. emergency departments for assault-related injuries each year.[3] Violence also erodes communities by reducing productivity, decreasing property values and disrupting social services.

Now, consider the impact of gangs on violence and other crime. Youth involved in gangs are far more likely than youth not involved in gangs to be both victims and perpetrators of violence.[4,5] In many U.S. communities, gang members (including youth and adult members of street, outlaw motorcycle and prison gangs) are responsible for more than half of the violent crimes and, in some jurisdictions, gang members are responsible for 90 percent of violent crimes.[6]

The consequences of youth gang membership extend beyond the risk for crime and violence. Gang-involved youth are more likely to engage in substance abuse and high-risk sexual behavior and to experience a wide range of potentially long-term health and social consequences, including school dropout, teen parenthood, family problems and unstable employment.[7]

Why Prevention?

The goal of this book is to provide practitioners and policymakers with knowledge about why kids become involved in gangs and to offer effective and promising strategies that *prevent* them from doing so. A significant proportion of local, state and federal budgets — in health, criminal justice, law enforcement and community services — is dedicated to dealing with gang-joining and its sequelae *after* it has occurred. We also know that a large majority of youth who join gangs do so very young — between ages 11 and 15 — and the peak ages for gang-joining are between 13 and 15 years old.[8]

Fortunately, we know that many early prevention programs provide taxpayers with significantly more benefits than costs. Nobel Prize-winning economist James Heckman, for example, has written about the economic benefits of targeting high-risk children before they start kindergarten.[9] Researchers at the Washington State Institute for Public Policy have done cost-benefit analyses of programs that show significant effects on a range of outcomes, including crime, educational attainment, substance abuse, child abuse and neglect, teen pregnancy and public assistance. One example is the Nurse-Family Partnership, which provides support during pregnancy to low-income women and helps them develop parenting skills during the child's first two years of life. Evaluations of the long-term effects of this program show significant reductions in child neglect and abuse, and sustained effects on the child through age 15, including less likelihood of running away, reduced alcohol consumption, and 56 percent fewer arrests. The Nurse-Family Partnership is estimated to provide $2.37 return on every dollar invested, resulting in approximately $13,181 in savings per child.[10]

Although such cost-benefit data provide decision-makers with the fiscal rationale for implementing early prevention programs, it is also important to consider the ethical responsibility that communities have to help children avoid gang membership. That said, no one who reads this book will be surprised to learn that there is no quick fix. Reducing gang activity and violence requires a combination of strategies, including prevention, enforcement and reentry services for those returning from confinement. Preventing gang membership in the first place holds promise for long-term success in reducing both violence and crime *and* the "downstream" societal problems that stem from gang activities.

What You Will Learn

Little scientific evidence specifically addresses gang-membership prevention; however, the body of research on youth delinquency and youth violence offers substantial insights. Where research specific to gang-joining exists, the experts who worked on this book discuss it, but we also asked them to consider research on youth violence, delinquency, developmental ecology and substance use to explore promising principles for gang-membership prevention.

We begin with a chapter by a pioneer in the field of youth gangs, James ("Buddy") Howell. Examining why preventing gang-joining is so important, Dr. Howell discusses the latest information about the magnitude and seriousness of the gang problem in the U.S. In chapter 2, Dr. Carl Taylor and Ms. Pamela Smith discuss aspects of gang life that are attractive to some youth. This chapter considers the perceptions that an adolescent may have about the personal, economic and social motives for joining a gang.

In chapter 3, Dr. Tamara Haegerich, Dr. James Mercy and Ms. Billie Weiss explore the public health impact of gang membership, and they encourage readers to consider the complementary roles of public health and law enforcement in helping to prevent kids from joining a gang. In chapter 4, Dr. Scott Decker describes the role that law enforcement can play in preventing youth from joining a gang and recommends an emphasis on prevention rather than suppression-only tactics. Together, these two chapters highlight the importance of collaboration and coordination across sectors, including health, law enforcement, education and business.

The next four chapters are structured according to the social ecological model for designing prevention strategies.

The social ecological model posits multiple levels at which risk factors can be reduced and protective factors can be enhanced — moving from within individuals and relationships to an entire community or society at large (see graphic, "Levels of Social Influence on Youth Violence: The Social Ecological Model"). First, in chapter 5, Dr. Nancy Guerra and colleagues describe the individual and family factors in early childhood (ages 0-5) and the elementary school years (ages 6-12) that increase the risk for gang-joining. They also explore opportunities for prevention when at-risk youth are identified and provided with age-appropriate prevention strategies that help them avoid a cascade of problems, including gang-joining, delinquency and violence. In chapter 6, Dr. Deborah Gorman-Smith and colleagues focus on how early prevention strategies increase the protective role of families by enhancing consistent and appropriate discipline, monitoring, communication and warmth. In chapter 7, Dr. Gary Gottfredson describes the need for strategies to enhance the willingness — and ability — of schools to assess gang problems accurately, implement prevention strategies, and address the fear in schools that contributes to the risk for gang-joining. In chapter 8, Dr. Jorja Leap emphasizes the opportunity to build on existing strengths within communities. She describes the need for community-based, multifaceted prevention efforts that work across the life span and are grounded in collaboration among the various stakeholders.

As the editors of this book, we felt strongly that — in addition to describing principles for gang-membership prevention at the individual, family, school and community levels — it was incumbent on us to consider head-on the need to reduce gang-joining among girls and the issues of race and ethnicity. In chapter 9, Dr. Meda Chesney-Lind explores how we can prevent girls from joining gangs. Her discussion includes the risks of child sexual abuse, poor family functioning, neighborhood safety, substance abuse and dating violence. In chapter 10, Drs. Adrienne Freng and T.J. Taylor look at the complex role that race and ethnicity can play in gang membership. Although there is no doubt that more research is needed in this area, they argue that, at this point, common underlying risk factors — such as poverty, challenges for immigrants, discrimination and social isolation — should be our focus.

In chapter 11, Drs. Finn Esbensen and Kristy Matsuda examine a subject that is critical to those responsible for making decisions about how limited resources for gang-membership prevention are allocated. Everyone — from federal and state policymakers to local school board members, and from health departments to police departments — is eager to answer the question: "How do we *know* if we are preventing gang membership?" Anecdotal success stories do not justify creating a new program or continuing the investment in an ongoing one. Decisions should be made on the best available evidence. We believe that it is crucial for decision-makers to understand the key principles of process, outcome and cost-effectiveness evaluations offered in this chapter.

Finally, in our Conclusion, we extend an invitation to policymakers and practitioners to engage in a new way of thinking about the intersection of public health and public safety strategies and leveraging public health and public safety resources. As a collaboration of international experts recently noted, "It may not be an easy invitation to accept."[11] We are accustomed to attacking problems such as gang-joining through "silos." These silos can exist in all levels of government and can be fairly entrenched. So, in addition to facing our nation's economic challenges, we must start breaking down silos — silos of thinking, silos of action. With this goal in mind, the Conclusion offers suggestions for strategic actions that can help prevent kids from joining a gang.

Making Research Useful to Practitioners and Policymakers

The chapters in this book have these common features to help readers determine what information may be most important to them, see the most critical information up front, and begin to connect research with real-world applications:

- The titles are framed as questions.

- Key principles are presented in bulleted form.

- An "In Brief" summary pulls together key findings and ideas.

- A Q&A interview with a practitioner offers a personalized illustration of the principles discussed.

- Implementation and policy challenges are explored.

The need to move beyond silos is one of the reasons we brought together diverse perspectives: public health and law enforcement, researchers and practitioners. Criminal justice and public health can collaborate at multiple levels to raise awareness about the importance of early prevention in helping to keep youth from joining gangs and to ensure that the best available evidence of what works is identified and fully used.

This book provides a foundation for that collaboration by describing the principles and promising practices for preventing gang-joining that practitioners and policymakers can use to guide decisions and long-term planning for reducing gang activity. NIJ and CDC are dedicated to this mission, and we hope that this collaboration will serve as an example of the way forward.

Vocabulary: Some Basic Definitions

Vocabulary can be a stumbling block for collaboration across sectors. To help avoid confusion and to facilitate consistency across chapters, we established a few basic operational definitions. In the same way that this book attempts to help break down silos between criminal justice and public health, we tried to remove some of the jargon that might get in the way of policymakers and practitioners understanding and embracing the principles in this book. Here, then, is some general guidance about what we mean when we use these terms:

Youth gang: Although there is no standard definition of what constitutes a gang, one of our authors, James C. ("Buddy") Howell, has offered a practical definition, which incorporates several widely accepted criteria for classifying a group as a youth gang:[12]

- Five or more members.

- Members share an identity, often linked to a name and other symbols.

- Members view themselves as a gang and are recognized by others as a gang.

- The group has some permanence and a degree of organization.

- The group is involved in an elevated level of delinquent or criminal activity.

Gang-joining: We use an operational perspective to define this as when a youth self-identifies as a member of a gang.

Gang-membership/Gang-joining prevention: This is the implementation of a strategy, program or policy that has the direct or indirect effect of reducing youth's risk of joining a gang. We use the term *primary prevention* to refer to preventing youth from joining a gang in the first place. We include strategies that either reduce known risk factors or enhance protective factors that reduce the likelihood of gang-joining.

Evidence: Principles or assertions made by the authors of the chapters in this book are based on systematic research. We have endeavored to ensure that an evaluation exists to support statements of effectiveness and that the rigor of an evaluation qualifies the strength of statements about a program's or principle's effectiveness. We have tried to ensure that the authors avoided (1) statements of opinion or observation that are not based on systematic research, (2) assessments or discussions of a strategy's effectiveness that are not based on an evaluation, and (3) overstatement of confidence in the results of evaluation.

Endnotes

1. Egley A Jr, Howell JC. *Highlights of the 2010 National Youth Gang Survey.* Washington, DC: U.S. Department of Justice, Office of Justice Programs, Office of Juvenile Justice and Delinquency Prevention, 2012.

2. Robers S, Zhang J, Truman J. Indicators of School Crime and Safety: 2011 (NCES 2012-002/NCJ 236021). Washington, DC: U.S. Department of Education, National Center for Education Statistics, and U.S. Department of Justice, Office of Justice Programs, Bureau of Justice Statistics, 2012.

3. Centers for Disease Control and Prevention. Web-based Injury Statistics Query and Reporting System (WISQARS) [online]. Centers for Disease Control and Prevention, National Center for Injury Prevention and Control, 2009. Available at http://www.cdc.gov/injury/wisqars/index.html. Accessed on September 6, 2012.

4. Thornberry TP, Krohn MD, Lizotte AJ, Smith CA, Tobin K. *Gangs and Delinquency in Developmental Perspective.* New York, NY: Cambridge University Press, 2003.

5. Peterson D, Taylor TJ, Esbensen F-A. Gang membership and violent victimization. *Justice Quarterly* 2004; 21:793-815.

6. Federal Bureau of Investigation. National Gang Threat Assessment: Emerging Trends; 2011. Available at http://www.fbi.gov/stats-services/publications/2011-national-gang-threat-assessment. This report is based on data from the National Drug Intelligence Center (through the National Drug Threat Survey), the U.S. Bureau of Prisons, state correctional facilities and the National Gang Intelligence Center law enforcement partners.

7. Krohn MD, Ward JT, Thornberry TP, Lizotte AJ, Chu R. The cascading effects of adolescent gang involvement across the life course. *Criminology* 2011; 49:991-1028.

8. Howell JC. *Gang Prevention: An Overview of Research and Programs.* Washington, DC: U.S. Department of Justice, Office of Justice Programs, Office of Juvenile Justice and Delinquency Prevention, 2010.

9. Heckman J. Skill formation and the economics in investing in disadvantaged children. *Science* 2006; 312:1900-1902.

10. Lee S, Aos S, Drake E, Pennucci A, Miller M, Anderson L. Return on investment: Evidence-based options to improve statewide outcomes (Document No. 12-04-1201). Olympia, WA: Washington State Institute for Public Policy, April 2012.

11. Violence Prevention: An Invitation to Intersectoral Action. Jointly published by the National Institute of Justice, Cardiff University, The Scottish Government, the Violence Prevention Alliance and the World Health Organization. Available at http://www.who.int/violenceprevention/about/intersectoral_action.pdf.

12. Howell JC. *Gangs in America's Communities.* Thousand Oaks, CA: Sage Publications, 2012.

Why Is Gang-Membership Prevention Important?

James C. Howell

- **Gangs are a serious, persistent problem in the United States; according to the National Youth Gang Survey, from 2002 to 2010 the estimated number of youth gangs increased by nearly 35 percent — from 21,800 to 29,400 nationwide.**

- **Because high-rate gang offenders impose enormous costs on society, successful prevention and early intervention programs potentially can produce large monetary cost savings to communities.**

- **Programs and strategies are most urgently needed with high-risk youth, families, schools and communities.**

- **The most successful comprehensive gang initiatives are communitywide in scope; have broad community involvement in planning and delivery; and employ integrated prevention, outreach, support and services.**

In Brief

Youth gangs are not a new social problem in the United States. They have been a serious problem since the early 19th century — and they remain a persistent problem. Overall, one-third (34 percent) of cities, towns and rural counties in this country reported gang problems in 2010.[1] Recent data indicate that nearly half of high school students report that there are students at their school who consider themselves to be part of a gang, and 1 in 5 students in grades 6-12 report that gangs are present in their school.[2, 3] Other data have found that nearly 1 in 12 youth said they belonged to a gang at some point during their teenage years.[4]

The consequences of joining a gang are potentially very serious, both for the youth and for their communities. The frequency with which someone commits serious and violent acts typically increases while they are gang members, compared with periods before and after gang involvement. Adolescents who are in a gang commit many more serious and violent offenses than nongang adolescents.[5, 6] In samples from several U.S. cities, gang members account for approximately three-fourths of the violent offenses committed by delinquents in those samples.[6] Gang involvement also elevates drug use and gun carrying, leading to arrest, conviction, incarceration and a greater likelihood of violent victimization. These experiences bring disorder to the life course through a cascading series of difficulties, including school dropout, teen parenthood and unstable employment.[7]

The total volume of crime costs Americans an estimated $655 billion each year.[8] Over his or her lifetime, each high-rate criminal offender can impose between $4.2 and $7.2 million in costs on society and their victims.[9, 10] Early prevention activities that target high-risk youth can have enormous payoffs *if* they are effective. Early prevention strategies are likely to produce other social and behavioral benefits in addition to reducing the risk for gang membership.

Universal prevention approaches are necessary to reach the entire youth population and reduce the number of youth who join gangs, particularly in high-crime and high-risk communities. More

7

intensive *"selected"* prevention programs are needed to reach youth who are most at risk of gang involvement.

To succeed, communities must first assess their gang problem and use that assessment to craft a continuum of responses that are communitywide in scope. These responses should involve the community in planning and delivering prevention and intervention programs and employ integrated outreach, support and services. A balanced approach that incorporates each of these components is most likely to have a significant impact.

This chapter draws on multiple data sources to provide a brief summary of the scope of youth gang problems in the United States. The second section considers the consequences of gang membership and calls attention to several issues of concern, particularly the enormous costs associated with gangs and criminal careers. The third section discusses the potential for gang-membership prevention activities. And, finally, the chapter concludes with a call for comprehensive, communitywide initiatives.

The gang problem in the United States persists, even though violent crime and property crime rates have dropped dramatically.[5, 11] An enduring concern for many large jurisdictions is the continued presence of gangs and gang activity, which are often associated with violence and serious crimes.[1,5] About one-quarter of all homicides in cities with populations of 100,000 or more were gang-related in 2009.[5,12] Gang activity and its associated violence remain significant components of the U.S. crime problem. It has been reasonably assumed that gang activity would follow the overall dramatic declines in violent crime nationally; however, the analyses provided in this report find overwhelming evidence to the contrary — that is, gang problems have continued at exceptional levels over the past decade despite the remarkable drop in crime overall.

Other data — regarding youth gangs, in particular — are equally compelling. In a 2010 national survey, 45 percent of high school students and 35 percent of middle school students said that there were gangs — or students who considered themselves to be part of a gang — in their school.[2]

Youth gangs are not a new phenomenon; they have been a serious crime problem in the United States since the early 19th century.[5,13] However, as described below, key indicators of youth-gang activity clearly show the persistence of this social problem over the past decade. These indicators include youth self-admission of gang membership and estimates of gang activity by knowledgeable observers of gangs, particularly law enforcement. Youth surveys are also a main source of information for gauging gang activity.

Although most youth never join a gang, 8 percent of youth reported in a national survey that they had belonged to a gang at some point between the ages of 12 and 17.[4] The proportion of youth that joins a gang during this age span is largest in high-crime areas and among high-risk youth in cities with gang problems. This proportion can vary considerably across cities — for example, 17 percent of youth in Denver, CO, and 32 percent in Rochester, NY, were members of a gang at some point during their teenage years.[5]

Assessments of patterns of gang membership and activity by racial and ethnic subgroups vary widely across data sources (official records vs. self-reports), locations, and how the questions are asked. Adrienne Freng and T.J. Taylor, in chapter 10, describe these patterns and the implications for prevention.

More girls are involved in gangs than most people realize. Nationwide, the male-to-female ratio is approximately 2:1 (11 percent of boys, 6 percent of girls).[4] However, in a nine-city survey published in 2008, researchers found that nearly identical proportions of girls and boys belonged to a gang — 9 percent of boys and 8 percent of girls.[14]

Among early adolescents, girl gang members commit crimes that are similar to those boy gang members commit, including assault, robbery and gang fights, although a smaller proportion of girls is involved.[15, 16] (For more information on girls and gang membership, see chapter 9.)

Presence of Gang Problems Over Time

Reported youth gang problems grew significantly in the United States during the 25 years before 1995, reaching the highest peak in our nation's history in the mid-1990s.[17] In the 1970s, only 19 states reported youth gang problems. Twenty-five years later, all 50 states and the District of Columbia reported youth gang problems. Formerly a problem only in large cities, youth gangs became present in many suburbs, small towns and rural areas during the 1990s. Thereafter, there was a significant decline in the number of jurisdictions reporting youth gang problems, which continued until 2001.[18]

As shown in the figure below, the percentage of localities reporting gang problems through the National Youth Gang Survey (NYGS) jumped almost 10 percentage points (23.9 percent to 33.6 percent) from 2001 to 2005. The estimate has remained elevated since 2005; slightly more than one in three cities, suburban areas, towns and rural counties reported gang problems in 2010.[1] The data from the NYGS also indicate that, during 2002-2010, the estimated number of gangs increased by nearly 35 percent, from 21,800 to 29,400 (special data analyses from the National Gang Center, Tallahassee, FL). Although the number of gang homicides has dropped in suburban areas and smaller cities, recent evidence has shown increases in gang violence in large urban areas. In cities with more than 100,000 people, for example, gang-related homicides increased by more than 10 percent from 2009 to 2010.[1]

Student reports of gang activity in the School Crime Supplement to the National Crime Victimization Survey show a similar pattern. In the mid-1990s, 28 percent of a national sample of students reported that gangs were present in their schools.[19] This dropped to 17 percent in

Percentage of Local Law Enforcement Agencies Reporting Youth Gang Problems, 1996-2010

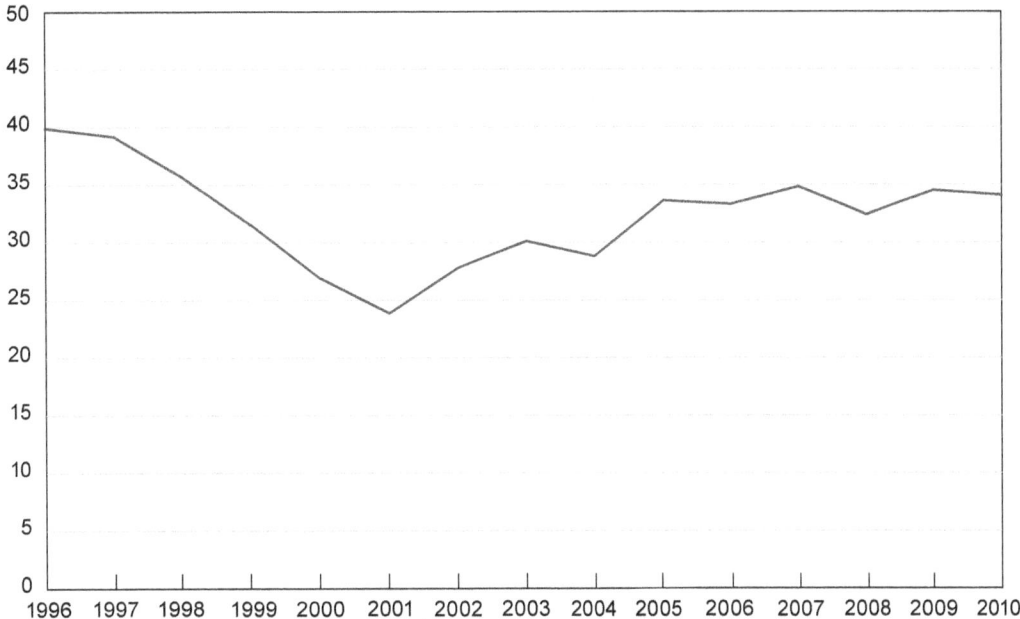

SOURCE: Data from National Gang Center Survey Analysis: Prevalence of Gang Problems in Study Population, 1996-2010. U.S. Department of Justice, Office of Justice Programs, Bureau of Justice Assistance and Office of Juvenile Justice and Delinquency Prevention. Available at http://www.nationalgangcenter.gov/Survey-Analysis/Prevalence-of-Gang-Problems#prevalenceyouthgang.

1999, then began to increase to 23 percent in 2007 — nearly the level reported a decade earlier — and dropped slightly in 2009.[3, 19]

Although there are some discrepancies in these data (largely because they come from different sources and are gathered using different methods), they clearly show that gang activity is widespread and that strategies for gang-membership prevention need to address all segments of the child and adolescent population in the United States.

Gang-Joining

Studies have shown that the gang-joining process is similar to how most of us would go about joining an organization — that is, gradually, as familiarity and acceptance grow. A youth typically begins hanging out with gang members at age 11 or 12 and joins the gang between ages 12 and 15. In other words, the process typically takes from 6 months to 1-2 years from the initial association with a gang.[20, 21, 22, 23]

Some widely held beliefs on why youth join gangs are misleading.[5, 24] For example, there is a common misperception that many youth are coerced into joining a gang. Quite to the contrary, most youth who join a gang very much *want* to belong to a gang but for reasons that may vary. The major reason youth give for joining a gang is the need for protection, followed by fun, respect, money, and because a friend was in the gang.[25, 26] (For more information about why youth join gangs, see chapter 2.)

Gang-joining typically has several steps, particularly in communities where gangs are well-established.[27] In elementary school, children may hear about gangs and some are in awe when they see gang members in middle school. Seeing gang members for the first time can validate their importance in a young adolescent's mind. Also, the schoolyard may have separate gang hangouts to which youngsters gravitate. In addition, the most vulnerable children enter middle school with poor academic achievement, and their street exposure renders them prime candidates for gang membership. Researcher Diego Vigil observes that "[a]s they become more and more involved in the oppositional subculture, they become increasingly disdainful of teachers and school officials — and in the process become budding dropouts."[27] Walking home from school with friends, a child might have a chance to bond with gang members with whom he had been hanging out during the school day. Perhaps he is invited to join them by older gang members who wish to make their group appear bigger and more menacing in the eyes of onlookers, particularly to rival gang members. The child or adolescent who joins the gang may feel compelled to do so. Faced with the prospect of belonging to nothing and feeling alone, youngsters in this situation may feel that they *must* join the gang, "even though," Vigil notes, "the requisites for membership are quite demanding and life threatening."[27]

The Consequences of Gang Membership

At the individual level, youth who join a gang develop an increased propensity for violence and, in turn, are more likely to be victims of violence. In addition, the likelihood of favorable life-course outcomes is significantly reduced. Communities are also negatively affected by gangs, particularly in terms of quality of life, crime, victimization and the economic costs.

Increased Involvement in Violence

Studies of large representative samples in several large U.S. cities show that many gang members are actively involved in violent crimes.[5, 28] Youth commit many more serious and violent acts while they are gang members than before they join and after they leave the gang. During the time they are actively involved in a gang, youth commit serious and violent offenses at a rate several times higher than youth who are not in a gang. In late adolescence, gang involvement leads to drug trafficking and persistent gun carrying.[29]

Gang members account for a disproportionate amount of crime in communities where gangs are particularly active.[5, 28] In several cities, gang members accounted for more than 7 in 10 self-reported violent offenses in the study sample.[6] The extensive criminal involvement of gang members — particularly in serious and violent crime — has been noted by Terence Thornberry, a highly respected gang researcher, to be "one of the most robust and consistent observations in criminological research."[6]

Life-Course Outcomes

Gang involvement encourages more active participation in delinquency, drug use, drug trafficking and violence, and in turn may result in arrest, conviction and incarceration.[28, 30] These effects of gang involvement also tend to bring disorder to the life course in a cumulative pattern of negative outcomes, including school dropout, cohabitation, teen parenthood and unstable employment.[7] These and other unfortunate impacts of gang involvement on youngsters' lives are particularly severe when they remain active in the gang for several years.[28]

Individual Victimization

The victimization cycle can begin at home, when children are abused or neglected. Youth who experience violent victimization — such as maltreatment at home or assaults outside the home — may experience a range of consequences: becoming more aggressive themselves, being rejected from prosocial peer groups, affiliating with high-risk youth, and consequently being at elevated risk of joining a gang.[5] According to researcher T.J. Taylor and his colleagues, "Although victimization preceding gang membership often comes from sources outside the gang, other gang members are often the ones inflicting the victimization once youth become involved with gangs."[31] It should come as no surprise, therefore, that active gang members are also more likely to be victimized themselves than are youth who do not belong to a gang.[26,31]

Frequent association with other gang members encourages and reinforces violent responses to situations and retaliation against others; this, in turn, elevates the risk of violent victimization in gangs.[32,33,34]

For girls, regularly associating with gang members increases the likelihood of very high-risk sexual activity, other problem behaviors and violent victimization.[35] (For more information on girls, see chapter 9.)

Community Decline and Costs

More than seven out of 10 very large cities reported a consistently high level or increasing proportion of gang-related homicides over the 14-year period, 1996-2009.[12] Fear of crime and gangs are immediate, daily experiences for many people who live in neighborhoods where gangs are the most prevalent.[36] Also, the intimidation of witnesses is serious — it undermines the judicial process, making it difficult for law enforcement to maintain order in gang-impacted areas.[37]

Other negative impacts of gangs on communities include the loss of property values, neighborhood businesses and tax revenue; weakened informal social-control mechanisms; and the exodus of families from gang-ridden neighborhoods.[38]

The total monetary burden of crime on Americans is estimated at $655 billion each year.[8] Researchers are now able to estimate the costs of crime to victims, to the criminal justice system, and those incurred by the offender.[9,10] Mark Cohen, at Vanderbilt University's Owen Graduate School of Management, and Alex Piquero, at the University of Texas at Dallas, have estimated the staggering cost of crime imposed on society by high-risk youth: A youth with six or more offenses over his or her lifetime imposes $4.2 to $7.2 million in costs on society and the victims.[9,10] These costs include $2.7 to $4.8 million resulting from crimes committed as well as costs due to drug abuse and the lost productivity due to dropping out of high school.

For young offenders who become chronic offenders (six or more police contacts through age 26), costs imposed in the early ages (through age 10) are relatively low — about $3,000 at age 10.[9] Over a lifetime, these costs aggregate to nearly $5.7 million. This demonstrates the costs and benefits of early interventions that target high-risk youth, which can have a high payoff *if* they are effective.[10] All too often, the initial intervention with high-risk youth occurs several years after the onset of an offender career — and at enormous cost to taxpayers.

The Comprehensive Gang Prevention, Intervention, and Suppression Model — supported by the Office of Juvenile Justice and Delinquency Prevention (OJJDP) — is one model that has demonstrated effectiveness in multiple cities.[39,40,41,42] Researchers looked at five cities in the initial evaluation of the model; they compared youth and neighborhoods that received Comprehensive Gang Model programming with matched comparison groups of youth and neighborhoods that did not receive the programming.[39] They found that the program was implemented with high fidelity in three of six sites (Chicago, IL, Riverside, CA, and Mesa, AZ). In these three sites, there were statistically significant reductions in gang violence, and in two of these sites, there were statistically significant reductions in drug-related offenses when compared with the control groups of youth and neighborhoods.[39]

In the most recent evaluation of the Comprehensive Gang Model in four cities (Los Angeles, CA, Richmond, VA, Milwaukee, WI, and North Miami Beach, FL), researchers concluded that the model was successfully implemented in all four sites despite substantial variation in the nature of the sites' gang problems, albeit with varying impacts.[41] The researchers also found that although results varied across outcomes, one or more indicators of crime reduction were seen. In sum, the Comprehensive Gang Model has demonstrated evidence of its effectiveness in reducing gang violence when fully implemented with program fidelity. Although the research to date has been primarily on the intervention and suppression components, the Comprehensive Gang Model holds promise for integrating prevention activities with intervention programs and suppression strategies.

The first step in implementing the Comprehensive Gang Model is for the community to take stock of its particular youth gang problem because the response must be tailored to fit the situation. No two gangs are alike, and no two communities' gang problems are alike. Assessing the nature and scope of a gang problem is the first step. The National Gang Center provides an assessment manual that identifies many of the social contexts in which gangs form and the elevated risk factors that can lead to child delinquency and gang involvement[43] (see http://www.nationalgangcenter. gov/Comprehensive-Gang-Model/ Implementation-Manual).

The second step is taking an inventory of existing programs that address risk factors for gang-joining and other conditions that give rise to gangs. Gaps in existing prevention activities can then be easily identified in the third step. Only then is a community prepared to consider programs and practices that need to be put into play in response to the local gang problem.

Questions to Guide the Assessment

Because information on what constitutes a gang is often misrepresented in broadcast media, each community should agree on a common definition to guide data collection and strategic planning. This practical definition could be considered as a guide:[5]

- The group has at least five members, generally ages 11-24.

- Members share an identity, typically linked to a name.

- Members view themselves as a gang and are recognized by others as a gang.

- The group has some permanence (at least 6 months).

Prevention Options

Because gang membership typically occurs along a pathway to serious and violent delinquency, delinquency prevention programs can help to prevent gang involvement. Involvement in juvenile delinquency — almost without exception — precedes gang-joining, and *very early involvement* in delinquency has been shown to be a precursor behavior for gang-joining in several independent studies.[21,28,44,45,46,47] In fact, one study suggests that fighting and other delinquent acts by age 10, and perhaps younger, may be a key factor leading to gang involvement.[45] Another study found that failure as early as in elementary school is a main risk factor for later gang involvement.[46]

Children who are on a trajectory of increasing anti-social behavior are more likely to join gangs during their late childhood or early adolescence.[45,48] In fact, we know that early onset of behavioral problems can escalate to gang involvement and, in turn, to serious and violent offending.[49,50]

There are multiple strategies for working with pre-delinquent and delinquent youth in early prevention of gang-joining. For example, it is possible to focus at the individual level on at-risk children, particularly disruptive children. Other strategies work at the family, school or community levels to reduce risk and to enhance protective influences. Other chapters in this book discuss the principles for gang-joining prevention that are

- The group has a degree of organization (for example, with initiation rites, established leaders, symbols or colors).

- The group is involved in an elevated level of criminal activity.

The last four criteria are particularly important when validating the existence of gangs in small cities, towns and rural areas because few gangs survive in less populated areas.[51]

To help communities determine the nature and scope of their gang problem, an assessment should answer these questions:

- Who is involved in gang-related activity and what is the history of the gang?

- What crimes are these individuals committing?

- When are these crimes committed?

- Where is gang-related activity primarily occurring?

- Why is the criminal activity happening (for example, individual conflicts, gang feuds, or gang members acting on their own)?

Answers to these questions help stakeholders focus on bona fide gangs.

The assessment should also identify:

- Neighborhoods with many risk factors for gang involvement.

- Schools and other community settings in which gangs are active.

- Hot spots of gang crime.

- Gang members with high rates of criminal offending.

- Violent gangs.

Identifying Program Gaps

After making an assessment, communities should identify program gaps and develop and coordinate a continuum of prevention and intervention program services and sanctions. These should work in concert with community and government agencies in responding to serious and violent gang activity. Prevention and intervention services should be directed to the neighborhoods, schools and families from which gangs emanate. An implementation guide is available at http://www.nationalgangcenter. gov/Comprehensive-Gang-Model/ Implementation-Manual.[52]

Planning and Development

To facilitate program planning and development guided by the Comprehensive Gang Model, OJJDP's Strategic Planning Tool — available at http://www.nationalgangcenter. gov/SPT — offers a variety of resources, including:

- A list of research-supported risk factors for delinquency and gang membership, organized by age, and strategies that address them.

- Data indicators (measures) of risk factors.

- Sources for finding relevant data.

- Hyperlinks connecting risk factors with effective programs that address them.

- A "Community Resource Inventory" for community planning groups to store and maintain up-to-date information on existing programs.

- A free software program ("Client Track") to track services and client outcomes.

relevant to each of these levels in more detail: chapter 5 looks specifically at the individual child, chapter 6 discusses the family, chapter 7 looks at school-based prevention strategies, and chapter 8 discusses community-level prevention programs.

Each of these strategies is a key component of communitywide programming that, of course, can be expanded to encompass cities, counties and entire states. It is important to recognize that although family and school settings are important, they are often not sufficient. Preventing gang involvement of children who are alienated from their own families and schools — particularly in communities characterized by concentrated disadvantage — is a formidable challenge. Consider, for example, an analysis of data, collected by the National Center for Education Statistics, on more than 17,000 kindergarteners nationwide. Looking at parent and teacher reports, the researchers identified 9.3 percent of the kindergarteners as "severely impaired" because of low levels of self-control and high levels of impulsivity.[53] These children are at risk for challenges at home and at school, suggesting the need for comprehensive programs beyond family and school settings if they are to have a significant impact.

This is why many of the chapters in this book address the range of contexts that are crucial for prevention activities — including gang-joining prevention. Every community should address youth violence as part of its continuum of prevention programs, including specific services for children who are exposed to violence and are victims themselves.[54] In addition, more attention needs to be given to within-gang victimization and victimization of nongang youth by gang members in the individual, family, school and community contexts. In this regard, here are some priorities:[54]

- Mental health professionals should be placed in schools to immediately identify children needing services and deliver or coordinate those services.

- Interventions must focus on families and peer group affiliations.

- Prevention services at multiple levels and across multiple systems must address youth at risk and in need of protection.

- Prevention services must also give priority to the development of positive coping skills, competencies and problem-solving skills in children and adolescents so they can deal effectively with high levels of exposure to violence and victimization.

A Communitywide Strategy for Gang Prevention

We know that the most successful comprehensive gang initiatives are communitywide in scope — with broad community involvement in the planning and delivery of interventions — and offer a wide variety of integrated programs and services from multiple agencies that are coordinated by an intervention team.[5,39] Statewide implementation of prevention programming also appears feasible, as suggested by progress in the implementation of the Comprehensive Gang Model by the North Carolina Department of Juvenile Justice and Delinquency Prevention.[30] Moreover, the Massachusetts Executive Office of Public Safety and Security is providing large-scale funding for prevention and intervention programs that support the model statewide in large urban areas.[55]

Universal prevention programs are needed to reach the entire youth population in high-crime and high-risk communities. *Selected prevention programs* are needed to reach youth at risk of gang involvement. Each of these types of programs can help to reduce the number of youth who join gangs.

Intervention programs are also needed to provide sanctions and services for younger youth who are actively involved in a gang to help them separate from the gang. Law enforcement *suppression strategies* and intensive services are needed to target and rehabilitate the most violent gang members as well as the older, criminally active gang members. In addition, *reentry programs* are needed to help offenders who are returning to the community after confinement.

All of these components are integrated in OJJDP's Comprehensive Gang Prevention, Intervention, and Suppression Model, which has shown positive effects in multiple cities.[39,41] See the sidebar, "In the Spotlight: The Comprehensive Gang Model," for more information on this communitywide approach that incorporates key gang-membership prevention strategies and principles.

Conclusion

Crimes committed by gang members have enormous costs — and beyond the cost of crime itself are the long-term consequences of gang membership, even when it lasts for as little as a single year during adolescence. Typically, drug use, gun carrying and involvement in drug sales increase with gang membership and decrease when youth leave gangs. Gang members are responsible for the majority of crimes committed by delinquents in many areas of large cities. Gangs account for about one-fourth of all homicides in very large U.S. cities[12] and for more than six out of 10 homicides among youth ages 15-24 years in some cities, such as Los Angeles and Long Beach, CA.[56] The individual impact of being a gang member — and the associated costs — are well-known, including school dropout, teen parenthood and unstable employment.

We must develop strategies and programs that reach high-risk youth, communities, families and schools. To be sure, preventing gang activity is not easy. But the good news is that gang crime can be reduced — even among some of the worst gangs — and communities can be protected from the social destruction that often follows in the wake of gangs.

Unfortunately, the typical first community response to gangs is suppression strategies, but these are not enough when gangs are rooted in the cracks of our society where core social institutions — like families and schools — are weak and fractured. The youngest gang members emerge from small groups of rejected, alienated and aggressive children and adolescents. They spend more time together and become actively involved in delinquency — when street socialization is substituted for the nurturing and guidance of parents, teachers, mentors, outreach workers, ministers, and other positive adult role models.

That is why we must implement early prevention strategies that keep youth from joining gangs in the first place. Prevention programs that divert youth from joining a gang can have enormous payoffs *if* they are effective. In fact, early prevention strategies are likely to produce other social and behavioral benefits in addition to reducing risk for gang membership. This is a smart investment that surely will pay large dividends.

Although there is no quick fix, once communities make a commitment to solving gang problems, they are in an excellent position to undertake strategic planning to thwart gang development and overcome established gangs. Each community needs to assess its own gang activity, prepare a strategic plan that fits its specific gang problem, and develop a continuum of programs and activities that parallels youth's gang involvement over time. Services must be directed where they are most needed in the community and to vulnerable youth and their families.

The evidence shows that the most successful gang initiatives are communitywide, have broad community involvement in planning and delivery, and provide integrated outreach, support and services. In other words, communities that organize and mobilize themselves using a data-driven strategy can direct their resources toward effectively preventing gang formation and its associated criminal activity.

About the Author

James C. (Buddy) Howell

James C. (Buddy) Howell has been conducting research on gangs for more than 30 years. Dr. Howell has published extensively on gangs in schools, risk factors, myths about gangs, drug trafficking, gang homicides, and "what works" in preventing gang-joining and reducing gang crime. In his new book, *Gangs in America's Communities,* Dr. Howell details a communitywide approach to gang prevention. He received his Ph.D. from the University of Colorado and is currently a Senior Research Associate at the National Gang Center.

Endnotes

1. Egley A Jr, Howell JC. *Highlights of the 2010 National Youth Gang Survey.* Washington, DC: U.S. Department of Justice, Office of Justice Programs, Office of Juvenile Justice and Delinquency Prevention, 2012.

2. National Center on Addiction and Substance Abuse at Columbia University. *National Survey of American Attitudes on Substance Abuse XV: Teens and Parents, 2010.* New York, NY: National Center on Addiction and Substance Abuse at Columbia University, 2010.

3. Robers S, Zhang J, Truman J. *Indicators of School Crime and Safety: 2011* (NCES 2012-002/ NCJ 236021). National Center for Education Statistics. Washington, DC: U.S. Department of Justice, Office of Justice Programs, Bureau of Justice Statistics, and U.S. Department of Education, 2012.

4. Snyder HN, Sickmund M. *Juvenile Offenders and Victims: 2006 National Report.* Bulletin. Washington, DC: U.S. Department of Justice, Office of Justice Programs, Office of Juvenile Justice and Delinquency Prevention, and National Center for Juvenile Justice, March 2006. Available at http://www.ojjdp.gov/ojstatbb/nr2006/downloads/NR2006.pdf.

5. Howell JC. *Gangs in America's Communities.* Thousand Oaks, CA: Sage Publications, 2012.

6. Thornberry TP. Membership in youth gangs and involvement in serious and violent offending. In: Loeber R, Farrington D, eds., *Serious and Violent Juvenile Offenders: Risk Factors and Successful Interventions.* Thousand Oaks, CA: Sage Publications, 1998:147-166.

7. Thornberry TP, Krohn MD, Lizotte AJ, Smith CA, Tobin K. *Gangs and Delinquency in Developmental Perspective.* New York, NY: Cambridge University Press, 2003.

8. Fight Crime: Invest in Kids. *Caught in the Crossfire: Arresting Gang Violence by Investing in Kids.* Washington, DC: Fight Crime: Invest in Kids, 2004.

9. Cohen MA, Piquero AR. New evidence on the monetary value of saving a high risk youth. *J Quant Criminol.* 2009; 25:25-49.

10. Cohen MA, Piquero AR, Jennings WG. Estimating the costs of bad outcomes for at-risk youth and the benefits of early childhood interventions to reduce them. *Crim Just Policy Rev.* 2010; 21:391-434.

11. Planty M, Truman, JL. Criminal Victimization, 2011. Washington, DC: U.S. Department of Justice, Office of Justice Programs, Bureau of Justice Statistics, 2012. Available at http://bjs.ojp.usdoj.gov/index.cfm?ty=pbdetail&iid=4494.

12. Howell JC, Egley A Jr, Tita G, Griffiths E. U.S. gang problem trends and seriousness. *National Gang Center Bulletin.* No. 6. Tallahassee, FL: Institute for Intergovernmental Research, National Gang Center, 2011.

13. Howell JC, Moore JP. History of street gangs in the United States. *National Gang Center Bulletin.* No. 4. Tallahassee, FL: Institute for Intergovernmental Research, National Gang Center, 2010.

14. Esbensen F-A, Brick BT, Melde C, Tusinski K, Taylor TJ. The role of race and ethnicity in gang membership. In: Genert FV, Peterson D, Lien I, eds., *Street Gangs, Migration and Ethnicity.* Portland, OR: Willan, 2008:117-139.

15. Esbensen F-A, Peterson D, Taylor TJ, Freng A. *Youth Violence: Sex and Race Differences in Offending, Victimization, and Gang Membership.* Philadelphia, PA: Temple University Press, 2010.

16. Bjerregaard B. Self-definitions of gang membership and involvement in delinquent activities. *Youth Soc.* 2002; 34:31-54.

17. Miller WB. *The Growth of Youth Gang Problems in the United States: 1970-98.* Report. Washington, DC: U.S. Department of Justice, Office of Justice Programs, Office of Juvenile Justice and Delinquency Prevention, April 2001.

18. Egley A Jr, Howell JC. *Highlights of the 2010 National Youth Gang Survey.* Fact Sheet. Washington, DC: U.S. Department of Justice, Office of

Justice Programs, Office of Juvenile Justice and Delinquency Prevention, 2012. Additional data are available at http://www.nationalgangcenter.gov/Survey-Analysis.

19. Chandler KA, Chapman CD, Rand MR, Taylor BM. *Students Reports of School Crime: 1989 and 1995.* Washington, DC: U.S. Department of Education and U.S. Department of Justice, 1998.

20. Decker SH, Van Winkle B. *Life in the Gang: Family, Friends, and Violence.* New York, NY: Cambridge University Press, 1996.

21. Esbensen F-A, Huizinga D. Gangs, drugs, and delinquency in a survey of urban youth. *Criminology* 1993; 31:565-589.

22. Huff CR. The criminal behavior of gang members and non-gang at-risk youth. In: Huff CR, ed., *Gangs in America.* 2nd ed. Thousand Oaks, CA: Sage Publications, 1996:75-102.

23. Huff CR. *Comparing the Criminal Behavior of Youth Gangs and At-Risk Youth.* Research in Brief. Washington, DC: U.S. Department of Justice, Office of Justice Programs, National Institute of Justice, 1998.

24. Howell JC. Menacing or mimicking? Realities of youth gangs. *Juvenile Fam Court J* 2007; 58:9-20.

25. Esbensen F-A, Deschenes EP, Winfree LT. Differences between gang girls and gang boys: Results from a multi-site survey. *Youth Soc.* 1999; 31:27-53.

26. Fleisher MS. *Dead End Kids: Gang Girls and the Boys They Know.* Madison, WI: University of Wisconsin, 1998.

27. Vigil JD. The established gang. In: Cummings S, Monti D, eds., *Gangs: The Origins and Impact of Contemporary Youth Gangs in the United States.* Albany, NY: State University of New York Press, 1993:95-112.

28. Krohn MD, Thornberry TP. Longitudinal perspectives on adolescent street gangs. In: Liberman A, ed., *The Long View of Crime: A Synthesis of Longitudinal Research.* New York, NY: Springer, 2008:128-160.

29. Lizotte AJ, Krohn MD, Howell JC, Tobin K, Howard GJ. Factors influencing gun carrying among young urban males over the adolescent-young adult life course. *Criminology* 2000; 38:811-834.

30. Howell MQ, Lassiter W. *Prevalence of Gang-Involved Youth in NC.* Raleigh, NC: North Carolina Department of Juvenile Justice and Delinquency Prevention, 2011.

31. Taylor TJ, Freng A, Esbensen F-A, Peterson D. Youth gang membership and serious violent victimization: The importance of lifestyles and routine activities. *J Interpers Violence* 2008; 23:1441-1464.

32. Decker SH. Youth gangs and violent behavior. In: Flannery DJ, Vazsonyi AT, Waldman ID, eds., *The Cambridge Handbook of Violent Behavior and Aggression.* New York, NY: Cambridge University Press, 2007:388-402.

33. DeLisi M, Barnes JC, Beaver KM, Gibson CL. Delinquent gangs and adolescent victimization revisited: A propensity score matching approach. *Crim Justice Behav.* 2009; 36:808-823.

34. Papachristos AV. Murder by structure: Dominance relations and the social structure of gang homicide. *Am J Sociol.* 2009; 115:74-128.

35. Valdez A. *Mexican American Girls and Gang Violence: Beyond Risk.* New York, NY: Palgrave Macmillan, 2007.

36. Lane J, Meeker JW. Subcultural diversity and the fear of crime and gangs. *Crime Delinq.* 2000; 46:497-521.

37. Troutman DR, Nugent-Borakove ME, Jansen S. *Prosecutor's Comprehensive Gang Response Model.* Alexandria, VA: National District Attorneys Association, 2007.

38. Decker SH, Pyrooz DC. Gang violence worldwide: Context, culture, and country. *Small Arms Survey 2010.* Geneva, Switzerland: Small Arms Survey, 2010.

39. Spergel IA, Wa KM, Sosa RV. The comprehensive, community-wide, gang program model: Success and failure. In: Short JF, Hughes LA,

eds., *Studying Youth Gangs.* Lanham, MD: AltaMira Press, 2006:203-224.

40. Spergel IA. *Reducing Youth Gang Violence: The Little Village Gang Project in Chicago.* Lanham, MD: AltaMira Press, 2007.

41. Hayeslip D, Cahill M. *Community Collaboratives Addressing Youth Gangs: Final Evaluation Findings From the Gang Reduction Program.* Washington, DC: Urban Institute, 2009.

42. Cahill M, Hayeslip D. *Findings From the Evaluation of OJJDP's Gang Reduction Program.* Bulletin. Washington, DC: U.S. Department of Justice, Office of Justice Programs, Office of Juvenile Justice and Delinquency Prevention, 2010.

43. Office of Juvenile Justice and Delinquency Prevention. *OJJDP Comprehensive Gang Model: A Guide to Assessing a Community's Youth Gang Problems.* Washington, DC: U.S. Department of Justice, Office of Juvenile Justice and Delinquency Prevention, 2009. Available at http://www.nationalgangcenter.gov/Comprehensive-Gang-Model/Assessment-Guide.

44. Howell JC, Egley A Jr. Moving risk factors into developmental theories of gang membership. *Youth Viol Juv Just.* 2005; 3:334-354.

45. Craig WM, Vitaro CG, Tremblay RE. The road to gang membership: Characteristics of male gang and non-gang members from ages 10 to 14. *Soc Dev.* 2002; 11:53-68.

46. Hill KG, Howell JC, Hawkins JD, Battin-Pearson SR. Childhood risk factors for adolescent gang membership: Results from the Seattle Social Development Project. *J Res Crime Delinq.* 1999; 26:300-322.

47. Gordon RA, Lahey BB, Kawai E, Loeber R, Stouthamer-Loeber M, Farrington DP. Antisocial behavior and youth gang membership: Selection and socialization. *Criminology* 2004; 42:55-88.

48. Lahey BB, Gordon RA, Loeber R, Stouthamer-Loeber M, Farrington DP. Boys who join gangs: A prospective study of predictors of first gang entry. *J Abnorm Child Psychol.* 1999; 27:261-276.

49. Howell JC. *Preventing and Reducing Juvenile Delinquency: A Comprehensive Framework.* 2nd ed. Thousand Oaks, CA: Sage Publications, 2009.

50. Loeber R, Farrington DP, Stouthamer-Loeber M, White HR. *Violence and Serious Theft: Development and Prediction from Childhood to Adulthood.* New York, NY: Routledge, 2008.

51. Howell JC, Egley A Jr. *Gangs in Small Towns and Rural Counties.* NYGC Bulletin 2005: No. 1. Tallahassee, FL: National Youth Gang Center, 2005.

52. Office of Juvenile Justice and Delinquency Prevention. *OJJDP Comprehensive Gang Model: Planning for Implementation.* Washington, DC: U.S. Department of Justice, Office of Justice Programs, Office of Juvenile Justice and Delinquency Prevention, 2009.

53. Vaughn MG, DeLisi M, Beaver KM, Wright JP. Identification of latent classes of behavioral risk based on early childhood manifestations of self control. *Youth Viol Juv Just.* 2009; 7:16-31.

54. Flannery DJ, Singer MI, Van Dulmen M, Kretschmar JM, Belliston LM. Exposure to violence, mental health, and violent behavior. In: Flannery D, Vazonsyi A, Waldman I, eds., *Cambridge Handbook of Violent Behavior.* New York, NY: Cambridge University Press, 2007:306-321.

55. Gebo E, Bond BJE. *Beyond Suppression: Community Strategies to Reduce Gang Violence.* Lanham, MD: Lexington Books, 2012.

56. Egley A, Logan J, McDaniel D. Gang homicides—five U.S. cities, 2003-2008. *Morbid Mortal Wk Rep.* 2012; 61:46-51.

The Attraction of Gangs: How Can We Reduce It?

Carl S. Taylor and Pamela R. Smith

- Because youth join gangs for various reasons — for money, a sense of support and belonging, status, a perceived sense of protection, or to exhibit an outlaw mentality — multiple strategies are needed to lessen the attractions.

- Youth, including those at risk for gang-joining, possess developmental assets that can be strengthened when aligned with positive community resources to help prevent gang-joining.

- Community partnerships are crucial to reducing the attraction of gangs; these should include youth, their families, law enforcement, public health, schools, faith-based organizations, and groups that offer recreational programs, employment and job-training skills.

- Deliberate effort is needed to counter the attractions of gangs that are often perpetuated among youth, in families, in neighborhoods and in the media; communities must provide prosocial alternatives to gang life that are attractive to youth.

In Brief

For many young people who are at risk for joining a gang, the perceived benefits of being in a gang seem to outweigh the potentially life-altering consequences that we know can be associated with gang life. Attractions for youth include economics, relationship to friends or family who are already in the gang, a sense of support and belonging, a perception that the gang will provide protection, and the status of being an "outlaw."

It is important that practitioners and policymakers understand what the evidence shows about why kids join gangs. Increasing our understanding of the attractions of gangs can also help families, schools and community groups who work with young people to better understand the motivations for gang-joining and to plan prevention strategies that provide alternative options for youth so that they do not become involved with gangs. With the right level of motivation and a commitment to evidence-based strategies, we can do many things to help prevent kids from joining a gang. Chief among these is providing youth with other options and opportunities. Ideally, prevention strategies should offer a "brand" for at-risk children that reflects youth culture and can rival the allure of gang glory.

In this chapter, we draw widely from research across geographical locations, racial and ethnic groups, and methodological approaches to discuss the attractions of gang-joining in the United States.

Why do youth join gangs? The first issue to consider is why youth are particularly *vulnerable* to the influence of gangs. Ages 11-14 are a transitional period for youth — a time when they are moving from childhood to adolescence. During this period, children begin spending less time with family and more time with friends.[1] They also start to become acutely aware of what others are thinking and the consequences for their actions.[1] Additionally, teens begin to form their identity by experimenting with clothes, hairstyles, friends, music and hobbies. They also begin to assert their independence by pressing the limits that adults put on them. (For more on the developmental factors that are pertinent to gang-joining, see chapter 5.)

During the teen years, it is common for youth to engage in some form of risk-taking behavior. For youth in an environment with healthy, prosocial alternatives, such risk-taking might seem tame. However, youth lacking such alternatives are more likely to take extreme risks such as drug use, shoplifting, fighting and gang-joining. Further, if gang-joining seems a "viable" alternative and the perceived attractions of gangs are reinforced — in families, by peers and neighborhood norms, and by the popular media — youth will be more likely to join a gang.

An important goal for prevention is to recognize the multiple perceived attractions that gangs offer youth and to develop alternative messages and options in urban, suburban and rural environments and across race, economic class and gender. The factors that we discuss in this chapter exist to varying degrees across communities, and the order in which we discuss them is not intended to reflect any kind of "ranking." Also, a youth's decision to join a gang cannot be summed up by a single factor. The decision often includes many reasons, reflecting the multiple influences faced by youth.[2] These include:

- Economics.

- Relationships with family and friends.

- Protection.

- Support and belonging.

- Status.

- An "outlaw" mentality.

Economics

Gangs often claim to offer economic benefits to their members.[3] Money is one of the perceived benefits that attract youth to gangs.[4,5,6,7] Many gangs engage in various aspects of an "informal economy" to generate cash flow among their members.[4,5] This can include stealing and reselling property[4,8,9] or involvement in the potentially more lucrative work of distributing drugs.[3]

The economic attraction of gangs also applies to females. Many young Detroit women whom I (Carl Taylor) interviewed, as a part of my research in the late 1980s, said that they had joined a gang to make money.[6] In fact, the economic opportunities that gangs are thought to provide can be regarded as acceptable alternatives to a low-wage job in the legitimate employment arena by many young men and women who feel disconnected from the "American Dream."[4,10,11]

Low-level "jobs" in gangs are generally much more readily available than a minimum-wage job in many areas of the U.S. — and they can give kids the sense that they are at least doing something to make some money. However, we know that most gang members do not get rich in the gang and, for older gang members, there is no real economic advancement.[12] And we know that young people who quit school rarely advance beyond a low-wage legitimate job.[3,4,6]

In a forthcoming book on the Michigan Gang Research Project (MGRP), I (Carl Taylor) describe how a gang economy can become part of a larger social and economic network of criminal enterprises directly connected to the mainstream culture. Members of this "underworld" do not abide by mainstream society's rules, orders or policies in their daily lives; their rules supersede those of the larger society. For youth who do not see viable alternatives — and whose families are struggling financially or are part of the underworld economy themselves — the financial opportunities in the underworld can be attractive, making gang-joining an easy transition.

Relationships With Family and Friends

Some youth find gangs appealing because of close relationships with family members and friends who are already involved in gang life.[7, 13] In fact, for young adolescents, close familial and peer relationships with gang members can be a significant attraction for gang-joining.[2,14,15] In a study published in 2002, researchers found that hanging out with friends "on the corner" was a highly significant activity among both male and female gang members — 50 percent of male and 52 percent of female gang members said they did this, compared with only 7 percent of males and 13 percent of females who were not in a gang.[16] Not surprisingly, gang members spent more time hanging out with their friends than with their families.[2]

Protection

Some youth join a gang for a feeling of protection that they believe the gang can provide against potentially violent attackers in their neighborhoods and schools.[2,16,17] In a longitudinal assessment of the Gang Resistance Education and Training (G.R.E.A.T.) program, youth consistently reported protection as a reason for joining a gang.[13] Violence is a regular occurrence in many of the environments where gangs exist, so, to avoid victimization, youth seek out gang membership for protection from rival gangs.

As Yusef Shakur, a former "Zone 8" gang member, said:

> The first corner we claimed to stick our Zone 8 "flag" on was [the streets of … and …], on the side of [a candy store]. During the school year at [a middle school], there was never a day that you didn't see one of us representing on that corner. We strategically placed ourselves at this spot because of its vantage point: the students going to [and] returning from school couldn't miss us. If we weren't there, it was merely because we were being detained [or] hunted down by law enforcement. While on the block where [the candy store] stood, we would also take turns catching guys from across the Boulevard and put classic ass whippings on them

as they also went to/returned from school. As for retribution, they could only retaliate by jumping us in the school. They were in our 'hood, so they were fair game. [An original Zone 8 gang member's] attitude was that if he couldn't catch one of *them,* he was gonna kick their sisters', brothers', cousins' or even girlfriends' asses. This strategy left the guys across the Boulevard with no choice but to join one of the gangs in their 'hood.[18]

Yusef Shakur's words illustrate a process of *protection through intimidation* that is common to many gangs. They show how the actions of one gang can motivate youth to join a rival gang for protection and also, in this instance, how the Zone 8 gang protected their neighborhood, which, in turn, kept bigger situations from erupting in which the police would be called.

Gang affiliation and the process of protecting territory can also foster a sense of identity and pride rooted in the connection to the community.[2, 4, 5] Researchers have found that many Chicano gang members in Chicago and Los Angeles viewed their membership as a commitment to protect their communities from outsiders and gang members from nearby communities.[4, 5] As one gang member from St. Louis stated, "You need someone to protect the people from coming in the neighborhood."[2]

The willingness to protect the community can also take on a practical function among gangs involved in drug distribution, for example. In this context, protecting the turf could also mean minimizing conflict and violence that would attract police to the community rather than the active public intimidation of potential rivals.[4]

Problems and conflict with family members in the home also lead some youth to seek protection within the gang.[17] We also know that gangs offer some girls the opportunity to learn fighting skills to protect themselves. Many of the girls involved in gangs in two Midwestern cities viewed gangs as a refuge from drug addiction and sexual abuse in their home environments.[19] (For more on the involvement of girls in gangs, see chapter 9.)

For youth living in violent families or neighborhoods, the ability to be proficient at violence is reinforced and becomes a part of one's identity.[20] The ability of youth to engage in an act of violence and be successful in that violence can create a form of internal validation of an identity of toughness. It is important to note that this identity may be validated not only by gangs themselves but also by the prevalence of gangs in many mainstream movies, video games, music and music videos. When it is validated, fighting — or engaging in other illicit or delinquent acts — can become part of a youth's identity.

Based on a sense of security provided by gang affiliation, gang members may feel that they are less likely to be victimized by members of the community.[8, 13] Youth may overlook the potential for violent encounters within and across gangs because of the *perception* that gang affiliation can provide protection from violence. Research indicates that the risk of being victimized is greater for gang members.[21] For example, we know that some gangs have violent rituals for joining, leaving or breaking the rules; being "beat in" is a ritual for joining some gangs. We also know that gang members can encounter a greater risk of violence, compared with nongang members, when they sell drugs and possess weapons.[22]

Support and Belonging

Many youth join a gang to build relationships with other people in their age group.[2] Some researchers believe that youth join gangs to address the needs associated with adolescent identity development and that they are looking for a sense of belonging.[5,7,8] Other researchers note that youth who join gangs are marginalized, rejected or ignored in other areas of their lives — family, school or church, for example — and therefore identify with a gang to fill a need for support.[7]

Gangs can allow youth to expand their social networks and make new friends.[2,5] Youth can regard a gang as offering a support system that addresses their social needs, and this attraction can even reduce a gang's need to actively recruit new members.[5,14]

The attractions of joining a gang can apply even when actual membership in a gang is short-lived. Findings from a Seattle study suggest that belonging to a gang is a generally short phase: 69 percent of youth in the study belonged to the gang for one year, and less than 1 percent had been gang members for the entire five-year duration of the study.[15] These findings were comparable to longitudinal studies in cities with similar demographics, such as Denver, CO,[23] and Rochester, NY.[24]

Status

Like most people, gang members desire the status associated with the "good life" in American society. Imagery of this type of success — clothes, cars, jewelry — is constantly reinforced through the media. However, many youth at the greatest risk for gang-joining are unable to access legitimate ladders of success. They often live in communities that have overlapping barriers to success, including high crime rates, dysfunctional households, underprivileged school systems, and lack of access to meaningful work. For some youth, it seems that one can "make it" only through illegitimate means.

Another reason youth join gangs is to enhance their status among their peers.[2] As one 15-year-old from Detroit said in an interview with researcher William Brown, the boost to his status and self-importance was directly tied to his gang membership: "I'm somebody now ... Now I got respect."[10] The boy also reported that his membership in a gang had raised his status in school. Other research has shown that some youth believe joining a gang will impress interested young women.[2,5]

Outlaw Mentality

Some young men join a gang for the excitement of street life,[2] whereas some girls join to build a reputation as being tough.[16] Of course, many kids — not only those at risk for gang membership — rebel against traditional "middle-class" values and ethics. And, when all else in society fails, gangs provide youth with a seeming "escape clause." Gangs can be seen as taking a stand against society, empowering their followers with a sense of independence.

This roguish attitude and image of the "outlaw culture" — running with an organization of gangsters, hoodlums, thugs or "banditos" — is crucial to understanding the allure of gangs for impressionable youth during this stage of social and cognitive development. And this is exacerbated by an entertainment industry that focuses, in marketing and programming, on the allure of the outlaw. Fast cars, fancy clothing, and sexy images of both female and male outlaws making their own way are pervasive in U.S. culture.

The media creates pop-culture images in print, film, art, radio and television that are often influenced by street culture. These images can be found everywhere: in music videos, popular television shows, video games, magazines, language, movies and cars. This pervasiveness impacts the social fabric and can affect the daily choices youth make. For example, the popularity of outlaw behavior may be reinforced by popular video games, including some that specifically replicate an urban community plagued with poverty, gangs, drugs and corrupt police officers.[25]

Reducing the Attractions of Gangs

To reduce the attractions of gangs, we must increase the attractiveness of other organizations. Our goal should be to offer youth access to organizations with a solid image and a strong brand or identity that matches or counters the popularity of the neighborhood gangs. Here are four key principles that practitioners and policymakers should keep in mind when developing evidence-based strategies and programs to help prevent gang-joining:

- Promote positive opportunities.

- Train and educate for meaningful employment.

- Ensure an active role for law enforcement.

- Make comprehensive strategies community-wide.

Promote Positive Opportunities

We know that healthy adolescent development is fostered when communities are able to provide what Peter Benson and his colleagues at Search Institute call "developmental assets." These include strong connections to schools, the presence of adult mentors, positive connections to family members, parental involvement in the lives of youth, neighborhood safety, and positive connections to schools and to other community organizations and institutions, such as youth

development programs like 4-H Clubs, Boys and Girls Clubs, Boy Scouts and Girl Scouts, and the YMCA.

In Detroit, I (Carl Taylor) studied Overcoming the Odds (OTO), a project based on the premises that:

- All young people have strengths.

- All communities have some kind of developmental assets for young people.

- When the strengths of young people and the assets of communities are aligned, positive, healthy development will result.

In the study, we compared a group of African-American male adolescent gang members from inner-city Detroit with a sample of African-American males who lived in the same neighborhoods but who were involved in community-based organizations (CBOs) aimed at promoting positive youth development, such as church groups, urban 4-H groups, and Boys and Girls Clubs.

Results from this longitudinal study show, in general, that adolescents in the comparison group (CBO youth) possess more developmental assets and exhibit more positive developmental changes than the gang-involved youth.[26,27,28,29] However, gang-involved youth also possess some developmental assets — and, when these assets approach the levels of the CBO youth, outcomes begin to converge. More positive development and lower levels of problem behaviors — such as violence and substance use and abuse — are found among gang-involved youth who possess developmental assets at levels that overlap with those seen among the CBO youth.

We believe the findings of the OTO study can be used to inform community actions that decrease youth gang-related behavior and that improve the lives of kids who are at risk of joining a gang. As OTO has shown, it is important that programs are not separate from the community but, rather, are built into the community. Unfortunately, many prevention programs are built and implemented separately from the community; this can lead to youth still having to negotiate the streets and avoid the attractions of gangs within their own community.

IN THE SPOTLIGHT: WORKING, BOOTS-ON-THE-GROUND, IN DETROIT

▶ *INTERVIEWS WITH ANTHONY HOLT, VIRGIL TAYLOR, TISHA JOHNSON, YUSUF SHAKUR AND MICHAEL WILLIAMS*

Detroit has been hit hard in recent years. The 2010 U.S. Census showed it to be the poorest big city in the nation. To take an in-depth look at how some of the city's boots-on-the-ground practitioners are working to help keep Detroit kids from joining a gang, we interviewed five people:

- Anthony Holt, Chief of Police and Assistant Vice President for Community Affairs at Wayne State University.

- Virgil Taylor, Executive Director of The Peace Project, a partnership of youth, universities, community organizations, law enforcement agencies, businesses and youth development agencies.

- Tisha Johnson with the Street-Side Development Academy.

- Yusuf Shakur, Director of the Urban Youth Leadership Group, and a community activist, entrepreneur and former gang leader.

- Michael Williams, President of Orchards Children's Services.

All five of our interviewees said that gang involvement and criminal behavior can be significantly reduced when young people have options and opportunities. They agreed that the most important ways to combat young people's attraction to gangs are to:

- Create a brand that will be considered "cool" and compelling to youth and that rivals the allure of gang and thug glory.

- Provide skills that translate into employment and growth potential.

- Establish a safe place for youth to find refuge and be able to interact in a healthy, positive fashion, and where the admissions and membership policies demand nonviolent, harmonious behavior and attitudes.

- Combat the normalization of ignorance and violence with an uncompromising, multifaceted community approach.

Here are excerpts from the interviews:

Chief Anthony Holt: Our greatest challenge today is unemployment, not just for youth but also for their families in many instances. Many young men are responsible for providing for their families and thus, without jobs or opportunity, they subscribe to street-culture values. When a young person accepts that street code is acceptable, that means that engaging in criminal activity is acceptable … . [N]aturally, this means that the police are the enemy. We are taking steps to engage youth before the streets grab them. If we can direct them towards constructive mechanisms, we can steer them away from the street game. I work closely with Virgil [Taylor] and The Peace Project to be part of the rescue effort. The youth we engage learn that the job of the police is to protect and serve, not just Mr. and Mrs. Citizen but them as well. Through engagement, education, training and caring, I strive to have young people see me as an adult that cares about them, not just the firm hand of the law.

Effective programs ideally marry the prevention strategy or program to improvements in the community. For example, a program might organize community service projects that include cleaning local parks and planning community events for families and youth. A 4-H event could include maintaining a community garden to provide vegetables to a local school or to low-income individuals. For youth working on these types of projects, a prosocial identity can be formed within — and reinforced by — the community itself.

Train and Educate for Meaningful Employment

For some time now, the U.S. has been transitioning from a manufacturing-based to a service-based economy. Most of the jobs that are emerging in today's economy — in the computer, medical, biological sciences and engineering fields, for example — require a degree or vocational experience.[30] Even many manufacturing jobs require specialized training, and this has led to an increase in the proportion of jobs for youth that are low-paying and offer no opportunities for advancement. One study found that jobs that do not offer living wages or opportunities for upward mobility are not sufficient to keep youth out of gang activity.[31]

Young people may find it necessary to supplement their income through the informal economy (babysitting, cleaning houses, fixing cars) or through the illicit economy (selling stolen goods or drugs) to maintain a livelihood.[3] Because gangs provide a social network that can allow people to participate in an informal or illicit economy, joining a gang can seem like a positive move for some young people.

Virgil ("Al") Taylor: Our objective is to reduce the attraction to gangs in our communities. Gang members are part of our communities. Working to understand the needs of at-risk youth — youth involved in gangs and undesirable behavior — we strive to make them stakeholders. It is imperative that affected youth also understand their community and their history. Through engagement and involvement, we seek to make them part of the solution — reclaiming their environment and being community partners. Chief Holt and his department have been instrumental in helping to engage these young people. Efforts include providing connection between youth and members of the community who are providing jobs, training for jobs and educational opportunities — for example, Focus Hope, The Peace Project, YouthVille and Mayor's Time. Chief Holt demonstrates that authority figures participating in this project are not individuals for youth to dread or fear … they are not the enemy.

Tisha Johnson: The best prevention is to have something for youth. Our city is hurting; we have a major problem since these kids have nothing constructive to do. I work with young girls, young women, some of them living in poverty with no one helping them with anything. They've been in failing schools; most of the time, they've made poor choices because they haven't known any better … and then there are the gangsters. For a lot of young women, a gangsta' or gang life is the only possible answer. To make matters worse, a lot of these so-called programs have unrealistic expectations for kids … . [K]ids see their friends participate in programs that fail them; it makes them feel hopeless and they stop believing. I think the failure of some key programs is one of the reasons we got lots of youth not in school; they don't believe it means anything for them … they've given up hope.

Yusuf Shakur: I was in the gang. What lured me was … there was guys who made me feel like I was something special. They were my brothers; they looked out for me. If you want change [lowering the risk of gang-joining], you have to compete with that fact. I was the leader; I know how to get folks to join. You can't do anything if you don't understand how they live, what they do. That is why so many organizations, especially the church, can't connect. Unless you have somebody who talks the gang talk, somebody who has suffered the streets, comes from the same experience, got street creds … otherwise it don't work.

Michael Williams: Many of our children have suffered extreme neglect and/or abuse. Children that are taken from their biological parents often struggle with emotional health issues that are overlooked by the system. We have scores of well-intentioned adults working to help our kids, but the numbers are exasperating. The street understands how to engage kids, how to make them feel that they belong, how to utilize their abilities. A child that feels they are failing in school — who is hurt and angry — can often find acceptance on the street, where they only find scorn in school and with the rest of society … we need to learn what the street knows.

It is critical that practitioners and policymakers understand that today's economy renders many low-wage jobs insufficient for meeting basic needs. Today, even employed youth who are engaged in a positive development activity are finding gang membership attractive. Even being employed does not exempt a young person from the lure of gang life.[32]

Therefore, a comprehensive program to help prevent gang-joining might include providing alternative identities to 11- to 14-year-olds by teaching them skills and exposing them to vocational environments. Youth who are interested in getting into the medical field, for example, might begin by being taught basic CPR and first aid, or they might be encouraged to volunteer in local hospitals or senior citizen homes.

Ensure an Active Role for Law Enforcement

Law enforcement must take an active role in working with young people to counter the lure of gang membership. When young people's interactions with law enforcement contradict a perception that police officers are a punitive authority, it is possible to establish a relationship of respect and trust. This strategy of officers serving as positive role models is not a new paradigm, but it must be reinforced. When Chief Holt, of the Wayne State University Public Safety Department, interacts with youth, he is effectively showing them an example of how they can also be successful. "I have made myself the example for our law enforcement team and the young men who are marginally enticed to join gangs," he said. "I show them that the police do not consider them the enemy. We fight criminals.

[Young people's] choice is not to become part of any negative activity in our communities. We help them see a better choice."

Make Comprehensive Strategies Communitywide

In its Comprehensive Gang Model, the Justice Department's Office of Juvenile Justice and Delinquency Prevention promotes five strategies:

- Community involvement.

- Education and training programs.

- Social outreach.

- Supervision of gang-involved youth.

- Development of policies and procedures.

Several states have used the Comprehensive Gang Model to develop anti-gang strategies and programs. In Richmond, VA, activities focus on the general population of youth who are at risk for gang-joining and on their families. A number of prevention activities — the "Class Action" summer camp, sports and life-skills activities and training, a theater group that showcases issues faced by gang-involved youth, and after-school programs for elementary and middle-school youth — have the potential to connect youth with prosocial friends and enhance their sense of belonging while providing safe places to have fun and learn.

Such strategies can be complemented by programs aimed at reducing the economic attraction of gangs. For example, programs that teach English as a second language to Hispanic residents and that provide mentoring or tutoring can help at-risk youth see other options to gang-joining.

Programs that keep kids off the streets are also important. School athletics help make young people feel that they are part of a team or family, and going to practices and games gives them a safe environment. Groups like the Boys and Girls Clubs of America (BGCA) offer after-school activities. In fact, BGCA is known for its gang-prevention strategies that strive to decrease the attraction to gangs.

As the handbook, *Targeted Outreach: Boys and Girls Clubs of America's Approach to Gang Prevention and Intervention,* states:[33]

> [M]any Clubs are located in areas identified with high rates of gang activity. As such, they are in a prime spot to reach out to those youth and offer easily accessible services, which is crucial because transportation issues can often be a major impediment.

A 2002 study of BGCA found that most youth who had participated in BGCA programs for one year said they felt safer in the Club than they did in school. In turn, they frequented the Club often and participated in programs that fostered healthy youth developmental practices. Additionally, the research found that some youth showed an indication "of positive changes in gang, delinquent, school and relationship behaviors, and attitudes."[33]

Establishing alternatives to gang membership that direct and influence the behavior of at-risk youth should involve youth, parents, law enforcement, schools, churches, policymakers and researchers. To counter the attraction of gangs, it is important to create a "brand" in the community. This can be done by ensuring that activities are not only highly visible and easily accessible but also in touch with youth culture, language, norms, values and symbols.

Implementation Challenges and Strategies

There is no magic strategy for preventing youth from joining gangs. Young people get involved with gangs for various reasons, and the length of involvement varies from person to person. Therefore, it is important to understand that prevention strategies which focus exclusively on making youth aware of the risks associated with gang-joining may not be sufficient to address the problem.[2,29] Rather, prevention strategies must identify and provide healthy alternatives to the reasons that youth join a gang.

The following principles can form the foundation of a strong initiative to help prevent gang-joining:

- Create a community-based task force to assess the community's resources, including grass-roots organizations, faith-based organizations, schools, law enforcement, public health, youth, parents and guardians, local businesses, policymakers, funding sources and researchers.

- Select team members for a subcommittee to oversee the development of activities and services for at-risk youth; subcommittee members could include community groups, social agents, government, youth and the church — for example, someone from the juvenile division of the court, schools (teachers, counselors, administrators), church (youth minister) and youth (gang and nongang).

- Determine a facility to house the project; ideally, it should be centrally located in the community and able to satisfy particular requirements with respect to structure, cost, size and hours of operation.

- Seek creative funding sources to support innovative strategies; for example, YouthVille, a community agency in Detroit, offers programs that overlap with The Peace Project and also partners with Michigan State University's Outreach and Engagement component.

- Use innovative strategies to reach youth who are not integrated into traditional community institutions — such as those who do not attend school or church, or are otherwise left out of mainstream society — and ensure that the admissions policies for such programs emphasize nonviolent, harmonious behavior and attitudes.

- Train youth and adults to be gang-prevention representatives; this empowers residents to play an active role in investing in their community. Adults should work together to understand and address the needs of youth — for excitement, protection, support and status, for example — which, when unmet, can increase the attraction of gangs.

- Develop prosocial opportunities for youth to start building the foundation for a fulfilling career.

- Send constructive and positive messages — through social media, local news and radio media — that help to create a balance of information to decrease the attraction of gangs; these messages could be designed to counter the pro-gang messages that kids receive in the popular media and to raise the status of the positive alternatives that exist in the community.

Conclusion

It is very important that local decision-makers who determine which gang-prevention strategies are implemented — and the practitioners who actually implement them — have solid information regarding what gang attractions are at play in their community. A one-size-fits-all approach to tackling the issues of gang attraction and recruitment will not work when constructing local, state or federal policy. The ability to understand exactly what young people are facing — in their respective cities, communities and neighborhoods — is key.

Youth can perceive that gangs offer empowerment — and the attraction of gangs to some youth is enhanced if they feel that gang members recognize and listen to them. Gangs can fill the void left by dysfunctional families and poor education, and some youth see them as providing protection, support, excitement, money and status. When all else in society fails at the time in their lives when they are willing to take risks, young people can regard a gang as providing an alternative to just accepting the socioeconomic challenges in their environment.

To counter the attractions of gang culture, society must be ready to understand that the gang problem — which is a threat to our suburban, rural and urban communities — goes beyond issues of race, class and gender. (For more on this issue, see chapter 10.) To counter the attractiveness of gangs, society must provide alternatives to gangs that youth will value. This can best be done through comprehensive, community-based strategies and programs that provide an alternative to gangs in a young person's life.

About the Authors

Carl S. Taylor

Carl S. Taylor has worked with communities in the areas of youth violence, gangs and youth development for 40 years. Dr. Taylor's focus on urban gangs is rooted in the Michigan Gang Research Project. He has worked with the City of Detroit Mayor's office on youth-violence reduction, and he was a member of the Governor's Committee on Juvenile Justice. He received his Ph.D. from Michigan State University, where he currently teaches.

Pamela R. Smith

Pamela R. Smith manages the female study for the Michigan Gang Research Project. Her research interests include gangs, adolescent development, and youth-violence prevention and intervention programs. Ms. Smith is currently a doctoral candidate in the Department of Sociology at Michigan State University.

Endnotes

1. Kroger J. *Identity in Adolescence: The Balance Between Self and Other.* New York, NY: Routledge, 2004.

2. Decker SH, Curry GD. Addressing key features of gang membership: Measuring the involvement of young members. *J Crim Just.* 2000; 28:473-482.

3. Hagedorn JM. Gangs in the informal economy. In: Huff CR, ed., *Gangs in America III.* Thousand Oaks, CA: Sage Publications, 2002:101-120.

4. Padilla F. *The Gang as an American Enterprise.* New Brunswick, NJ: Rutgers University Press, 1992.

5. Shelden RG, Tracy SK, Brown W. *Youth Gangs in American Society.* Belmont, CA: Wadsworth, 2004.

6. Taylor CS. *Dangerous Society.* East Lansing, MI: Michigan State University Press, 1990.

7. Wiener V. *Winning the War Against Youth Gangs: A Guide for Teens, Families, and Communities.* Westport, CT: Greenwood Press, 1999.

8. Howell CJ. *Youth Gangs: An Overview.* Bulletin. Washington, DC: U.S. Department of Justice, Office of Justice Programs, Office of Juvenile Justice and Delinquency Prevention, 1998.

9. Pih KK, de la Rosa M, Rugh D, Mao K. Different strokes for different gangs? An analysis of capital among Latino and Asian gang members. *Sociol Perspect.* 2008; 51:473-494.

10. Brown WB. The fight for survival: African-American gang members and their families in a segregated society. *Juv Fam Court J.* 1998; 49:1-14.

11. Cureton SR. Introducing Hoover: I'll ride for you gangsta'. In: Huff CR, ed., *Gangs in America III.* Thousand Oaks, CA: Sage Publications, 2002:83-100.

12. Venkatesh S. Community-based interventions into street gang activity. *J Commun Psychol.* 1999; 27:551-568.

13. Peterson D, Taylor TJ, Esbensen F-A. Gang membership and violent victimization. *Justice Q.* 2004; 21:793-815.

14. Greene J, Pranis K. *Gang Wars: The Failure of Enforcement Tactics and the Need for Effective Public Safety Strategies.* Washington, DC: Justice Policy Institute, 2007.

15. Hill KG, Lui C, Hawkins JD. *Early Precursors of Gang Membership: A Study of Seattle Youth.* Bulletin. Washington, DC: U.S. Department of Justice, Office of Justice Programs, Office of Juvenile Justice and Delinquency Prevention, 2001.

16. Maxson C, Whitlock ML. Joining the gang: Gender differences in risk factors for gang membership. In: Huff CR, ed., *Gangs in America III.* Thousand Oaks, CA: Sage Publications, 2002:19-36.

17. Shelden RG, Tracy SK, Brown W. Girls and gangs: A review of recent research. *Juv Fam Court J.* 1996; 47:21-39.

18. Shakur Y. *The Window 2 My Soul.* Detroit, MI: Urban Guerrilla Publishing, 2008:31.

19. Miller J. The girls in the gang: What we've learned from two decades of research. In: Huff CR, ed., *Gangs in America III.* Thousand Oaks, CA: Sage Publications, 2002:183.

20. Anderson E. *Code of the Street: Decency, Violence, and the Moral Life of the Inner City.* New York, NY: W.W. Norton, 1999.

21. Peterson D, Taylor TJ, Esbensen F-A. Gang membership and violent victimization. *Justice Q.* 2004; 21:793-815.

22. Taylor TJ, Freng A, Esbensen F-A, Peterson D. Youth gang membership and serious violent victimization: The importance of lifestyles and routine activities. *J Interpers Viol.* 2008; 23:1441-1464.

23. Esbensen F-A, Huizinga D, Weiher AW. 1993. Gang and non-gang youth: Differences in explanatory factors. *J Contemp Crim Just.* 1993; 9:94-116.

24. Thornberry TP, Krohn MD, Lizotte AJ, Chard-Wierschem D. The role of juvenile gangs in facilitating delinquent behavior. *J Res Crime Delinq.* 1993; 301:55-87.

25. Taylor CS, Lerner RM, von Eye A, Bobek PL, Balsano AB, Dowling E, Anderson PM. Positive individual and social behavior among gang and nongang African American male adolescents. *J Adolesc Res.* 2003; 18:548-574.

26. Taylor CS, Lerner RM, von Eye A, Balsano AB, Dowling EM, Anderson PM, Bobek DL, Bjelobrk D. Individual and ecological assets and positive developmental trajectories among gang and community-based organization youth. In: Lerner RM, Taylor CS, von Eye A, eds., *Pathways to Positive Development Among Diverse Youth.* In: Noam G, series ed., *New Directions for Youth Development: Theory, Practice, and Research,* Vol. 95. San Francisco, CA: Jossey-Bass, 2002:57-72.

27. Taylor CS, Lerner RM, von Eye A, Bobek DL, Balsano AB, Dowling E, Anderson PM. Positive individual and social behavior among gang and non-gang African American male adolescents. *J Adolesc Res.* 2003; 18:548-574.

28. Taylor CS, Lerner RM, von Eye A, Bobek D, Balsano AB, Dowling E, Anderson PM. Internal and external developmental assets among African American male gang members. *J Adolesc Res.* 2004; 19:303-322.

29. Taylor CS, Smith PR, Taylor VA, Lerner RM, von Eye A, Balsano AB, Dowling E, Anderson PM, Banik R, Almerigi J. Individual and ecological assets and thriving among African American adolescent male gang and community-based organization members: A report from wave 3 of the "Overcoming the Odds" study. *J Early Adolesc.* 2005; 25:77-93.

30. U.S. Department of Labor, Bureau of Labor Statistics. *Occupational Outlook Handbook 2010-11.* Washington, DC: U.S. Department of Labor, Bureau of Labor Statistics, 2010.

31. Sassen S. The global city: One setting for new types of gang work. In: Sassen S, ed., *Gangs in the Global City: Alternatives to Traditional Criminology.* Chicago, IL: University of Illinois Press, 2007:97-119.

32. Gandara P, Contreras F. *The Latino Education Crisis.* Cambridge, MA: Harvard University Press, 2009.

33. Arbreton AJ, McClanahan WS. *Targeted Outreach: Boys and Girls Clubs of America's Approach to Gang Prevention and Intervention.* Philadelphia, PA; Public/Private Ventures, 2002.

What Is the Role of Public Health in Gang-Membership Prevention?

Tamara M. Haegerich, James Mercy and Billie Weiss

- Gang membership has been viewed as a criminal justice problem rather than a public health problem. The public health approach to monitoring trends, researching risk and protective factors, evaluating interventions, and supporting the dissemination and implementation of evidence-based strategies is an important complement to law enforcement strategies.

- Often, communities do not have a comprehensive strategy to address gang membership that includes public health departments. Interdisciplinary collaborations among partners in multiple sectors such as health, education, criminal justice, labor and urban planning are critical. Because of its focus on enhancing community wellness, public health is uniquely positioned to convene partners, encourage collaboration across disciplines and sectors, and develop and evaluate comprehensive strategies.

- Key challenges to building and expanding the role of public health in gang-membership prevention include a lack of focus on primary prevention, an underdeveloped system for supporting and sustaining preventive interventions and programs, a lack of uniform definitions and data systems to adequately monitor the problem, and limited attention to the underlying environmental and social forces that drive gang involvement.

- Fundamental operational changes in agencies and systems, and coordination of funding streams, are needed to facilitate collaboration across sectors and generate sufficient resources to monitor gang membership adequately, implement prevention strategies, and evaluate those strategies' effectiveness. Because there is limited evidence of effectiveness for prevention programs, to be successful we must place a high priority on using collaboration and coordinating resources to identify effective prevention programs and policies and to build a body of knowledge to guide future policies and programs.

In Brief

Communities have most often turned to law enforcement to address the burden of gang membership and violence, yet public health has much to offer for the prevention of death, injuries, and other health and social consequences associated with youth involvement in gangs. Public health can contribute to the development of definitions, data elements and data systems necessary to adequately understand the magnitude of gang-joining, membership and violence. For example, we highlight the contributions of the National Violent Death Reporting System, a state-based surveillance system that links data from health and law enforcement sources on violent deaths, to understanding gang-related homicide and points for intervention. Furthermore, with its scientific epidemiological approach, public health can assist in identifying the factors and conditions that place youth at risk for gang involvement or, alternatively, lead youth away from gang involvement. By learning about risk and protection, prevention strategies can be developed that change these processes and, in turn, result in positive outcomes for youth.

We provide some examples of the types of prevention strategies that are likely to be successful in preventing youth-gang membership and describe efforts under way to identify new strategies. For example, programs that have been shown to be effective in preventing youth violence, highlighted by the Blueprints for Healthy Youth Development Initiative, are currently being adapted to address gang membership. We describe the importance of rigorously evaluating these adapted programs, in addition to newly developed prevention programs, and then disseminating proven programs for implementation in communities. We also review public health efforts to further the implementation of strategies based on the best available evidence by synthesizing the scientific information about prevention, building the capacity of communities to implement prevention strategies through training and technical assistance, and forming multisector collaborations to develop an infrastructure to deliver prevention strategies.

To achieve these goals, public health must overcome key challenges, including a less than adequate focus on primary prevention, and a lack of comprehensive strategies in communities to address gang-membership and gang-violence prevention that integrate primary prevention and community development with law enforcement approaches. Strengthened by its integration of multiple complementary disciplines, public health can make valuable contributions to overcoming these challenges through efforts such as strengthening data systems, developing the evidence base for effective programs and policies, and convening partners for prevention.

Youth involvement in gangs and violence has traditionally been viewed as a criminal justice problem, that is, as a public safety issue to be addressed by police and the legal system reactively, after problems occur, rather than a public health issue to be addressed proactively, before problems occur, by multiple sectors that influence health (including health and human services, education, housing, labor and urban development as well as justice).[1] Yet, gang-joining and gang membership take their toll on public health through violence that results in death, injuries, long-term disability, and related health care and psychosocial costs.

Youth are often the victims of violence. In 2010, the latest year for which mortality data are available, 4,828 young people ages 10 to 24 were murdered (an average of 13 youth each day, resulting from both gang- and non-gang-related events).[2] Yet, deaths are only part of the problem. More than 738,000 assault-related injuries young people ages 10 to 24 were treated in emergency departments in 2010.[2] Although the number of youth victims of gang violence cannot be determined by these statistics, based on death certificates and hospital data, other studies have illustrated that gang-involved youth are many times more likely to be victimized than youth who are not in a gang.[3]

The Bureau of Justice Statistics reports approximately 1,000 gang killings each year; this is likely an underestimate because the definition of "gang" varies across jurisdictions, in addition to the difficulties in determining whether a crime is gang-related.[4] Gang members perpetrate a disproportionate amount of violence at both the individual and the community levels. For example, the Rochester Youth Development Study and the Denver Youth Survey showed that gang members were involved in more than 80 percent of serious and violent crimes committed, although the percentage of youth in the samples that were gang members was much smaller (less than 20-30 percent).[5] A study of homicides in Los Angeles in 1993 and 1994 showed that four out of five adolescent homicides involved gang participants or gang motives. Furthermore, compared to homicides with adult participants, homicides with adolescent participants were more than twice as likely to include gang dynamics as a precipitating factor.[6] Communities with a large number of in gangs in a concentrated area experience a greater homicide burden than other communities.[7]

Injury and death are only some of the impacts on health: Youth involved in gangs engage in a variety of other health-risk behaviors, such as substance use and high-risk sexual behavior.[5,8,9,10]

Exposure to gangs and violence in a community can lead to high levels of chronic stress and mental health problems among youth that may, in turn, lead to chronic health conditions.[11,12] Violence and gang membership are also associated more broadly with social and economic determinants of health, such as community structural characteristics (for example, concentrated disadvantage, economic opportunity and property value) and community social processes (such as the willingness of people to be involved in the community or to help others).[13,14] It is unclear whether social characteristics and structural processes influence gang violence, vice versa, or both. It is likely that the mechanism is reciprocal.

The Public Health Perspective

Public health plays a critical role in addressing gang membership and violence through its multidisciplinary perspective, which values applied science, an understanding of the social determinants of health, and utilization and mobilization of the best evidence from epidemiologic studies for prevention. The Centers for Disease Control and Prevention (CDC) has focused on youth violence as a public health issue since the 1980s. The Division of Violence Prevention (DVP), in the Injury Center at CDC, emphasizes the primary prevention of violence perpetration: that is, stopping violence before it starts. DVP has a commitment to developing and applying a rigorous science base, including monitoring and tracking violent trends, researching risk and protective factors, using that information to develop and rigorously evaluate prevention strategies, and disseminating the most promising new strategies. A cross-cutting perspective is employed that includes multiple disciplines and multiple sectors. Finally, there is a focus on the health of groups of people and entire communities (population health), not just the health of individuals.

Public health includes the work of health and mental health professionals in state and local health departments, social service agencies, and community-based organizations as well as the work of researchers who have adopted the public health approach to prevention. It is important to recognize, however, that because of their cross-disciplinary nature, public health approaches also include the prevention work of professionals from multiple sectors (for example, health, justice and education) and multiple disciplines (for example, medicine, epidemiology, psychology, sociology, criminology, urban studies and economics), so public health can serve as an effective convener within communities. One of the strengths of public health is its established record of convening partners from different sectors and disciplines, and building community coalitions to advance prevention efforts in many areas of health. Its success in bringing multiple perspectives to the table may be due, in part, to the view that public health is oriented toward providing helpful services that enhance community wellness without focusing on retribution or punishment. Hence, public health can be quite effective at bringing a neutral, community-friendly atmosphere to collaboration.

There has been increasing national recognition of the role of public health in violence prevention, and the prevention of gang membership and gang violence in turn. This recognition is evidenced by the 2001 Surgeon General's *Report on Youth Violence,* the Healthy People 2010 and 2020 national health objectives, reports from the World Health Organization[15] — including the 2011 *Violence Prevention: An Invitation to Intersectoral Action*[16] — and policy statements released by professional societies such as the Academy of Pediatrics and the American Public Health Association, and the work of national advocacy organizations and think tanks, such as the Advancement Project and the Justice Policy Institute (see the sidebar, "Recognizing the Role of Public Health").

What, specifically, is the public health approach to youth violence? The steps include: (1) describing and monitoring the problem; (2) identifying the factors that place youth at risk for, or protect youth from, engaging in gang membership and violence; (3) development and testing of prevention approaches; and (4) dissemination, implementation and widespread adoption of prevention approaches. The illustration "The Public Health Approach to Gang-Membership and Gang-Violence Prevention" (see next page) shows the public health approach to gang-membership and gang-violence prevention.[17]

Although this approach has been applied to the prevention of violence, we believe that it can be equally applied to the prevention of gang-joining and gang membership, although there may be some unique considerations (see the sidebar "What Youth- and Gang-Violence Strategies May

The Public Health Approach to Gang-Membership and Gang-Violence Prevention

Disseminate prevention strategies

Develop and evaluate prevention strategies

- Assists in ensuring widespread adoption of strategies that work.
- Includes building capacity of a community through training and technical assistance.

Identify risk and protective factors

- Assists in determining what works best in preventing gang membership.
- Conducted by comparing individuals or communities exposed to a prevention approach with those not exposed using a strong research design (for example, experimental, quasi-experimental).

Describe the problem

- Assists in understanding the characteristics of individuals, families and communities that place youth at risk for, or protect them from engaging in, gang membership and violence.
- Conducted through longitudinal, cross-sectional, ecological and qualitative studies.

- Assists in determining how many youth are gang-involved and engage in violence, where activity is occurring in the community, and how rates of activity change over time.
- Conducted through community surveys, compiling data on homicides and other incidents through public health (for example, coroner, hospital) and law enforcement records.

Problem   **Response**

SOURCE: Adapted from Mercy JA, Rosenberg ML, Powell KE, Bromme CV, Roper WL. Public health policy for preventing violence. *Health Aff.* 1993; Winter:7-29.

Teach Us About Preventing Gang-Joining"). Note that the public health model has some similarities to the problem-oriented policing SARA model[18] (see chapter 4). The steps in the SARA model include: **S**canning (identifying and prioritizing problems), **A**nalysis (utilization of data sources to inform response plans), **R**esponse (development and implementation of interventions), and **A**ssessment (evaluating how well the response works). The SARA model highlights the importance of using data to identify, implement and evaluate appropriate policing interventions.

However, the public health model and approach more broadly provides a greater emphasis on primary prevention, the routine inclusion of multiple sectors and disciplines in addressing problems, the use of strategies that affect the health of entire populations, identifying risk and protective factors to inform prevention approaches, and

facilitating the widespread adoption of programs, practices and policies. Next, we illustrate how each of the public health principles can be applied to gang-membership and gang-violence prevention.

Public Health Principle #1: Monitoring the Problem

To understand the magnitude of the problems of gang membership and gang violence, it is critical to have agreed-upon definitions of gangs, gang-joining and gang membership (see Introduction). Equally important are the development and maintenance of systems to track the prevalence of gang membership — where gang saturation in a community is the strongest, where and when gang-involved violence and related behaviors take place — and the health consequences of such violence and behaviors, including injury

Recognizing the Role of Public Health

The role of public health in preventing violence has long been recognized. The World Health Organization has recently published reports that highlight the magnitude and impact of violence worldwide, the opportunities for prevention, and the crucial role of public health.[15, 16] Here are a few examples of U.S. agencies, professional associations and expert groups that have highlighted the role of public health in the last few years:

• **Surgeon General's Report on Youth Violence:** This landmark report designated youth violence as a public health issue and described how gang membership increases the risk for violence among youth.[19]

• **Healthy People 2010 and 2020:** This U.S. Department of Health and Human Services framework provides national health objectives surrounding the most preventable threats to health and includes multiple objectives related to youth violence, illustrating a focus on violence as a public health issue.

• **American Academy of Pediatrics Policy Statements:** These policy statements, issued in 1999 and 2009, discussed the role of the pediatrician in youth violence prevention, focusing on the need to include violence prevention in routine health maintenance and preventive care practice.[20]

• **American Public Health Association Policy Statement on Youth Violence:** This policy statement, issued in 2009, promotes the importance of building public health infrastructure for youth violence prevention, highlighting that "most cities do not have a comprehensive strategy to address youth violence, and public health departments are not generally included

in current city strategies," but that "public health is uniquely positioned to convene, collaborate, and coordinate the multidisciplinary teams to work together to prevent youth violence."[21]

• **Advancement Project:** In 2008, this civil rights law, policy, and communications "action tank" developed gang reduction approaches for Los Angeles. *A Call to Action: A Case for a Comprehensive Solution to L.A.'s Gang Violence Epidemic* (commissioned by the Los Angeles City Council's Ad Hoc Committee on Gang Violence and Youth Development) recommended a sustained political mandate on the part of leadership to reduce gang activity and violence, and a comprehensive strategy of prevention, intervention, community development and investment, and community policing and strategic suppression.[22]

• **Justice Policy Institute:** Dedicated to promoting effective solutions to social problems and ending reliance on incarceration through accessible research, public education, and communications advocacy, the Justice Policy Institute published *Gang Wars* in 2007, which recommended that more funding be directed toward gang-membership prevention strategies implemented by health and human service agencies because — compared to law enforcement suppression programs — health and human service programs focus on long-term solutions to social problems, reducing risk and building competencies. The report stated that such programs are also evidence-based and cost-effective, and that health and human service agencies have a good track record of monitoring the outcomes of prevention programs.[23]

and death. These data can be obtained from population-based surveys as well as existing data sources such as police reports, health records and death records. With its strong foundation in epidemiological methods, public health is well-suited for the development of standard definitions, data elements, and surveillance systems to track

prevalence and trends. It is critical, however, to share data across sectors to maximize the potential for the data to be used to inform practice.

The National Youth Gang Survey is conducted by the National Gang Center with support from the Office of Juvenile Justice and Delinquency

Prevention (OJJDP). Since 1995, the survey has gathered gang data from more than 2,500 law enforcement agencies each year. Respondents answer questions about youth gangs, defined as "a group of youths or young adults in your jurisdiction that you or other responsible persons in your agency or community are willing to identify as a 'gang.'" These data have been used to estimate the number, characteristics and distribution of gangs by area; trends in the number of gangs and gang members; gang-member migration; and the number of gang-related homicides and other violent crimes. The survey documents a surge in gang problems in recent years, following a decline from the mid-1990s to early in this century.[24] Questions have been raised, however, about the reliability and validity of these data, given that the reports are from law enforcement agencies that use different definitions of "gang member" and different strategies for tracking gang involvement, reports of gang involvement are subject to local political considerations, and reports include only those membership ties that rise to the attention of law enforcement officers.

CDC's National Violent Death Reporting System (NVDRS) is an example of how health data have been integrated with criminal justice data to provide detailed information on violent deaths, including gang-related homicides. NVDRS is a state-based surveillance system (in 18 states as of 2012, with a goal of all 50 states) that links data on violent deaths (that is, homicide and suicide) from law enforcement, coroners and medical examiners, vital statistics, and crime laboratories. By combining these data sources, a more comprehensive picture of the circumstances surrounding violent deaths can be achieved, extending beyond the narrow context that these data sources provide individually.[25, 26] NVDRS data can provide insight into the points for intervention and, in turn, improve violence-prevention efforts. Each homicide record in NVDRS includes a detailed narrative of the incident and information about victims, suspects, the relationship between the victim and the suspect, the circumstances surrounding the death, and the method of injury. The records in NVDRS are incident-based so that multiple forms of violence that occur as part of one incident can be linked together (for example, multiple homicides or homicide followed by suicide). One of the incident circumstances coded is whether a homicide is gang-related; this is indicated if the medical examiner or law enforcement report

indicates that the homicide resulted, or is suspected to have resulted, from gang rivalry or gang activity.

In 2002, CDC funded the New Jersey Department of Health and Senior Services to participate in the NVDRS. The Office of Injury Surveillance and Prevention, Center for Health Statistics, Public Health Services Branch, has used NJVDRS data to develop a measure of "gang and gang-like homicide," which includes gang homicides as defined by NVDRS in addition to homicides that have characteristics similar to gang homicides in terms of weapon used, location, and types of suspects and victims. Using this new measure of gang-style homicides, NJVDRS data were used to determine the number of homicides and map their location through Geographic Information Systems (GIS) technology. They determined that the increases in homicides in the state were due to an increase in gang-like homicides. These maps are being used to inform police departments so that violence-reduction efforts can be targeted to affected locales.[27]

These two examples illustrate the benefits of collecting consistent, longitudinal data from multiple sources to adequately understand the complexity of the gang problem. By adequately understanding the nature of the problem over time, we are better able to direct prevention strategies to the most appropriate contexts and settings. (For more information about how data sources have provided an understanding of the prevalence and trends of gang membership and gang violence in the United States, see chapter 1.)

Public Health Principle #2: Identifying Risk and Protective Factors

The second step of the public health approach focuses on identifying the factors that place youth at risk for engaging in gang membership. It also focuses on identifying factors that may protect youth from engaging in gang membership and gang violence. By learning about risk and protection, we can develop prevention strategies that change these processes and, in turn, result in positive outcomes for youth. Risk and protective factors exist at all levels of the "social ecology": the individual level (such as personal characteristics of youth), the relationship level (for example, characteristics of relationships between youth and their caregivers and other adults in the community); the community level (such as characteristics of youth's neighborhoods and schools) and the societal level (for example, characteristics of social norms and policies). The figure below depicts the relationships within the social ecological model.

One method for measuring risk and protective factors is surveying youth, their families and other influential adults (teachers) about youth themselves, their relationships, and the environments that they grow up in. Below, we review some key self-report studies that have contributed to our understanding of youth risk. However, for a detailed review of risk and protective factors for gang membership and gang violence, and using multiple methodologies across the developmental phases, see chapter 5.

Longitudinal studies represent one of the most advanced approaches to determining risk and protective factors because of the ability of these studies to determine the effects of early risk and protective factors on later behavior, including gang membership, rather than examining behavior at one point in time after gang-joining. In the 1990s, the Office of Juvenile Justice and Delinquency Prevention funded a series of longitudinal studies to determine the causes and correlates (that is, the risk and protective factors) of serious delinquency, violence and substance use of youth, including factors at the individual, family, peer, school and community levels. The Causes

and Correlates studies included the Denver Youth Survey, the Pittsburgh Youth Study and the Rochester Youth Development study; they focused on assessing youth from childhood into adolescence and early adulthood.[28] In addition to studying delinquency and violence more broadly, these studies focused on gang membership and gang violence. Key findings from these studies indicate that early conduct problems, violence, delinquency, substance use, involvement with delinquent peers, beliefs that involvement in delinquent behavior is normal and acceptable, poor school performance and poor parent-child relationships predict gang membership.[5,8]

Additional longitudinal studies — including the Montreal Longitudinal Study and the Seattle Social Development Project — have complementary findings, showing that the following factors predict gang-joining: early engagement in violence, oppositional behavior (for example, questioning rules and authority, and refusal to comply), low popularity, inattention/hyperactivity, early substance use, low academic achievement, learning disabilities, easy availability of substances in the neighborhood, a large number of youth in trouble in the neighborhood, and only one parent or other adult in the household.[29, 30, 31]

Much of the research has focused on factors that increase the risk for violence rather than for gang-joining. Therefore, we know much more about what increases the likelihood that youth

What Youth- and Gang-Violence Strategies May Teach Us About Preventing Gang-Joining

Some of what we have learned from the youth-violence field may be applied to gang-membership prevention, but it is critical that the contextual and social factors that influence gang presence in a community — such as residential instability, changes in population composition and culture, economic deprivation, relative social isolation, presence of drug markets, social identity and social networks — be considered in developing strategies to help prevent kids from joining a gang. We know, for example, that the presence of gangs in a community poses unique risks to youth that must be considered beyond the traditional factors considered in the youth-violence field, such as the degree of saturation of gangs in a community, and gang membership of family relatives.[5]

As this chapter discusses, the public health model may be a fruitful approach for the prevention of gang violence in addition to gang-joining and gang membership. However, although there is a strong history behind the public health approach to youth violence, gang-joining and gang-membership prevention have not received as much attention from the public health community. Gang-membership prevention efforts in many communities have focused primarily on criminal justice approaches.

This may be because of limited resources, insufficient access to health data, a lack of collaboration across sectors, and a feeling that something must be done quickly and visibly to address existing high levels of gang violence. Nonetheless, many of the public health approaches used to understand youth violence can provide insight into preventing youth from joining gangs.

For example, some factors that increase risk for violent behavior are shared among violent gang-involved and violent non-gang-involved youth, such as attitudes and beliefs about violence, early conduct problems, association with aggressive peers, poor school performance, family poverty, lack of parental monitoring, and neighborhood disorganization.[34] It is clear that, compared with non-gang-involved youth, youth involved in gangs tend to have a greater number of risk factors, and risk factors at multiple levels — individual, family and community — of the social ecology.[35] Although additional research is needed to confirm this hypothesis, approaches to evidence-based public health prevention that address the important risk factors for youth violence may also be effective at reducing risk for gang-joining and gang-related violence.

will become involved in violence than we do about what increases the likelihood that youth will become involved in a gang. Furthermore, of the research that has focused on gang-joining, most studies have investigated the factors that *increase* risk. The factors that protect youth from joining gangs and engaging in gang violence are less well-understood.[32] An emerging area of scientific research is suggesting that policies and programs for youth-violence prevention should focus on both reducing risk and promoting protective influences in communities.[32,33] Factors that have the potential to be protective include, for example, pre- and perinatal exposures (for example, adequate prenatal care, healthy behaviors during pregnancy, and early parenting support), family environment (such as safe, stable and nurturing relationships without maltreatment; consistency in discipline and supervision; and positive role modeling), school factors (for example,

connectedness with school and achievement), peer relationships (such as bonding with prosocial peers and support from friends), community environment (including advantaged socioeconomic context and high collective efficacy), and cultural factors (such as a value for prosocial conflict resolution or for a morality of cooperation).[32]

Public Health Principle #3: Developing and Evaluating Interventions

Once risk and protective factors for gang membership have been identified, programs that address these factors need to be developed, implemented and evaluated. Prevention programs can focus on primary, secondary or tertiary prevention. In lay terms, as described by Philadelphia youth in a meeting with city officials, primary prevention occurs "up front," before gang membership and violence begins; secondary prevention occurs "in the thick" of the problem, when youth are at high risk; and tertiary prevention occurs in the "aftermath" to deal with the consequences. Prevention strategies can be implemented for all youth in a population regardless of risk (universal populations), for youth who are at risk for gang membership (selected populations), or for youth who are already deeply engaged in gang life (indicated populations). Regardless of the timing and targets of prevention efforts, programs need to address the key risk and protective factors for gang-joining. Only by addressing these factors can prevention programs be expected to be effective. It is critical to focus on individual- and family-level factors, in addition to broader community-level factors, either through multi-component programs or through separate but complementary strategies that focus on different levels of the social ecology.

One example of a multicomponent, community-wide approach for youth development that could potentially be protective against gang member-ship — given its focus on the risk factors that predict gang membership — is the Harlem Chil-dren's Zone, initiated by Geoffrey Canada. The approach has been widely cited, although under-evaluated, and represents a variety of integrated programs that have been implemented within an area of Harlem.[36] The programs address all levels of the social ecology — for families with children at all developmental levels — creating a preven-tion pipeline and safety net for children. Programs include, among others, Baby College parenting workshops for parents of children ages 3 and younger, Peacemakers social development pro-grams for elementary and middle school children, an Employment and Technology Center for high school-age youth, and a variety of other family and community health programs to address pov-erty, truancy, and mental health and substance use problems. It is yet to be determined whether this program prevents gang-joining and gang membership; this should be a priority for future evaluation efforts.

Overall, programmatic efforts have been focused more on *violence* than on *gang-joining* and *gang membership*. Furthermore, a greater priority has been placed on developing and evaluating *intervention* approaches than on *prevention* ap-proaches. Therefore, we know much more about how to intervene in youth violence after it starts than about how to prevent gang-joining and gang

membership before it begins. However, we can learn from public health programmatic efforts that have focused on the risk factors related to gang-joining and gang membership and on the prevention of violence that often co-occurs with gang membership. Two programs that illustrate the potential of the public health approach are highlighted below: Barrios Unidos in Santa Cruz, CA, and CeaseFire in Chicago, IL.

Barrios Unidos is an example of a primary pre-vention approach that uses both universal and selected strategies and emphasizes the commu-nity-level factors that contribute to youth joining gangs and perpetrating violence (see http://www.barriosunidos.net/). Daniel "Nane" Alejandrez — the Executive Director of Barrios Unidos, who has been conducting gang-intervention and gang-membership prevention work since 1977 — describes the approach as one that "affects people's lives and their health; it affects them emotionally, economically, every part of their life."

Based in Santa Cruz, CA, Barrios Unidos was founded to promote peace and justice and to end gang warfare among inner-city ethnic youth. It is an evolving grass-roots organization that focuses on culture and spirituality to support at-risk youth, provides ways to suppress and end gang war-fare, and offers a promising model for building healthy and vibrant multicultural communities. Chapters have been established in San Francisco, Venice-Los Angeles, Salinas and San Diego, CA; Washington, DC; Yakima, WA; San Antonio, TX; Phoenix, AZ; and Chicago, IL. Programmatic efforts include leadership and human capital development, community economic develop-ment, civic participation and community mobiliza-tion, cultural arts and recreational activities, and coalition building.

For example, in Santa Cruz, the youth program of-fers leadership development training to selected youth to develop skills that foster personal and civic responsibility, and self-improvement pro-grams that empower youth to serve as agents of social change in the community. These activities are complemented with vocational counseling and job training. Youth are selected by program staff for leadership development training based on leadership qualities displayed by the youth as they mature through early childhood and family programs in the community. Although evaluation

IN THE SPOTLIGHT: The Advancement Project

▶ INTERVIEW WITH CONNIE RICE

Connie Rice is a civil rights lawyer and co-director of the Advancement Project, an innovative civil rights law, policy and communications "action tank" that advances universal opportunity and a just democracy in America for those left behind. In 2005, the Advancement Project began a three-phase Gang Activity Reduction Strategy Project in the city of Los Angeles and produced a highly regarded report, *A Call to Action: A Case for a Comprehensive Solution to L.A.'s Gang Violence Epidemic*, which was commissioned by the City Council's Ad Hoc Committee on Gang Violence and Youth Development. The report recommended that the city would have to "replace its current efforts with a comprehensive, multi-sectored, multi-disciplined, schools-centered, and highly coordinated, carefully targeted, neighborhood-based gang and violence reduction system" that would "have to use the public health, child development, and community development models — approaches designed to reverse the underlying driving conditions that spawn and fuel neighborhood violence problems of which gangs are one factor."[22]

Ms. Rice was a critical force behind development of the gang-reduction strategy in Los Angeles. We asked her to reflect on her experience and discuss what role she sees for public health and public health professionals in gang-membership and gang-violence prevention.

How did you begin recognizing some of the advantages of the public health approach?

As a civil rights lawyer, I was winning my cases, but I was sending my clients home to communities where kids were dodging bullets and still dying. I learned that law is not the answer. It wasn't a matter of civil rights, or enforcement, or fully changing the culture of entertainment. Gang membership and violence was an entrenched problem and was complex. We needed another paradigm, or lens, to address this problem. The public health perspective gave us a fresh start. Because the health professionals were leading, everybody could come to the table without the baggage of the past. Everybody was starting out at the same place, and we could begin as partners as opposed to past opponents.

You use an analogy of fighting malaria to help understand public health principles that apply to preventing gang membership and youth violence. Can you explain that?

Epidemiologists have such a great vocabulary and great concepts. It makes it easy for people to understand how they have to change their thinking. For example, if you have a malaria epidemic, you can keep swatting mosquitoes, but this isn't going to end the epidemic. You have to use a vector control model and go after all the vectors that cause

a disease at an epidemic level. If you don't, you are going to be swatting mosquitoes forever and people are going to keep dying of the disease. So instead, you have to go to the source of the disease and its widespread nature. You have to change norms and behaviors. You have to pass out nets. You have to drain the swamp. You have to make sure the mosquitoes aren't multiplying. With malaria, people get this. Epidemiology, public health concepts and public health terminology really translate well to the problem of gang violence because people can start to think about violence as a disease, as an epidemic.

What are some specific roles that public health professionals can play in preventing gang membership and gang violence?

In terms of research, policy and best practices, there is still a lot we don't know. We need to convince policymakers to move to action based on experiments that document what works and does not work with different populations of kids, levels of membership and types of violence. Public health research expertise is critical because we don't know a lot about what works. If we don't get the right menu of choices, we can't make policymakers understand which programs and policies to put in place. Because there are a lot of unknowns, gang membership and violence is a scary issue, politically. So you have to have the public health sector with you to help you

is challenging, Barrios Unidos is committed to more intensive evaluation of its programs. A qualitative study of the youth program conducted by the Ceres Policy Institute revealed that health care, academic commitment and community engagement improved. Mr. Alejandrez explains, "The children involved were going out into the community and were more involved in the community, and the parents were more involved and they had their own group. Cultural and spiritual improvement was marked." Preventing violence is a struggle in impoverished, disenfranchised communities. The communities within which Barrios

Unidos operates have been neglected for generations, resources have not been available to provide the jobs that are needed, and approaches to violence have been very law enforcement-based. Yet, Barrios Unidos has made a commitment to continuing activities and securing further funding for prevention. "What we are doing here is developing the foundation for peace in our young people," Mr. Alejandrez continued. "We're still trying to undo what's been there for generations. Since we started, foundations have learned a lot about communities. People understand cultural and spiritual work in a way that they didn't, years design programs and policies, carry them out, and evaluate them. This is an area that needs to be driven by the experts.

What are the primary drivers behind gang membership and what do you see as promising strategies to prevent gang-joining?

We haven't really attacked membership directly — we've just been stabilizing the violence. But because the public health approach focuses on changing norms, attitudes and behaviors, similar approaches may be used to prevent gang membership and to prevent gang violence. The idea of reducing membership is like a tug-of-war. Do you attack the gang? Do you directly intervene and close off the entrance ramps to the gang? Do you make resources available for the exit ramp? Or do you indirectly deflect membership by creating another center of gravity that is more attractive? Attractiveness of the gang culture is what is important. Adolescents have to go through a passage into adulthood and they have to declare their independence, and they have to find power and validation in their independence. We can either find a positive way to affirm their independence and their passage from adolescence into adulthood or they will create one for themselves. And they have created it — in gangs. When we don't give them a positive way to become young adults, they find their power — their own way — that validates the reality they

face. We have to make a more attractive alternative available and without directly attacking the gang, which may reinforce the power of the gang. So gang-membership prevention is changing the way youth think of themselves, how they imagine their passage into adulthood, and how they get power. As long as the gang model is out there, we['d] better be able to offer something that reduces the attraction of gang membership, and that creates a different norm of power for the kids that is safer, more rewarding, gives them money, and gives the ability to stand on their own two feet. We need different sets of strategies to get kids out who are in, and to keep the kids out who are in danger of being recruited. We need to try some experiments and see what works for what kinds of kids and what kinds of gangs.

In addition to focusing strategies on individual-level change by directly intervening with youth, what do we need to do at the community and societal levels?

It is critical to get people to participate in a holistic strategy, but operational changes are needed to cross jurisdictions. It is a leap for agencies to rethink their missions. There is every reason in the world not to cooperate. We need to force a culture change in bureaucratic norms, but the incentives are all wrong. I have come to the conclusion that it's going to have to be done through money.

Funding should not be available for initiatives unless you put teams together that are fully collaborative and you have outsiders evaluate the level of collaboration. Otherwise, the barriers won't come down, and the silos won't open up. We can get jurisdictions to work together on initiatives, if there is funding available for collaborative work on specific projects. Further[more], the work of the civic and private sector is not enough. We need to produce changes at the ecological and systems levels. We need to get government to engage in a smarter way. This is the new horizon.

It seems as if you are very personally invested in preventing gang membership and gang violence. Why is that?

I became involved in gang-violence prevention because I didn't have a choice. I am a civil rights lawyer, but I learned that the law is not the answer. There are no civil rights without the right to safety. If there is no freedom from violence, there are no other freedoms. All rights are based on the unspoken freedom of being free from violence. If kids can't walk to school safely, stay in school safely, get to their tutor safely, and walk home safely, no other promises we make to them are viable. The agenda needs to end the epidemic of violence and create safe environments. To have that opportunity is their right — that is their path to freedom.

ago. We are talking about generations and healing in a way that folks seem to understand now."

The CeaseFire project, from the Chicago Project for Violence Prevention, is a program that can best be described as being implemented "in the thick" with selected populations (now known as "Cure Violence;" see http://www.cureviolence. org).[37] It is grounded in disease-control and behavior-change strategies. "There is a need to have a scientific approach and understanding. We need to look at behaviors, how they are formed, how they are maintained, and how they

spread," says Gary Slutkin, Executive Director and Professor of Epidemiology and International Health at the University of Illinois at Chicago. "Violence behaves like an infectious disease — one fight leads to another; one killing leads to another. In order to reverse the epidemic, we need to interrupt transmission, identify and redirect those at highest risk, and change behavioral norms." CeaseFire focuses on street-level outreach, conflict mediation, and changing community norms to reduce violence, particularly shootings. CeaseFire relies on highly trained outreach workers and "violence interrupters," faith leaders, and other community leaders to intervene in conflicts, or potential conflicts, and promote alternatives to violence. One component of the program includes hospital responders — who work with emergency room staff, hospital spiritual care, and social workers when gunshot and other violence-related trauma cases present in the emergency room — to intervene in conflicts and prevent retaliatory violence. CeaseFire also involves cooperation with police, public education campaigns to instill the message that violence is not acceptable, and strengthening communities to build capacity to exercise informal social control and mobilize forces to reduce violence. Different models of the program have been adapted and adopted in locations across the country, including the Safe Streets adaptation by the Baltimore City Health Department.[38] The program was evaluated in Chicago with a longitudinal, matched comparison-group design examining hot spots for violent crime; data were collected from seven CeaseFire communities. The evaluation results were promising yet variable, signaling a reduction of homicides in some of the CeaseFire communities.[37] Findings from a longitudinal evaluation of Safe Streets in Baltimore — in which four implementation communities were compared with neighboring and other violent communities without the intervention — have been mixed, with different patterns of findings for homicides and nonfatal shootings across communities.[38] As CeaseFire approaches are implemented in other U.S. cities, it is critical that rigorous evaluations (such as those with randomized or strong quasi-experimental designs, large sample sizes, and longitudinal data collection) be conducted to determine their ultimate effectiveness in changing social norms around gang membership and gang violence as well as preventing injuries and death.

Given that public health approaches to gang membership and gang violence are limited and newly developing, it is critical that the approaches are evaluated to determine their efficacy. Without rigorous evaluation, it is unclear whether the approaches are truly effective, or if changes in individuals, families and communities are occurring because of other ongoing events, programs, practices or policies. (For more information about the evaluation of gang-membership prevention programs, see chapter 11.)

Public Health Principle #4: Ensuring Widespread Adoption of Evidence-Based Strategies

Once strategies for gang-membership and gang-violence prevention are found to be efficacious through rigorous study, the next challenge is getting those strategies implemented in practice. CDC scientists and their colleagues have identified three key mechanisms, or systems, that need to be used to bridge the gap between research and practice, as defined by the Interactive Systems Framework for Dissemination and Implementation (ISF):

1. Synthesizing evidence and translating that evidence into user-friendly tools, programs and strategies (through a Prevention Synthesis and Translation System).

2. Building general and innovation-specific capacity for implementation through training and technical assistance (through a Prevention Support System).

3. Getting programs, practices and policies implemented at the organizational, community, state or national level (through a Prevention Delivery System).[39]

Optimally, these three systems interact to facilitate implementation of innovations.

To assist in building a prevention support system to help communities reduce youth violence, CDC has developed the STRYVE initiative: Striving To Reduce Youth Violence Everywhere. STRYVE aims to raise awareness that youth violence is a preventable public health problem, promote the use of prevention strategies based on the best available evidence, and guide communities on how to implement, evaluate and sustain prevention strategies. STRYVE includes online resources and tools (see http://www.safeyouth.gov), and a national, multisector partnership that includes justice, health, education, law enforcement, social service agencies and youth-serving organizations to support local action. One component of STRYVE is UNITY: Urban Networks to Increase Thriving Youth. UNITY is a national initiative led by the Prevention Institute, the Harvard School of Public Health, and the Southern California Injury Prevention Research Center at the University of California at Los Angeles, supported in part by the

California Wellness Foundation. There are currently more than 200 members from cities and national, state and community-based organizations. UNITY focuses on fostering effective communication, conducting needs assessments, developing violence-prevention roadmaps, supporting peer (city) networks, conducting training and technical assistance, and developing a strategy to articulate the policies and resources that are needed to support urban areas in violence prevention.

The primary tool utilized by UNITY to build capacity for prevention is the UNITY RoadMap.[40] The RoadMap is a resource that assists cities in understanding the current status of their efforts and the key elements of prevention, and it provides resources and examples to help cities in planning, implementation and evaluation. The RoadMap focuses on the *Who* (partnerships), the *What* (prevention capacity, practices and policies) and the *How* (strategic planning, evaluation and funding) of prevention. Although the RoadMap and UNITY's efforts focus more broadly on youth violence, a city assessment conducted in 2008 with a representative sample of the largest cities found that respondents identified gang violence as the major type of youth violence that needs to be addressed.[41] Thus, capacity-building and assistance provided through the UNITY network include a focus on issues surrounding gang violence. This assistance could also be useful in focusing on strategies that prevent gang-joining. As of April 2012, ten city mayors had signed Memorandums of Understanding (MOUs) indicating that they will work with UNITY to develop multijurisdictional teams in their cities and use a coordinated public health approach to violence prevention. Future plans for UNITY include disseminating the UNITY RoadMap and recruiting additional cities to participate in the network and inform prevention planning at a national level. For more on UNITY, go to http://www.preventioninstitute.org/unity.html.

Another initiative that is assisting in building communities' capacity for gang prevention is the OJJDP Strategic Planning Tool (see http://www.nationalgangcenter.gov/SPT). Sponsored by the U.S. Department of Justice, the tool illustrates the utility of the public health approach to addressing gang membership and gang violence. The tool includes resources that support communities in conducting an inventory of organizations, programs and services that could be leveraged to develop a comprehensive, coordinated approach to gang-membership prevention and intervention; identifying data sources to assess risk and protective factors for gang involvement in a community; and identifying programs, policies and practices for community-based prevention and intervention.

Implementation Challenges

There are a number of key challenges to building and expanding the role of public health in research and programs designed for gang-membership prevention. One clear challenge is that, from a societal point of view, a focus on prevention — keeping kids from joining a gang in the first place — is not well-understood or highly valued. Policymakers and the public are strongly invested in programs and strategies that focus on punishment and that supposedly yield immediate results. This may be the most pronounced when youth are labeled as gang-involved and may not be seen as having the capacity for rehabilitation. Preventing gang violence through reductions in gang membership will require a long-term investment in research and program development and evaluation, which may prove difficult for policymakers and the public to support.

Another key challenge is that the system for supporting and sustaining preventive interventions and programs to reduce gang-joining is underdeveloped. With some notable exceptions, state and local health departments have been reluctant to tackle the issue of violence prevention, much less gang-violence prevention or gang-joining prevention. This is probably due to a combination of the limited availability of funding support and their relative lack of experience in addressing this type of public health problem. As a consequence, the prevention system needed to support and sustain successful dissemination and implementation of programs and policies does not presently exist in most locales.

The availability of accurate and uniform data to monitor the problems of gang membership and gang violence is also an important challenge. Federal, state and local governments, and communities, need to be accountable for the impact of programs and policies intended to address the problem of gang membership and gang violence. This emphasis on accountability requires that timely, reliable and useful data be collected systematically and on an ongoing basis. At present, we lack uniform definitions and data systems for gang membership and gang violence across the U.S., other than the National Youth Gang Survey mentioned previously, which is limited in scope. Lessons can be learned through methods utilized by CDC to develop standard definitions and recommended data elements for surveillance systems. CDC uses an expert panel process that brings together experts in epidemiology research, prevention and surveillance — who represent universities, health departments, hospitals, federal agencies and other organizations — to discuss operational definitions and to draft recommendations for measuring specific forms of violence. Through this process, uniform definitions and recommended data elements have been developed for sexual violence, self-directed violence, child maltreatment and intimate partner violence.[42,43,44,45] A similar process might be considered for developing uniform definitions and recommended data elements related to gang membership and gang violence that could be used across law enforcement records, emergency department records, coroner/medical examiner records, and in research. Lessons can also be learned through public health surveillance methods used for tracking diseases, such as the *International Statistical Classification of Diseases, 10th Revision* (ICD-10). This classification system allows for consistent coding of medical diagnoses of health problems and causes of death on health and vital records used throughout the healthcare industry (see http://www.cdc.gov/nchs/icd/icd10. htm for more information). Such a system could ideally be created and used by justice, health and social service agencies to standardize the way gang membership, violence, and associated activities are tracked and coded into case files. In this way, data would be more easily triangulated to obtain a more comprehensive perspective on gang involvement and activity. Creating such systems is a challenge — given the need to come to agreement on definitions and measurement at a national level, and the need to update databases constantly to ensure accuracy — but will facilitate efforts at accountability in two key ways. First, they can provide a tool for goal management. Second, as uniform systems are implemented across more and more states and data are accumulated over time, these systems will become increasingly useful for directly evaluating the impact of state and local violence-prevention policies and programs. It is important to note,

however, that communities should not wait to act on the data that they currently have available locally to address gang membership and gang violence. Even when uniform data systems are implemented, communities must continue to take into consideration the local context and tailor their prevention strategies appropriately.

A particularly difficult challenge is addressing the underlying social forces that play a key role in fueling gang membership and associated violence. Most gang-related violence, drug sales and turf wars occur between gang youth from similar marginal areas.[46] The complex interplay between poverty, competition over scarce resources and crime creates environments that are conducive to the formation of gangs and their attractiveness to youth. Success in reducing gang membership and violence will require attention to these underlying social determinants, including, for example, the investigation of prevention strategies that focus on reducing the levels of economic stress (for example, through business development and improvements), reducing the concentration of poverty (for example, through urban planning approaches), and improving educational attainment and job skills to enhance success in the labor market and reduce the attraction of gangs.

Policy Issues and Future Directions

There are many opportunities to overcome the challenges described here and to make measurable progress in reducing gang membership and gang violence. Public health can make valuable contributions to overcoming these challenges in several tangible ways. In particular, public health has tremendous experience in establishing data systems to systematically track and monitor health problems. As mentioned earlier, NVDRS is one of these systems. A future direction that would enable better documentation of gang-related homicides would be expanding NVDRS to all 50 states; developing, testing and integrating a common set of measures for gang-related homicide into the system; and training law enforcement officials in how to apply these common measures in their primary collection of data on homicide cases. Creating such a national system would fill an important gap in the availability of comparable and accurate data on the magnitude and nature of gang homicide in the U.S. As indicated earlier, such a system would provide data for the establishment of goals and, thereby, enable states and communities to measure progress in reducing homicide, the most serious consequence of gang membership. It is also important for other data systems to be developed to complement NVDRS and to allow for the collection of information on gang behavior and nonfatal consequences, including assaults and injuries.

Public health also has an extensive track record in applying scientific methods to identify risk and protective factors for health problems, which have led to effective policy and programmatic actions. The factors that contribute to the risk of joining gangs and being involved in gang violence are fairly well-understood; however, less attention has been devoted to understanding the factors that protect youth.[32] Thus, we know little about what keeps youth on the positive path away from gang membership and gang violence. Public health researchers — again in collaboration with their colleagues in criminal justice — could significantly strengthen the scientific foundation for developing effective programs and policies for gang-membership and gang-violence prevention by investing in studies to better understand factors that protect youth from gang membership and gang violence. In particular, more attention is needed to determine the critical protective factors at the community and societal levels.

An important role that public health can play in advancing efforts to prevent gang membership and gang violence is to help strengthen the evidence base for effective programs and policies. Although numerous gang-membership prevention programs have been implemented in the past, few have been proven to be effective.[47,48,49,50] An important reason for this is that few gang-membership prevention programs have been rigorously evaluated. Consequently, there may be effective programs that are currently being implemented, but we do not know which ones are effective because few have been evaluated. Moreover, among prominent programs that have been evaluated — such as the G.R.E.A.T. program or the Spergel model, which has evolved the Comprehensive Gang Model, funded by OJJDP — there is mixed evidence of effectiveness.[51,52,53]

A potentially useful approach for accelerating efforts to identify effective programs to prevent

gang membership and gang-related violence is currently being applied by the Blueprints for Gang Prevention Project at the University of Maryland. This project is developing potentially viable prevention programs for gang membership and gang-related violence that are based on prevention and intervention programs the Blueprints for Healthy Youth Development Project (formerly known as Blueprints for Violence Prevention) has identified as effective with delinquency and youth violence.[49] The basic strategy is to bring together the literature on effective programs for youth-violence prevention with what we know about gang membership and gang-related violence, modify evidence-based programs to maximize their ability to address risk factors for gang membership and gang-related violence, and then subject those programs to a rigorous evaluation. This approach will hopefully lead to new and effective programs for the prevention of gang membership and gang violence.

Finally, public health has demonstrated an ability to build infrastructures that can support the successful dissemination and implementation of evidence-based and evidence-informed policies, programs, practices and processes. Such an infrastructure is needed if we want to succeed in implementing sustainable interventions and reducing gang membership and gang violence. Developing evidence-based policies and programs is insufficient to stem this problem if we do not also develop systems to support their successful implementation. We should start by building the necessary infrastructure to move effective gang-membership and gang-violence prevention interventions from research to action, even before we have established a strong evidence base.

The first part of this infrastructure, the Prevention Synthesis and Translation System, would best be organized through the collaboration of the public health and criminal justice sectors within communities.[39] It would involve, for example, establishing easily accessible, user-friendly and one-stop sources of information that coalesce existing knowledge about gangs, gang membership and gang-violence prevention. These information gram sources would enable communities to have direct into access to state-of-the-art information on prevention of gang membership and gang violence.

The second dimension of this system is a Prevention Support System, which would build the general skills and motivations of communities and organizations, and strengthen their capacity to successfully implement specific interventions.[39] This requires building a strong network of technical assistance that can provide direct assistance to communities as they formulate and implement programs and policies to address this problem.

Third, it is necessary to build a Prevention Delivery System that can deliver high-quality implementation of specific interventions at the national, state or local level.[39] This aspect of a system of dissemination and implementation is perhaps the most difficult because of the widespread nature of the gang problem and the need for local expertise in prevention delivery. One important dimension of this system is the need to establish training programs that can increase the capacity of local prevention practitioners to implement evidence-based policies, practices and programs successfully. If such an infrastructure existed, it would enable us to add new discoveries as they were made, ensuring that the best available scientific evidence was being

immediately translated, supported and delivered in a sustainable way.[54] The essential benefit of establishing such a system is that it would shorten the time lag between discovery and practice, and ensure the sustainability of policies, practices and programs.

Public health has much to provide to researchers who are investigating gang membership and gang violence as well as practitioners who are grappling with this problem in their communities. For future efforts in gang-membership and gang-violence prevention to be successful, the public health approach needs to be represented, with a focus on:

- Primary prevention.

- Practice informed by data, research and evaluation.

- Cross-sector collaboration among multiple sectors, including public health, criminal justice, education and social services.

About the Authors

Tamara M. Haegerich
Tamara M. Haegerich has been researching youth-violence prevention for more than 10 years. She has assisted in determining whether and how justice and education programs work, and her expertise has contributed to the development of federal initiatives that aim to prevent violence before it starts. Dr. Haegerich received her Ph.D. from the University of Illinois at Chicago. She is currently a senior health scientist at the Centers for Disease Control and Prevention.

James A. Mercy
James A. Mercy has been addressing violence as a public health issue for 30 years. A frequently published author, Dr. Mercy's work has spanned the areas of child maltreatment, youth and intimate partner violence, homicide, and firearm injuries. He received his Ph.D. from Emory University, and he currently oversees global violence prevention activities at the Division of Violence Prevention of the Centers for Disease Control and Prevention.

Billie P. Weiss
Billie P. Weiss is an epidemiologist who has worked in injury and violence prevention for more than 25 years. She is the founder of the Violence Prevention Coalition of Greater Los Angeles and co-author of *A Call to Action: A Case for a Comprehensive Solution to LA's Gang Violence Epidemic.* Currently the Associate Director of the Injury Prevention Research Program at the University of California, Los Angeles, School of Public Health, Ms. Weiss is particularly interested in the nexus between intimate-partner violence and gang violence. She holds a master's degree in Public Health from UCLA.

Endnotes

1. Moore MH, Prothrow-Stith D, Guyer B, Spivak H. Violence and intentional injuries: Criminal justice and public health perspectives on an urgent national problem. In: Reiss AJ, Roth JA, eds., *Understanding and Preventing Violence, Volume 4: Consequences and Control.* Washington, DC: National Academies of Science, 1994.

2. Centers for Disease Control and Prevention, National Center for Injury Prevention and Control. Web-based Injury Statistics Query and Reporting System (WISQARS™). Available at http://www.cdc.gov/injury/wisqars/index.html. Accessed on May 16, 2012.

3. Glessmann C, Krisberg B, Marchionna S. *Youth in Gangs: Who Is at Risk?* Oakland, CA: National Council on Crime and Delinquency, 2009.

4. Bureau of Justice Statistics. Homicide Trends in the U.S.: Homicide Circumstances. Available at http://www.bjs.gov/content/pub/pdf/htius.pdf.

5. Thornberry TP, Huizinga D, Loeber R. The causes and correlates studies: Findings and policy implications. *Juv Justice* 2004; 9:3-19.

6. Maxson CL, Klein MW, Sternheimer K. *Homicide in Los Angeles: An Analysis of the Differential Character of Adolescent and Other Homicides.* Los Angeles, CA: Center for the Study of Crime and Social Control, Social Science Research Institute, University of Southern California, 2000.

7. Robinson PL, Boscardin WJ, George SM, Teklehaimanot S, Heslin KC, Bluthenthal RN. The effect of urban street gang densities on small area homicide incidence in a large metropolitan county, 1994-2002. *J Urban Health* 2009; 86:511-523.

8. Gordon RA, Lahey BB, Kawai E, Loeber R, Stouthamer-Loeber M, Farrington DP. Antisocial behavior and youth gang membership: Selection and socialization. *Criminology* 2004; 42:55-87.

9. Harper GW, Robinson WL. Pathways to risk among inner-city African-American adolescent females: The influence of gang membership. *Am J Community Psychol.* 1999; 27:383-404.

10. Thornberry TP, Krohn MD, Lizotte AJ, Chard-Wierschem D. The role of juvenile gangs in facilitating delinquent behavior. *J Res Crime Delinq.* 1993; 30:55-87.

11. Fowler PJ, Tompsett CJ, Braciszewski JM, Jacques-Tiura AJ, Baltes BB. Community violence: A meta-analysis on the effect of exposure and mental health outcomes of children and adolescents. *Dev Psychopathol.* 2009; 21:227-259.

12. Wright R. Health effects of socially toxic neighborhoods: The violence and urban asthma paradigm. *Clin Chest Med.* 2006; 27:413-421.

13. Sampson R, Raudenbush S, Earls F. Neighborhood and violent crime: A multilevel study of collective efficacy. *Science* 1997; 277:918-924.

14. Tolan PH, Gorman-Smith D, Henry DB. The developmental ecology of urban males' youth violence. *Dev Psychol.* 2003; 39:274-291.

15. Krug EG, Dahlberg LL, Mercy JA, Zwi AB, Lozano R. *World Report on Violence and Health.* Geneva, Switzerland: World Health Organization, 2002.

16. Available at http://www.who.int/violenceprevention/about/intersectoral_action.pdf.

17. Mercy JA, Rosenberg ML, Powell KE, Broome CV, Roper WL. Public health policy for preventing violence. *Health Aff.* 1993; Winter:7-29.

18. Eck JE, Spelman W. *Problem Solving: Problem-Oriented Policing in Newport News.* Washington, DC: Police Executive Research Forum, 1987.

19. U.S. Department of Health and Human Services. *Youth Violence: A Report of the Surgeon General.* Rockville, MD: U.S. Department of Health and Human Services, Centers for Disease Control and Prevention, National Center for Injury Prevention and Control; Substance Abuse and Mental Health Services Administration, Center for Mental Health Services; and National Institutes of Health, National Institute of Mental Health, 2001.

20. Committee on Injury, Violence, and Poison Prevention. Policy statement: Role of the pediatrician in youth violence prevention. *Pediatrics* 2009; 124:393-402.

21. American Public Health Association. Building Public Health Infrastructure for Youth Violence Prevention. Policy Statement Database (policy number 200914, policy date November 10, 2009). Available at http://www.apha.org/advocacy/policy/policysearch/. Accessed on May 16, 2012.

22. Los Angeles City Council Ad Hoc Committee on Gang Violence and Youth Development. *City-wide Gang Activity Reduction Strategy: Phase III Report.* Los Angeles, CA: Advancement Project, 2008:1.

23. Greene J, Pranis K. *Gang Wars: The Failure of Enforcement Tactics and the Need for Effective Public Safety Strategies.* Washington, DC: Justice Policy Institute, 2007.

24. Egley A, O'Donnell CE. *Highlights of the 2007 National Youth Gang Survey.* Washington, DC: U.S. Department of Justice, Office of Justice Programs, Office of Juvenile Justice and Delinquency Prevention, 2009.

25. Paulozzi LJ, Mercy JA, Frazier L Jr., Annest JL. CDC's National Violent Death Reporting System: Background and methodology. *Inj Prev.* 2004; 10:47-52.

26. Mercy JA, Barker L, Frazier L. The secrets of the National Violent Death Reporting System. *Inj Prev.* 2006; 12(S-2):1-2.

27. Jacquemin B, Crabtree DL, Kelly LA. *Violent Deaths in New Jersey, 2003-2005.* Trenton, NJ: Office of Injury Surveillance and Prevention, Center for Health Statistics, New Jersey Department of Health and Senior Services, 2008.

28. Browning K, Huizinga D, Loeber R, Thornberry TP. *Causes and Correlates of Delinquency Program.* Washington, DC: U.S. Department of Justice, Office of Justice Programs, Office of Juvenile Justice and Delinquency Prevention, 1999.

29. Craig WM, Vitaro F, Gagnon C, Tremblay RE. The road to gang membership: Characteristics of male gang and nongang members from ages 10 to 14. *Soc Dev.* 2002; 11:53-68.

30. Haviland A, Nagin DS, Rosenbaum PR. Combining propensity score matching and group-based trajectory analysis in an observational study. *Psychol Methods* 2007; 12:247-267.

31. Hill KG, Howell JC, Hawkins JD, Battin-Pearson SR. Childhood risk factors for adolescent gang membership: Results from the Seattle Social Development Project. *J Res Crime Delinq.* 1999; 36:300-322.

32. Losel F, Bender D. Protective factors and resilience. In: Farrington DP, Coid JW, eds., *Early Prevention of Adult Antisocial Behaviour.* Cambridge, England: Cambridge University Press. 2003.

33. Pollard JA, Hawkins JD, Arthur MW. Risk and protection: Are both necessary to understand diverse behavioral outcomes in adolescence? *Soc Work Res.* 1999; 23:145-158.

34. Thornberry TP. Membership in youth gangs and involvement in serious and violent offending. In: Loeber R, Farrington D, eds., *Serious and Violent Juvenile Offenders: Risk Factors and Successful Interventions.* Thousand Oaks, CA: Sage Publications, 1998:147-166.

35. Howell JC, Egley A. Moving risk factors into developmental theories of gang membership. *Youth Violence Juv Justice* 2005; 3:334-354.

36. Tough P. *Whatever It Takes: Geoffrey Canada's Quest to Change Harlem and America.* New York, NY: Mariner Books, 2008.

37. Skogan WG, Hartnett SM, Bump N, Dubois J, Hollan R, Morris D. *Evaluation of CeaseFire Chicago.* Chicago, IL: Institute for Policy Research, Northwestern University, 2009.

38. Webster DW, Whitehill JM, Vernick JS. Effects of Baltimore's Safe Streets Program on gun violence: A replication of Chicago's CeaseFire Program. *J Urban Health* 2012 (ePub 2012, June 14).

39. Wandersman A, Duffy J, Flaspohler P, Noonan R, Lubell K, Stillman L, Blachman M, Dunville R, Saul J. Bridging the gap between prevention research and practice: The interactive systems

framework for dissemination and implementation. *Am J Community Psychol.* 2008; 41:171-181.

40. Prevention Institute. *Overview of the UNITY RoadMap: A Framework for Effective and Sus- Efforts.* Oakland, CA: UNITY RoadMap, 2008.

41. Weiss B. *An Assessment of Youth Violence Prevention Activities in USA Cities.* Los Ange- les, CA: Southern California Injury Prevention Research Center, University of California at Los Angeles, School of Public Health, 2008.

42. Basile KC, Saltzman LE. *Sexual Violence Sur- veillance: Uniform Definitions and Recommended Data Elements.* Atlanta, GA: Centers for Disease Control and Prevention, National Center for Injury Prevention and Control, 2002.

43. Crosby AE, Ortega L, Melanson C. *Self- Directed Violence Surveillance: Uniform Defini- tions and Recommended Data Elements, Version 1.0.* Atlanta, GA: Centers for Disease Control and National Center for Injury Prevention and Control, 2011. Available at http://www.cdc. gov/violenceprevention/pdf/Self-Directed- Violence-a.pdf. Accessed on May 18, 2012.

44. Leeb RT, Paulozzi L, Melanson C, Simon T, Arias I. *Child Maltreatment Surveillance: Uniform Definitions for Public Health and Recommended Data Elements, Version 1.0.* Atlanta, GA: Centers for Disease Control and Prevention, National Cen- ter for Injury Prevention and Control, 2008.

45. Saltzman LE, Fanslow JL, McMahon PM, Shelley GA. *Intimate Partner Violence Surveil- lance: Uniform Definitions and Recommended Data Elements, Version 1.0.* Atlanta, GA: Centers for Disease Control and Prevention, National Cen- ter for Injury Prevention and Control, 2002.

46. Vigil JD. Urban violence and street gangs. *Annu Rev Anthropol.* 2003; 32:225-42.

47. Klein M. *The American Street Gang.* New York, NY: Oxford University Press, 1995. *tainable*

48. Klein M, Maxson CL. *Street Gang Patterns and Policies.* New York, NY: Oxford University Press, 2006.

49. Mihalic S, Fagan A, Irwin K, Ballard D, Elliott D. *Blueprints for Violence Prevention Replica- tions: Factors for Implementation Success.* Boul- der, CO: University of Colorado, Center for the Study and Prevention of Violence, 2002.

50. Thornberry TP, Krohn MD, Lizotte AJ, Smith CA, Tobin K. *Gangs and Delinquency in Develop- mental Perspective.* New York, NY: Cambridge University Press, 2003.

51. Spergel IA, Grossman SF. The Little Village Project: A community approach to the gang prob- lem. *Soc Work* 1997; 42:456-470. Prevention,

52. Esbensen F-A, Osgood W, Taylor T, Peterson D, Freng A. How great is G.R.E.A.T.? Results from a longitudinal quasi-experimental design. *Criminol Public Policy* 2001; 1:87-118.

53. Cahill M, Hayeslip D. *Findings From the Evalu- ation of OJJDP's Gang Reduction Program.* Bulle- tin. Washington, DC: U.S. Department of Justice, Office of Justice Programs, Office of Juvenile Justice and Delinquency Prevention, 2010.

54. Mercy JA, Saul J. Creating a healthier future through early interventions for children. *JAMA* 2009; 301:2262-64.

What Is the Role of Police in Preventing Gang Membership?

Scott Decker

- **Based on their knowledge of youth in their communities — who is in trouble, and who is on the brink of trouble — the police are in a unique position to make an early identification of youth who are at risk of joining a gang.**

- **Because they are active in neighborhoods at times when (and in places where) other adults are not, the police can play a vital role in efforts to prevent gang-joining, including referrals to services.**

- **SARA — Scanning, Analysis, Response and Assessment, the primary problem-solving model used by law enforcement — and the public health prevention model share complementary data-driven components, which can be used in building initiatives and partnerships that prevent youth from joining gangs.**

- **Police legitimacy can be increased through partnerships with community groups and agencies that are trying to reduce the attraction of gangs; when police play a more active, visible role in gang-prevention activities, it builds trust and improves community efficacy.**

- **Law enforcement leaders should place more emphasis on recognizing gang-prevention work of patrol officers and making that work more visible to the public.**

In Brief

The role of law enforcement in addressing the nation's gang problem must move beyond a "hook 'em and book 'em" mentality. To do this, practitioners and policymakers should look beyond the traditional role of police officers as "crime fighters" through suppression of criminal activities. Suppression alone is only a Band-Aid; it has no lasting effect on gang membership and, over the long run, it costs too much to sustain.

The police have a vital role in *preventing* youth from joining gangs in the first place. In fact, they have a true mandate with respect to efforts to prevent gang-joining: It is, quite simply, a part of their job to serve and protect.

Controlling gang membership is key to serving and protecting, based on clear evidence that gangs and their members:

- Disrupt the important socializing power of institutions — schools, families and communities — that help young people learn and abide by the appropriate rules of a society.

- Commit crimes, victimizing innocents and each other.

- Detract from the quality of life in neighborhoods and cities.

- Divert important resources — money, personnel and programs — from other initiatives that could help create healthier, more productive communities.

The police literally are — or should be — on the front line of gang-membership prevention. They are highly visible in the community. They are active in neighborhoods at times and in places that other adults who engage in activities to keep youth out of gangs are not. Police know the trouble spots. They have extensive knowledge of individuals in a neighborhood, including youth who are in trouble or — most important in efforts to prevent gang-joining — are on the brink of trouble.

Therefore, the police can help identify kids who are at risk for joining a gang. They can collaborate with community, school, public health, and other public- and private-sector partners to work on primary, front-end prevention strategies. Police officers can work directly in programs that provide alternatives to gangs. They can help develop support systems for young people and thereby increase the accountability of youth to social institutions such as their families, schools and communities.

Although the police already engage in a considerable number of prevention activities, their role in gang-membership prevention should be enhanced. These measures include targeting at-risk youth with the appropriate response, avoiding suppression-only tactics, and understanding the following:

- Gang-joining is part of the gang problem.

- How the SARA and public health prevention models complement each other.

- The role of police in assessing the nature and magnitude of an actual or potential gang problem.

- The role of police in identifying at-risk youth.

- The role of police in partnerships.

To understand the roles that police can play in gang-membership prevention, it is useful to consider the Gang Response and Involvement Pyramid below.

Gang Response and Involvement Pyramid

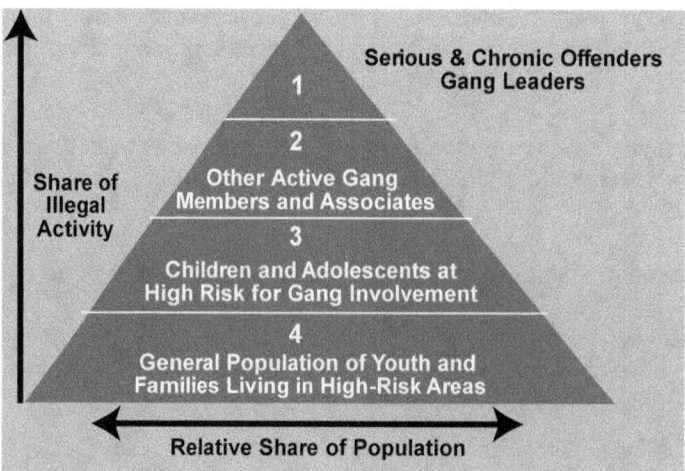

SOURCE: Phelan Wyrick, Ph.D., Gang prevention: How to make the "front end" of your anti-gang effort work, *U.S Attorneys' Bull.* 2006; 4(3):52–60.[1]

Here, we see that the widest part of the pyramid — 4, at the bottom — represents members of the general public who live in high-risk neighborhoods. Going up the pyramid, 3 represents a smaller portion of the population — youth who are at risk of joining a gang. Both of these groups are appropriate for targeting gang-membership prevention efforts. (*Note:* The top two tiers — active gang members, and serious and chronic offenders — represent those who are already gang members and, therefore, are not the focus of this book, which is *preventing* youth from joining gangs.)

As policymakers and law enforcement leaders consider the roles that police can play in preventing kids from joining a gang, the overarching issue of accountability is paramount. Getting out in front of the problem — preventing it from developing in the first place — is an important aspect of public agency accountability.

How the SARA and the Public Health Prevention Models Complement Each Other

Preventing youth from joining a gang is about much more than *crime* prevention — it is also about public health. Being in a gang exposes an individual to violence that can result in death and injuries, not only of the gang member and other members of the gang but also the general public.

Because keeping kids from joining a gang has criminal justice *and* public health ramifications, it is important to look at the problem-solving models used by professionals in both of these fields.

The Public Health Model

There are four basic steps in the public health model for prevention:

1. Using surveillance to better understand the scope, characteristics and consequences of the issue.

2. Identifying the risk and protective factors.

3. Designing and evaluating prevention strategies.

4. Disseminating and implementing the best   strategies.

For more information on public health's role in preventing youth-gang membership, see chapter 3.

The SARA Model

In law enforcement, the primary problem-solving model is called SARA: **S**canning, **A**nalysis, **Re**sponse and **A**ssessment. SARA grew out of problem-oriented policing, which focuses on *preventing* crime and, in fact, has been used in response to gang activity.[2] The four steps of SARA are:

1. Scanning the environment to identify the problem.

2. Analyzing the problem, using multiple sources of information.

3. Developing a response consistent with the information gathered.

4. Assessing the effectiveness of the response.

For more on the SARA model, see http://www. popcenter.org/about/?p=sara.

Similar Principles and Goals

Both the public health and the SARA models focus on the systematic collection of data to inform action. In addition to sharing similar problem-solving steps, they share some underlying assumptions. For example, with respect to violence prevention, both SARA and the public health model are based on the premise that the problem (violence) is not rare and that it occurs far more often than comes to the attention of official data sources (for example, emergency room records and police records).

This same principle could be applied to gang-joining: With nearly 1 in 12 youth saying that they belonged to a gang at some point during their teens, the problem is not a rare phenomenon.[3] Because of similarities in some key principles and the shared goal of reducing gang activity, police and public health professionals should find much in common. The similarities between the two approaches provide optimism about the potential for increasing collaboration between law enforcement and public health regarding gang-membership prevention.

Violence Prevention Is Possible

Another underlying principle of the public health approach to violence prevention — which also should inform principles of gang-membership prevention — is that the problem is not inevitable: There *are* ways to prevent it. This principle is entirely consistent with law enforcement's use of SARA to gather better knowledge of where gang problems exist (surveillance) and who is vulnerable to gang-joining (risk factors).

Differences in Data and Responses

Although there are parallels between law enforcement's SARA model and the public health model, there are important differences in the data used and the nature of the responses. The public health model generally draws on more data resources — such as community- or school-based youth surveys — than law enforcement typically does when using SARA. The goal when applying the public health model to violence prevention is to understand the individual-, family-, school- and community-level risk and protective factors that influence violence to inform prevention programs and policies that can change behavior. On the other hand, SARA emphasizes the use of data about the timing, location and nature of activity to inform a response to reduce that activity.

Also, law enforcement does not typically use efficacy trials, in the way that public health research does, to determine the success of a strategy. However, the importance of evaluation is gaining credibility in the law enforcement culture. Public health professionals also use the public health model to guide prevention work at the local, county, state and national levels. Police, on the other hand, generally use the SARA model locally.

Complementary Strategies

Overall, the SARA and the public health problem-solving models are complementary, and there are various ways they can be applied to strategies for gang-membership prevention.

With respect to the first step in each model — *surveillance* or *information-gathering* — a comprehensive strategy to keep kids from joining a gang would use law enforcement data, emergency room and other medical records, and surveys of the community, for example. Communities would use this information to plan comprehensive prevention strategies that reduce the attractions to gangs, provide alternatives to gang-joining, and provide youth with the competencies needed to avoid gangs (including, for example, communication, problem-solving and study skills). Law enforcement officers would contribute by helping to inform these strategies, advocating for their support and implementation, and referring appropriate youth and families to programs.

The bottom line is this: When it comes to creating sound strategies and programs to help prevent youth from joining gangs, it is important to understand the *complementary* aspects of the law enforcement (SARA) and public health models. Yes, there can be tensions between the two problem-solving approaches, based on deeply rooted philosophical traditions and social mandates of each professional group. However, any initiative for gang-membership prevention will only be enriched by moving beyond a single perspective to solving a social problem as complex as why kids join gangs.

To quote Dr. Deborah Prothrow-Stith, who broke new ground in her efforts to define youth violence as a public health — not just a criminal justice — issue:

> When a kid enters the emergency room with a gunshot wound to his thigh after having been shot in a dispute over a jacket, I want him to be as well treated for the "disease" of violence as he is for the traumatic injury he has sustained. When that young man is blanketed in therapeutic intervention that involves his parents, his pregnant girlfriend, the probation officer assigned to him on a previous case, the kid who shot him with whom perhaps he has had a long-standing feud, his school, which is about to expel him, and perhaps even his younger brother who has just started to act out violently — that's when we will start to make a difference.[4]

Increasing the role and visibility of police in initiatives to prevent gang membership — from assessment of the problem, to identification of at-risk youth, to development and implementation of programs — is consistent with public health's goal of implementing a comprehensive (addressing individual-, family-, school-, and community-level risk and protective factors), multisectoral (law enforcement, health, education and social services) plan to prevent the violence and the negative health outcomes associated with gang-joining.

The Role of Police in Assessment

The police should play a key role in providing a sober, realistic assessment of any gang problem — or *potential* gang problem — in a community. Such an assessment includes the nature (characteristics) and magnitude of the problem.

In fact, policymakers and practitioners should understand that sometimes school and elected officials engage in *denial* at the early stages of a gang problem.[5] This only allows things to get worse, increasing the potential that more kids will be recruited into a gang. On the other hand, officials may engage in *overidentification* of a gang problem, believing that there are more gang members than there really are. This can create public panic and a knee-jerk response that emphasizes suppression to the exclusion of other responses. Such an approach can also make things worse, criminalizing individuals at the fringe of gang membership and diverting resources from prevention activities.

One way to help avoid overcriminalizing youth is to have a validated, consistent definition (with specific criteria) of what constitutes gang membership. Consistent definitions that are uniformly applied across agencies and settings will prevent the use of misleading and sensationalized assessments of the size or extent of a gang problem. The use of a consistent approach will also lead to cooperation across law enforcement and public health agencies. (For more information about definitions of gang membership, see Introduction. For more information about the need for definitions in conducting effective surveillance, see chapter 3.)

There are a number of resources to help a community assess a gang problem or a potential gang problem. In many cases, the police use these tools already, and it is a matter of applying a problem-solving tool like the SARA model to gangs. Such tools are particularly important in helping to understand the gang problem better in ways that lead to effective strategies. For example:

- The Office of Community Oriented Policing Services (COPS) published *Strategies to Address Gang Crime: A Guidebook for Local Law Enforcement:* http://www.cops.usdoj.gov/files/RIC/Publications/e060810142Gang-book-web.pdf.

- The National Youth Gang Center has a number of analytic tools: http://www.nationalgangcenter.gov.

- The principles of Crime Prevention Through Environmental Design (CPTED) are familiar to law enforcement officials and can be used to develop strategies for gang-membership prevention. CPTED involves the assessment of physical structure and characteristics of a neighborhood as the first step in removing criminogenic elements, including, for example, targeting unlit alleys and other places with a low level of public surveillance, and increasing opportunities for prosocial interactions. Diane Zahm's excellent 2007 guide, *Using Crime Prevention Through Environmental Design in Problem Solving,* documents the utility of the CPTED model in a number of settings that apply to gangs, including responding to graffiti and repeat victimizations. (For more information, see http://www.popcenter.org/tools/cpted/.)

Of course, the best assessment of the nature and magnitude of a gang problem will use multiple sources of information and put that information in an appropriate analytic framework. Practitioners and policymakers would be well-advised to remember that — although calls for service, arrests, and other forms of gang documentation are certainly useful in assessing a gang problem — these data should be augmented by information from schools and other community organizations to develop the most comprehensive picture of a gang problem, particularly if it is to be used in developing strategies for gang-membership prevention.

The Role of Police in Identifying At-Risk Youth

There is evidence of effectiveness for a range of violence-prevention strategies (see model and promising programs at the Center for the Study and Prevention of Violence, http://www.colorado.edu/cspv/blueprints), including "universal" programs provided to an entire group of youth regardless of risk; many school-based programs are an example of this.[6]

There are also strategies directed specifically ("targeted") at the youth at highest risk for violence. Although targeting youth who are at the highest risk for joining a gang seems, on its face, to be a wise approach, we have little empirical evidence of the success of targeted (as opposed to general youth population) programs and strategies specifically for preventing gang-joining. This, unfortunately, is because rigorous evaluations have not been conducted or evaluations have failed to show significant effects. (For more on the importance of evaluations, see chapter 11.)

That said, it is likely that both types of approaches — universal and targeted — would influence risk for gang-joining. However, given scarce time, funds and other resources, as well as their unique expertise, it makes sense for law enforcement to include a specific focus on youth who we know are particularly at risk for joining a gang.

The differences in offending and victimization between gang members and nongang members make a compelling case for gang-prevention efforts.[7] And police officers may be in a unique position — arguably distinct from parents, school officials and neighbors — to engage in the early identification of youth who are at risk of becoming gang members.

Police Contact With Youth

Consider all of the ways that police come into contact with youth. Police officers are active in neighborhoods at times and in places that other adults who might engage in activities for gang-membership prevention are not. They know the trouble spots and have extensive knowledge of individuals in a neighborhood, including youth who are in trouble or — most important for efforts to prevent gang-joining — who are on the brink of trouble.

Much of this knowledge, which is crucial to a community's efforts to get in front of an emerging problem, comes from patrol. Using patrol as a strategy for gang-membership prevention costs

no additional money because officers are already engaged in patrol.

But, as Joe Mollner observed in my interview of him (see the sidebar "In the Spotlight: The Boys and Girls Clubs of America"), it is important that when patrol officers encounter groups of young people on the streets, they stop and talk to them, not harass or search them. This builds relationships that can provide a heads-up about at-risk individuals and gang problems that may be emerging.

The police also have contact with youth through enforcement of curfew and truancy laws, which may lead to filing of a Field Interrogation (FI) card, where information about a youth is recorded for possible future reference.

The police also have contact with youth through "custody and release," in which the juvenile is taken into custody, held and released.

Police officers also come into contact with juveniles through school-based programs such as G.R.E.A.T. (Gang Resistance Education and Training) and the School Resource Officer (SRO) program.

Finally, the police interact with juveniles through gang units. In fact, many gang units are primarily information-gathering, not enforcement-oriented, entities.[8] During the process of gathering intelligence on gang members, these special units also gain a good deal of information about individuals on the fringe of full gang membership. This information can be used for gang-prevention efforts, particularly when police in gang units work in partnership with schools, families, nongovernmental organizations and social service agencies.

Indeed, through every type of contact with youth, police gather information that allows them to identify those who are at risk for gang membership and to make referrals. In the St. Louis Consent to Search program, for example, officers referred at-risk youth to clergy and social services (see http://www.ncjrs.gov/pdffiles1/nij/191332.pdf).

The ability of police officers to do this well, however, depends on their ability to recognize at-risk families and youth and on their awareness of services and programs for referral. When they do recognize at-risk youth, police are an important conduit for directing adolescents to a variety of governmental and nongovernmental agencies, including school and after-school programs, social service programs, job training, recreational activities and mentoring programs (such as Big Brothers and Sisters of America). The information that police glean about youth at risk for gang membership also benefits the prevention-focused activities of outreach workers and other youth-serving groups.

Understanding the Risk Factors

For the police to engage in effective gang-membership prevention, they must understand the risk factors — the "pushes and pulls" — that make gangs attractive to some youth. "Pushes" are the negative factors that push youth into gangs; they are found in characteristics or conditions of neighborhoods, families, schools, peer groups and individuals. "Pulls" draw or attract youth to gangs; these include being part of a group and the perceived benefits of a gang lifestyle, such as excitement, the chance to make money, and the perception of protection.

What do we know about gangs and gang members that informs prevention efforts? First, membership in a gang usually lasts for a relatively short period of time, generally less than two years.[9] Second, the age of joining frequently coincides with early adolescence.[9]

Specific risk factors (which are discussed at length in other chapters of this book) include:

- Poor parental supervision.

- Early childhood aggression.

- Believing that it is acceptable to engage in delinquency.

- Significant negative life events, such as death of a parent.

- Peers who are gang members.

Because they are aware of the identity of gang members in their community, the police can play a role in keeping nongang members away from active gang members. Here are four specific measures that police agencies can take to help prevent youth from joining a gang:

1. Use the SARA model to assess gang problems and potential gang problems.

2. Work with other partners inside and outside the criminal justice system, including school resource officers (SROs), or through other school- and community-based programs that address the key risk and protective factors for gang-joining, such as drug abuse, mentoring and employment opportunities, delinquency and violence.

3. Target the appropriate youth with the appropriate response — and avoid suppression-only approaches; the "Gang Response and Involvement Pyramid" helps in understanding target populations.

4. Don't assume that gang membership or gang activities are the same in every jurisdiction; gangs vary across communities and require prevention activities that are tailored to the local population.

The Role of Police in Partnerships

Police partnerships with other community groups are crucial in preventing kids from joining gangs. Police can partner with schools, public health and community agencies, nongovernmental organizations, and youth service agencies in a wide range of gang-membership prevention activities. In fact, such partnerships can increase police legitimacy and credibility, particularly in at-risk communities and among at-risk youth.

The police can play a variety of roles in such partnerships. It is important for practitioners and policymakers to understand, however, that law enforcement might not take the lead in many prevention efforts. This could require a cultural shift for an organization that is used to leading suppression efforts, such as making arrests, serving search warrants, conducting investigations and engaging in directed patrols.

Regardless of the role that police play in trying to keep youth from joining gangs, it is important that the organizational culture of local law

IN THE SPOTLIGHT: THE BOYS AND GIRLS CLUBS OF AMERICA

▸ INTERVIEW WITH JOE MOLLNER

"We cannot arrest our way out of the gang problem. Over the years, I have seen that this [gangs] is a community-wide problem that needs a community-wide initiative to have any effect on it."

— Joe Mollner, veteran of 27 years at the St. Paul (MN) Police Department

As Senior Director of Delinquency and Gang Initiatives for the Boys and Girls Clubs of America (BGCA), Joe Mollner oversees gang and delinquency prevention as well as intervention and re-entry efforts across the country. Mollner began his career as a patrol officer in the St. Paul, MN, police department and left the force as a commander. In 1992, as a sergeant, he began working with BGCA on a gang-membership prevention initiative in the Twin Cities. Mollner has served as President of the Minnesota Midwest Gang Investigators Association and as Chairman of the Ten State Midwest Gang Investigators Association. He was a founding member of the Minnesota-Wisconsin Asian Gang Investigators Association and has served on the board of the National Gang Investigators Association.

How did you get started working with gangs?

I was a lieutenant. A young girl was wounded in a drive-by shooting on a street corner while waiting for the school bus. She was not the intended victim. The community was up in arms, and pressure was put on the mayor and the police chief. A 13-officer task force was asked to address the problem. The task force worked for eight weeks, doing home searches, serving warrants, car stops and surveillance work on known gang members. In short, they did heavy suppression work.

Did that approach work?

Gang members responded by moving guns out of the city and lying low ... for a few weeks. Then the guns came back. This il-lustrates that suppression alone is a Band-Aid that won't have a lasting effect. The costs of suppression are too great to keep it up for very long and, when suppression ends, you are back to where you started. By itself, suppression does nothing.

Why is it important for the police to work in gang-membership prevention efforts?

It is part of the job. When an officer joins the department, it is to serve and protect. Controlling gang membership and working to get gangs out of the community is a big part of serving and protecting. Routine patrol officers should start to build a network on the street that builds relationships with individuals and community agencies. Officers need to look at what is available on the resource side and get to know people in the community. This applies to individuals as well as the business community who will build community support.

The SARA model is excellent for developing partnerships as well because it provides information that the police can act on in developing strategies and responses to gangs and other problems.

What advice would you have about *assessing* potential gang problems — and how does that factor into actually preventing kids from joining a gang?

Denial is a big-time problem with many police departments. We need to be realistic in our assessment of how big a gang problem is — and is not. In many cities, the extent of the gang problem is overestimated, and lots of kids are stigmatized who shouldn't be. Sometimes, departments go overboard in developing lists of gang members. Developing lists in itself is not useful to law enforcement. Developing lists misses the point about most gang members, who have families and children or siblings who may or may not be gang-involved but are at high risk of becoming gang involved. The police may be able to identify those individuals at high risk of joining a gang and keep them out of gang activity. They are a tremendous source of knowledge and resources.

What can the police do to support gang-prevention activities?

First, patrol can play an important role in prevention. It doesn't cost any additional money, because the police already do patrol, but

enforcement agencies values prevention activities, which:

- Provide attractive alternatives to joining a gang.

- Develop support systems for young people.

- Increase the accountability of youth to social institutions, including family, schools and communities.

Of course, many police departments are already involved in gang-membership prevention efforts, including after-school programs, SRO programs, preventive patrols, and problem-solving or community-oriented policing. Expanding these efforts to include parents, teachers and neighborhood groups will be important to their success.

For example, the police can sponsor an athletic league or a team in an athletic league. They can provide safety for after-school activity centers, safe havens and athletic contests that offer alternatives to gang-joining. In many communities, the police participate in career days, help younger children learn to read or do math, or make referrals for youth who are at high risk for gang-joining. Some jurisdictions are thinking outside the box, using police officers as mentors who they need to consider the role of prevention activities during patrol. To do this, officers must know what the goals are and how they are to be accomplished. Prevention needs to be emphasized, reinforced and rewarded. When patrol officers see groups of young people on the streets, they need to stop and talk to them — not to harass or search — but to stop and talk and see what is going on, have a conversation. This builds relationships that can provide a heads-up about problems that may be emerging. Another important step that can be taken is to include community policing, particularly community meetings and community forums.

What about school-based prevention efforts?

School-based prevention activities are important. For example, a School Resource Officer (SRO) gets to know kids on a first-name basis. They can do gang awareness training in schools, which can build trust between juveniles and the police. They also can gather a large amount of information and intelligence when kids provide information about things before they take place. This information can be useful to others within and outside the school who are planning or implementing prevention strategies.

What role can police play in partnerships?

Partnerships are very important, and the police can contribute to or help form community partnerships — like a gang prevention task force — with police, schools, neighborhood organizations, and faith-based and other groups. In this way, the police can come together, not as a suppression tactic but as part of a good cross section of the community. The task force can identify the nature of the problem with a good community gang assessment and then identify what is available as far as services and interventions. The police need to be one of many members in such a group. That includes thinking outside the box. In this context, it may be necessary to look outside of city or county resources for support. When I was an officer, this led to partnerships with juvenile probation that added special caseloads with gang members and violent offenders. This approach led to increased accountability of gang members to their probation officers. On their own initiative, officers took youth from public housing to a variety of activities, such as rock climbing, picnics, and demonstrations of canine and horse patrol units. The key to this was that police officers worked with the community to show that there are other things the police do than arrest. In this context, the police can work with Parks and Recreation. They can build relationships with youth in supportive roles. Building trust is an important part of

these activities and makes prevention more successful.

Can you expand a bit on the importance of building trust?

Routine patrol officers can build their own network on the street — with individuals and community agencies. The element of building trust is critical, and how officers conduct themselves on the street can go a long way toward doing that. Officers need to look at what is available on the resource side and get to know people in the community. This applies to individuals as well as the business community. By using the SARA model, problems can be solved in the community, and officers won't just respond to calls for service. The biggest thing is for officers to learn to be community-minded.

When did you make the transition from law enforcement to the Boys and Girls Clubs of America?

I joined the Boys and Girls Clubs of America (BGCA) in 2002 as Director of Delinquency Prevention. BGCA began in 1906, and received a Congressional Charter in 1956. Today, BGCA serves more than 4 million boys and girls in over 4,000 club locations. There are more than 50,000 trained staff who provide services in all 50 states, the District of Columbia, Puerto Rico and the Virgin Islands.

engage youth who live in public housing in a variety of activities.

The Danes have an interesting collaboration between the police and the parents of children who are suspected of being involved — or about to become involved — in gang or other criminal activity. In what are called "worrying conversations," police officers talk with parents who often are unaware of (or unwilling to confront) the activities of their children and who may not know what resources are available, such as tutoring or free after-school supervised activities.[10] The police can include social service and nongovernmental organization

(NGO) representatives on their visits for the "conversations." Referrals to services or activities often result from such conversations and can create an alliance between parents, police and others in prevention efforts.

Through partnerships with other agencies and groups, law enforcement can help increase youth accountability, an important principle in gang prevention. In a number of communities throughout the U.S., the Juvenile Accountability Incentive Block Grant program (JAIBG) works to increase the accountability of young people to their schools and families.

In St. Louis, MO, for example, juvenile police officers partnered with juvenile probation officers to conduct more than 10,000 home visits per year.[11] These home visits not only increased youth accountability to their conditions of probation; they also offered probation and police officers new insights into family conditions. In some cases, the police became aware of potential abuse or neglect and took appropriate action. In other cases, the police learned of siblings who would benefit from prevention services and made referrals to social service and school agencies.

Another collaborative role for police in preventing gang-joining is disseminating information through presentations about gangs to schools, businesses and community groups. These opportunities raise the level of knowledge and awareness of gang problems among a variety of groups. Such presentations can also help to identify and enlist additional partners who may contribute their services or support gang-membership prevention efforts.

Finally, it is important that practitioners and policy-makers understand that when the police collaborate with other agencies and community groups in preventing gang-joining, they can become more successful in increasing public safety.

A relatively straightforward focus for collaboration is data sharing. Cardiff (Wales) and Oakland (CA) have innovative programs that create partnerships between law enforcement and emergency room departments to share information on better policing efforts and to develop novel strategies to prevent violence-related injuries.[12,13] Such partnerships are an example of how law enforcement and public health groups can work together.

Another example of collaboration is the Boston Gun Project, in which the police, probation officers, prosecutors and the clergy worked together to reduce youth firearm violence over a sustained period of time. Although the goal of the project was not to prevent youth from joining gangs, it is a good example of the role that law enforcement can play in a broad-based partnership. In the Boston Gun Project, police officers conducted home visits, made referrals across agencies, and held neighborhood meetings to make clear the consequences of involvement in gangs and violence. This collaborative, problem-solving model became the basis for other successful programs that stressed partnerships, including the Strategic Approaches to Community Safety Initiative (http://www.ojp.usdoj.gov/nij/topics/crime/gun-violence/prevention/sacsi.htm) and Project Safe Neighborhoods (http://www.psn.gov).

The Comprehensive Strategy, advocated by the National Youth Gang Center and the Office of Juvenile Justice and Delinquency Prevention (http://www.ojjdp.ncjrs.gov/pubs/gun_violence/sect08-b.html), is a good organizing tool for groups working to reduce the formation of gangs and address existing gang problems. This model can be used to place the police in multifaceted roles — including prevention — while partnering with other groups and agencies.

A few final words about partnerships are important here. Some prevention programs require substantial time to ramp up their activities, build momentum within communities, and show effects. For example, programs that are working with elementary school children to teach problem-solving skills and change attitudes about violence will not show effects on gang-joining for several years because youth generally do not join a gang until they are older.

When comprehensive gang-membership prevention responses are implemented, it is easy for the police to grow impatient with the pace of other activities. Patience, timing and partnerships are important but they aren't easy to attain. Strong leaders can commit their organizations (law enforcement, schools, social service agencies, neighborhoods) to courses of action that can overcome hurdles and pay dividends over the long haul. It is important to set near- and long-term goals and to sustain activities that can achieve both.

Bringing Law Enforcement and Public Health Together

Despite important differences in orientation, there are many benefits in bringing law enforcement and public health together to develop policies to help prevent kids from joining gangs. Each field derives from a distinct intellectual tradition:

- Law enforcement is part of the classical tradition that conceives of human action as a product of rational and moral choices.

- Public health is rooted in positivist conceptions of human behavior as influenced by internal and external forces that, in principle, are subject to modification.

Despite these differences, both fields depend on an accurate assessment of the problem that is based on solid evidence about the causes and consequences of the problem. Each field uses that assessment to build a response and, ideally, to monitor results of that response over time to see if things are getting better.

For decades, public health and law enforcement officials alike have linked high levels of violence in American society with social conditions such as joblessness, family disruption and educational disadvantage. Based on everything we know about gang-joining, these same risk factors apply to why kids join gangs.

Conclusion

It is difficult to imagine a successful gang-membership prevention program without police involvement. Police officers have unique knowledge of — and access to — individual citizens, including at-risk youth. Although the police are already engaged in a large number of prevention activities, they should be looking for opportunities to collaborate with other agencies and groups in the community. Such collaborations can assist the police in developing and expanding community trust and in making their prevention activities more visible in the community.

As police become more active and visible in efforts to prevent gang membership, their legitimacy within a community grows. It is no surprise that law enforcement — particularly in economically poor areas where other institutions, such as schools, also may have broken down — often lacks the confidence of the community.

Building trust has clear benefits: broader cooperation in the community and strengthening ties between citizens and public agencies. This strengthening of ties is part of a concept called *collective efficacy,* which is the tendency of residents to work together for the common good of the neighborhood. The evidence is clear that neighborhoods and communities with high collective efficacy have the ability to regulate and control the behavior of their juveniles. (For more on the role of the community in preventing youth from joining gangs, see chapter 8.)

Finally, it is important for practitioners and policymakers to take heart: Gangs do *not* overpower all other social institutions — and youth who are at risk, or are on the brink, of joining a gang have ongoing relationships with their families, neighbors, schools and other groups that are not involved in gang activity. Enhancing those relationships is an important part of prevention, and the police have an important role to play in that effort.

About the Author

Scott H. Decker

Scott H. Decker has been conducting research on gangs and gang members for more than two decades. He has been a keynote speaker at the national meetings of the Boys and Girls Clubs of America and at a White House conference on gangs. Dr. Decker's specific areas of research include gang organization, desistance from gangs and gang prevention. He received his Ph.D. from Florida State University and currently teaches at Arizona State University.

Endnotes

1. Wyrick P. Gang prevention: How to make the "front end" of your anti-gang effort work. *U.S. Attorneys' Bull.* 2006; 54(3):52–60. Available at http://www.nationalgangcenter.gov/Content/Documents/Front-End.pdf. Accessed on May 30, 2012.

2. Decker SH. *Strategies to Address Gang Crime: A Guidebook for Local Law Enforcement.* Washington, DC: U.S. Department of Justice, Office of Community Oriented Policing Services, 2008. Available at http://www.cops.usdoj.gov/Publications/e060810142Gang-book-web.pdf. Accessed on May 30, 2012.

3. Snyder HN, Sickmund M. *Juvenile Offenders and Victims: 2006 National Report.* Washington, DC: U.S. Department of Justice, Office of Justice Programs, Office of Juvenile Justice and Delinquency Prevention, 2006. Available at http://www.ojjdp.gov/ojstatbb/nr2006.

4. Prothrow-Stith D. *Deadly Consequences.* New York, NY: Harper-Collins, 1991:139.

5. Huff CR. Denial, overreaction and misidentification: A postscript on public policy. In: CR Huff, ed., *Gangs in America.* Newbury Park, CA: Sage Publications, 1991.

6. Centers for Disease Control. The effectiveness of universal school-based programs for the prevention of violent and aggressive behavior: A report on Recommendations of the Task Force on Community Preventive Services. *MMWR Morbidity & Mortality Wkly Rep.* 2007;56(RR-7):1-16.

7. Decker SH, Pyrooz DC. Gang violence around the world: Context, culture and country. In: G McDonald, ed., *Small Arms Survey 2010.* London, England: Oxford University Press, 2010.

8. Katz C, Webb VJ. *Policing Gangs in America.* Cambridge, England: Cambridge University Press, 2006.

9. Thornberry T, Krohn MD, Lizotte A, Smith C, Tobin K. *Gangs and Delinquency in Developmental Perspective.* Cambridge, England: Cambridge University Press, 2003.

10. Stevens A. Street gangs and crime prevention in Copenhagen. In: M Klein, H-J Kerner, CL Maxson, EGM Weitekamp, eds., *The Eurogang Paradox.* Boston, MA: Kluwer Academic Publishers, 2001.

11. Decker SH, Curry GD. *JAIBG, St. Louis.* Third Year Evaluation Report. University of Missouri-St. Louis: Department of Criminology and Criminal Justice, 2001.

12. Martin-Mollard M., Becker M. Key components of hospital based violence intervention programs. Oakland, CA: Youth ALIVE!, 2009. Available at http://violenceprevention.surgery.ucsf.edu/media/1067570/key.pdf. Accessed on May 30, 2012.

13. Florence C, Shepherd J, Brennan I, Simon T. Effectiveness of anonymised information sharing and use in health service, police, and local government partnership for preventing violence related injury: Experimental study and time series analysis. *BMJ* 2011; June (342):d3313.

How Should We Identify and Intervene With Youth at Risk of Joining Gangs?

A Developmental Approach for Children Ages 0-12

Nancy G. Guerra, Carly B. Dierkhising and Pedro R. Payne

- **Youth who grow up in poor, marginalized urban communities are more likely than other children to join gangs; however, only a relatively small minority of children in these neighborhoods join a gang.**

- **The most common age for gang-joining is 13 to 15 years old, and boys are more likely than girls to join a gang. Joining a gang should be understood as part of a life course that begins from the time a child is born (or even before).**

- **The early risk and protective factors (for children ages 0-12) for gang-joining are very similar to those for aggressive and delinquent behaviors; these behaviors increase the chances that youth will join gangs, particularly in neighborhoods with many gangs.**

- **Important risk factors for children ages 0-5 include hypervigilance to threat, cognitive impairments, insecure attachment to a caregiver and early aggressive behavior. For children ages 6-12, important risk factors include poor school performance, social information-processing skill deficits and antisocial beliefs, poor parental monitoring, and negative relationships with peers, including being rejected and victimized by peers.**

- **Protective factors for youth growing up in high-risk communities include higher levels of social-emotional competence, academic success, secure attachment and effective parenting.**

- **Only a handful of programs are specifically designed to prevent gang-joining from a young age; however, because of what we know about risk and protective factors — and how they overlap with other problems — prevention programs designed around other risky behaviors may also help prevent youth from joining a gang.**

In Brief

Gang-intervention strategies often focus on adolescents, but to help prevent youth from joining a gang, it is important that practitioners and policymakers address the developmental needs of youth from birth (or even prenatally) to age 12. In the U.S., age 12 corresponds roughly with both the start of adolescence and the transition from elementary school to middle school. Because it can be a crucial *turning point* for youth when lifestyle decisions are made, it is extremely important to begin prevention early in life — before harmful lifestyle decisions are made and before transient behaviors in childhood, such as aggression, turn into habits that are hard to break.

Early prevention is also important because risk factors during early ages can set in motion a cascade of problems that essentially shut the door to future prevention opportunities and increase risk for later problems, including delinquency, violence and gang-joining. We know that children are at risk for joining a gang from an early age if they are hypersensitive to threat because they regularly see shootings in the neighborhood, have fallen behind in school because they can't read, or live in neighborhoods where gangs and "easy money" seem to go hand-in-hand. Because risk factors for gang-joining and other related problems start so early in life and cut across different contexts — such as communities, families, schools and peers — it is important for prevention efforts to address these many influences simultaneously through multiple coordinated strategies.

The best solution is to intervene early to prevent or overcome risk factors associated with gang-joining. A compatible strategy is to identify young at-risk teens who may be considering joining a gang but have not yet become actively involved.

In this chapter, we highlight a newly developed, innovative program for families that targets these young teens: Gang Intervention for Teens (GIFT). GIFT provides home visits and family counseling for parents of 11- and 12-year-old youth who are acting out in school and show signs of gang involvement. A joint effort between schools, law enforcement and public health, GIFT is an example of a gang-membership prevention strategy that is based on solid data regarding risk and protective factors.

Teenage boys who live in poor, inner-city neighborhoods can become "street-socialized" — as an aggressor or as a victim — to norms of violence.[1] This risk is even greater for boys who belong to gangs. Studies have shown that self-reported gang members are more often shot, shot at and involved in violent assaults than nongang members.[2] This is true for both boys and girls who claim full gang membership as well as for those who claim only an affiliation with gangs (that is, a loose connection but not actual membership).[3]

Of course, most children growing up in poor communities do *not* become gang members. Research suggests that 6 percent to 30 percent of youth from economically disadvantaged neighborhoods actually affiliate with or join a gang during their lifetime. Involvement typically begins between the ages of 13 and 15, and most gang members stay involved for only one to two years.[4] It is this subgroup of youth — those who join gangs — that commit most crime and are put at the highest risk for serious injury and death.

Because gang involvement begins in the early teenage years, it is critical for prevention programs and policies to start early, before young people join gangs. In other words, a 13-year-old does not wake up one day and decide out of the blue to join a gang: The decision is a consequence of a particular life environment, behavior and way of thinking that leads a child to adopt the gang lifestyle later on. A child whose parents are in a gang, who falls behind in elementary school, who hangs around with aggressive friends, and who lives in a neighborhood with many gangs was started on this course from a very early age.

To illustrate this downward spiral, imagine a boy who is born in a high-gang, high-violence neighborhood to a poor, young mother and a gang-involved father. Imagine that his mother did not receive adequate prenatal care and that his father went to prison shortly after his birth. His mother struggled to make ends meet, tried working multiple jobs, and had little time or patience for her child. There were no books in the house, and his mother was always too tired or too stressed to talk to him or play with him. He often heard gunshots on his block and actually saw some fights and shootings, leading him to be very jumpy and easily startled (sometimes referred to as hyper-vigilance). Unfortunately, the young boy also had very poor verbal skills. When he began elementary school, he clearly was not ready to learn. His language development was delayed, and he had a hard time communicating with others. He fell further and further behind his classmates, making school frustrating rather than enjoyable. He started skipping school and hanging out with members of a neighborhood gang. He would get money from them for watching out for police, hiding guns and holding drugs — all before he was 10 years old.

It is not difficult to imagine how this young boy could soon become a full-fledged gang member. It is also not difficult to understand how many different events — witnessing violence in his neighborhood, inadequate support from his family, problems in school, and the lure of an antisocial peer group — contribute to the decision to join a gang. For some youth, joining a gang is not just one possible course: It may be the only course they can see with their young eyes and limited vision.

Here is how one boy, Sanyika Shakur — also known as "Monster Kody Scott" — describes his experience:

> I first sensed my radical departure from childhood when I was suspended a month before [elementary school] graduation ... not allowed to go on the grad-class outing for flashing a gang sign [in a class picture]. [The principal] was appalled and accused me of destroying a perfectly good picture. ... I wasn't listening and, besides, my mind had been made up [to join a gang] weeks prior to my having gotten caught flashing the sign on the panorama picture. How I expected to get away with flashing on a photograph is beyond me! But, too, it points up my serious intent even then. For I was completely sold on becoming a gang member.[5]

Although Shakur was barely 12 years old when he joined a gang, his decision represented the culmination of his experiences to date and reflected what he saw, at the time, as the best path for his future: a path that began somewhere much earlier in his development. His initiation was a rite of passage — a formal ritual marking the transition from child to man — that solidified this path in life, at least at that moment. But how did he get "completely sold" on becoming a gang member when he was only 12 years old? What could have been done earlier in this young man's life to change his destiny?

The answer to these questions is both simple and complex. The simple answer is: Start early and prevent risk. The complex part is determining *how* best to do this across different ages and the various contexts of community, family, school and peers.

As the figure below illustrates, children's individual development is embedded in and influenced by relationships in which they are involved, community opportunities and resources, and societal norms and practices. The influence of these different contexts also varies by age — for very young children, for example, families are the most important context; peers gain more influence later on.

To prevent youth from joining a gang, it is important to understand the most important risk factors — by

IN THE SPOTLIGHT: GANG INTERVENTION FOR TEENS PROGRAM

▶ *INTERVIEW WITH RAUL VERGARA AND JOE DELGUIDICE*

Although early prevention is the best strategy for preventing youth from joining gangs, it also is important to reach out to young teens who, for whatever reasons, are still on a path to gang involvement. Because youth join gangs around age 12 or 13, programs should reach youth during these *turning points,* when they may be contemplating joining a gang. To highlight this concept — reaching youth during a specific developmental turning point — we interviewed Sergeant Raul Vergara, with the Riverside County (CA) Gang Task Force (RCGTF), and Commander Joe DelGuidice, Assistant Director of the RCGTF and a member of the Riverside County District Attorney's Office Bureau of Investigations.

It is important to note that the Gang Intervention for Teens (GIFT) program has not yet been formally evaluated. We have chosen to highlight the program because of its innovative focus on influencing a young person's *decision* to join a gang. Also, unlike traditional delinquency-focused programs, the goal of GIFT is to prevent youth from joining gangs by identifying youth *immediately at risk of gang-joining,* and by targeting some of the risk factors that we discuss in this chapter and that are discussed in other chapters in this book.

As of September 2008, there were 391 documented gangs and more than 10,620 gang members in Riverside County; to respond to this pressing need to decrease gang activity — including keeping youth from joining gangs in the first place — the RCGTF was created. Here is a summary of our interviews with Sergeant Vergara and Commander DelGuidice.

What was the idea behind creating a new task force?

The goal was to have a countywide gang task force rather than small local task forces operating individually throughout the county. The RCGTF was designed with a three-pronged approach: prevention, intervention and suppression operations. It consists of 25 different federal, state, county and local law enforcement agencies, including the Riverside County District Attorney's Office, the Riverside County Sheriff and the Riverside County Probation Department.

We understand that you, Sergeant Vergara, spearheaded the expansion of the prevention component into Moreno Valley, a section of Riverside County.

Right. After two years of operation, we decided to expand prevention operations in Moreno Valley. Our pilot prevention program — called GIFT, Gang Intervention for Teens — was based on identifying middle school kids, beginning at age 11 or 12, who were at risk of joining a gang. It consists of four distinct phases: training, identification, home visits and documentation. In Phase One (training), gang task force officers work with school resource officers (SROs), school staff and district administrators on the goals and implementation plan of the program. A unique aspect of this program is the participation of the SROs. Because they're on school grounds, SROs are in a position to witness student fights or altercations and monitor shifts in peer groups. In fact, SROs gain valuable surveillance information about the students and their behavior patterns.

Why is that so important for prevention?

Understanding students and their behavior patterns is crucial. In Phase Two of GIFT, gang task force officers, assisted by school officials and SROs, identify at-risk juveniles. We focus mainly on children who are "on the fence" of joining a gang. For example, if a kid begins to hang out with identified gang members who they were not associated with before, they are targeted for intervention. SROs also regularly conduct large town-hall-type meetings and forums at the schools. Through these multiple techniques, they look for signs of gang association and try to identify at-risk students.

After at-risk kids have been identified, what are the next prevention strategies?

We use a personalized approach to really reach these kids by conducting home visits. This is Phase Three of the GIFT program. During these visits, members of the RCGTF and SROs sit down with the parents of the at-risk youth and provide personalized gang-awareness education. This includes showing parents what to look for in their children's behavior that may indicate an association or an attraction to the gang subculture. The students and their siblings are present during these home visitations, where they are counseled about the dangers and pitfalls of the gang lifestyle. At the conclusion of the visit, the parents are given information pamphlets containing referrals to county, state and federal resources that may provide assistance to meet the parents' particular needs in dealing with their children. Based on anecdotal feedback to the SROs, parents feel empowered by this information and report that they are better able to monitor their children, now that they know what to look for.

Explain more about the education-of-parents component of GIFT's prevention strategy.

Many parents are unaware of the full extent of their children's activities — especially as they relate to gangs. Many parents do not recognize the signs and indications of gang affiliation because they do not know what to look for. The home visitation teams often have to explain to parents that certain tattoos and markings, hand signs and gestures are associated with gang activity. Many of the tattoos are in areas of the body not readily visible. Parents have not seen these tattoos or markings because they never see their children with their T-shirts off. Similarly, notebook drawings and scribblings may be dismissed as innocuous doodles. The officers note that, by educating the parents about common gang signs and activities, the parents are more adept to appropriately monitor their children for these risk factors. An important next step would be to provide more extensive parent training.

What happens after these home visits?

The SROs prepare detailed reports based on the home visitations, including information about the nature of the referral, the number of siblings in the house, whether or not parents have discovered gang paraphernalia in the child's room, basic information about the parents or legal guardians, intervention actions, whether the parents were cooperative during the home visit, specific gangs that youth may become involved with, and type of resource materials issued to the parents. The reports also summarize what occurred during the home visit and whether or not the child already claims to be a gangster. Although this phase of the GIFT program is still in development, the information in these reports will be used to monitor program progress and to measure the effectiveness of the program.

What challenges have you encountered in implementing prevention strategies such as those used in the GIFT program?

In terms of operations and logistics, GIFT currently uses regular duty-time wages. Materials and supplies are relatively inexpensive, but the primary cost is the time that officers are out implementing this intervention versus carrying out their regular duties. Because the home visitation is conducted mostly in the early evening when parents are back from work, the RCGTF has to use overtime wages or employ flex time.

How do you know if GIFT is working?

Determining the success of any program is always an important challenge. Although GIFT has not been formally evaluated, we do know that the program incorporates strategies that help cultivate positive and beneficial community-police relations. Once parents understand why we are there — that we are trying to prevent the kids from joining gangs — we have never had anybody shut the door in our face. That has never occurred once in the 200 or so homes we've visited. Now, people may be hesitant to let us come in, but once they do, it really breaks down the barriers. One time, for example, one of our officers was visiting parents to talk about preventing a child from joining a gang — and he was the same officer who arrested and helped incarcerate the older sibling for homicide. When the parents saw the same officer trying to prevent the tragedy from happening to the younger sibling, they began to see that officer in a different light.

What other outcomes are you seeing?

Officers have also been able to solve additional crimes by obtaining criminal intelligence as a result of their home visits. At times, crucial information is learned about other violent crimes due to the willingness of parents and children to open up and trust some of the gang task force officers. We believe that this willingness to cooperate stems primarily from the relationships that are being forged through the home visitation program. Plus, our SROs have helped us learn so much about gang signs, symbols and the gang lifestyle among families they visited.

What other prevention strategies does GIFT use?

At this point, GIFT uses a single home visit, where information about gang activities and agency referrals are provided. Although

this is a lot better than what we had been doing, we know there is room to enhance the program. We need to develop a risk-driven logic model that incorporates both identification and intervention for youth at risk of joining gangs. We would also like to have a full-time SRO in each of the eight regions who's dedicated to coordinating GIFT. That person would be in charge of the liaison duties between the law enforcement agencies and the school districts as well as regular and intensive follow-up of at-risk youth on their caseload. We also see the need for increased access to mentoring and remedial programs for identified youth — and, as we learn more about unique risk factors for gang-joining, it may also be possible for the SROs to address these through additional focused activities, perhaps using an extended home visitation strategy with a more structured curriculum.

Do you have plans to formally evaluate GIFT?

We would like to see this program formally evaluated. Our goal is to prevent youth from joining gangs, and we need to know whether that is happening. We should also be aware of other valuable outcomes. For example, building relationships between the police and the community may empower families to be more proactive in preventing their children from joining gangs — and we need to capture these new relational dynamics when evaluating the effects. It's not just the specific prevention strategies we are using, like parental education and referrals, but the bond that we are forming with the community. We go in and basically talk to families from the heart, breaking down those barriers that separate us, so families see you as a human being — where, perhaps, in other situations in law enforcement, that just doesn't happen.

age and across contexts — from birth through age 12. However, because very little research has focused specifically on gang-joining from a very young age, we must rely on lessons drawn from research on related problems, such as aggression, violence and delinquency.

Risk Factors During the Very Early Years: Ages 0-5

There are no research studies of children in this age group that try to predict whether or not they will join a gang. On the other hand, there have been many studies examining early predictors of aggression, violence, delinquency, antisocial behavior and other youth problems. We believe, however, that early predictors of antisocial behavior correspond fairly well with predictors of joining gangs, particularly for children who grow up in high-crime neighborhoods with a strong gang presence.

Why consider risk for such young children, when other influences are likely to follow and shape their behavior? One important reason lies in the influence of very early developmental experiences on the wiring of the brain.[6] During the early years of life, biological "memories" are created through gene-environment interactions; in some cases, this begins as early as the prenatal period.

From an evolutionary perspective, the develop-ing child learns to read relevant environmental features to adapt to the environment. Safe, stable and nurturing relationships with adults protect youth from adversity and enhance the long-term physical and emotional health of children. However, studies show that disruptions occur when a young child experiences threat, neglect, abuse or heightened stress.[7] This can lead young children to develop certain ways of thinking about relationships and situations that are likely to reflect a heightened sensitivity to threat or danger, lack of trust in others, and support for aggression and violence, particularly for children who regularly witness violence in their families or communities. Over time, children can learn to feel "at home" in settings where violence is acceptable — and this is an obvious path to gang-joining later on.[8]

What do we know about the most influential early risk and protective factors for antisocial behavior that should also be important for gang-joining? Several important *individual and family risk factors*

develop from birth through age 5 that can increase risk for antisocial behavior. Some of the most important risk factors for ages 0-5 are:

- Hypervigilance to threat.
- Cognitive impairment, including verbal deficits.
- Insecure attachment to a primary caregiver.
- Early aggression and acting-out behavior.

These risk factors result from the interaction between a child's biological characteristics, his or her personality, and the most relevant developmental contexts; for very young children, these are the family and the community. We briefly discuss each risk factor as it develops in these contexts. Although we discuss these separately, we want to emphasize that these risks often overlap and cumulate.

Hypervigilance to Threat

Research shows that children who witness or are victims of repeated violence before age 5 are more likely to develop a heightened sensitivity to perceived threats. This can lead to a persistently active stress-response apparatus in the central nervous system, including an increased startle response. It can also lead children to develop ways of thinking that are overly sensitive to perceived hostility and threat, even when no threat exists. Children who live in violent neighborhoods are more likely to be aware of violence, hear gunshots, or witness violent events. Children who live in families with high levels of domestic violence, who receive excessive corporal punishment or who are victims of child abuse are more likely not only to witness violence but also to experience ongoing victimization. Indeed, the link between being a victim of early child abuse and later being the perpetrator of delinquency and violent crime is well-documented.[9]

Cognitive Impairments

Chronic poverty and disadvantage increase the likelihood that children will suffer from cognitive and learning problems such as poor verbal skills, inattention and lack of school readiness. For example, inadequate prenatal care for mothers, including poor nutrition (one potential consequence of poverty), has been shown to increase the likelihood that children will be born with lower birth weights and develop resultant neurological problems and cognitive impairments years later. Lack of early stimulation and learning opportunities — often seen in children who are neglected or have few opportunities for preschool enrichment — can lead to changes in brain development that can affect behavior.

Insecure Attachment to a Primary Caregiver

It is very important developmentally for an infant to establish a secure attachment relationship with a caregiver. This requires a nurturing and responsive parent or caregiver who can meet the child's needs. Children who are insecure in these relationships are more likely to develop later aggression and violence. Researchers recently looked at 69 studies of the association between *insecure* attachment and subsequent aggression and violence. They found that children (particularly boys) with insecure maternal attachments and difficulty coping with separation were at elevated risk for later behavior problems and aggression.[10] This pattern of insecure attachment can also lead to *internal working models* of relationships that may limit a young child's ability to develop trusting and stable friendships and long-term intimate relationships later in life.[11]

Early Aggression and Acting-Out Behavior

Children develop certain styles of behavior very early in life. Without prevention efforts, an aggressive 3-year-old is likely to become an aggressive 13-year-old. In fact, early aggression and acting-out behaviors are among the best predictors of later behavioral problems. This association has been documented in many studies in the U.S. and internationally. Retrospective studies of youth in gangs have found that youth who remained in gangs for longer than one year were also more likely to have displayed very early signs of aggression, oppositional behavior and hyperactivity than those who left the gang.[12]

Prevention During the Early Years

Given the importance of family life for early child development, prevention programs for infants and young children typically provide enrichment for children and enhance family functioning and parenting skills. These programs are designed to prevent early aggression and associated factors (such as hypervigilance to threat), provide cognitive enrichment opportunities, and help families interact more positively with children.

For example, the Family Development Research Project (FDRP) worked with families with economic disadvantage and limited education from before a child was born to age 5. The FDRP was based on principles of child development and consisted of frequent home visitation, family problem-solving, and child empowerment and educational activities. Parent training emphasized the development of appropriate interactive skills, prosocial interaction modeling, and involvement in educational activities. This type of program reduces risk factors and simultaneously fosters protective factors. An evaluation study with a 10-year follow-up found fewer probation cases among participants compared with the control group.[13] Other well-known preschool/parent partnerships, enrichment programs and family engagement programs have shown long-term effects on preventing delinquency and promoting adjustment.[14]

Another promising approach that has been shown to reduce risk for child maltreatment is early home visitation for high-risk families. These programs empower families and strengthen the foundation for children by providing support and training around prenatal and infant care as well as parenting skills to young parents.[15]

Risk Factors During the Elementary School Years: Ages 6-12

Studies of elementary school children have looked at risk factors for later antisocial behavior, delinquency and gang-joining. Although children's aggressive and acting-out behavior patterns tend to continue as they get older, other factors can increase risk for problem behaviors. It is also during this time that schools and peers become influential contexts in addition to the ongoing influence of families and communities. Four primary risk factors for problem behaviors, including gang-joining, stand out:

- Poor school performance.

- Social information-processing deficits and antisocial beliefs.

- Peer social status, including being rejected and victimized by peers.

- Poor parental monitoring.

These risk factors are also related to earlier problems that children may experience. For instance, a young boy with cognitive impairments and poor verbal skills is unlikely to be ready to learn when he enters school, leading to poor school performance. We briefly discuss each risk factor and how it is influenced by contexts during ages 6-12.

Poor School Performance

Low levels of school achievement and low attachment to school in elementary school predict gang involvement and other types of antisocial behavior later on.[16] For children who are unprepared to learn and enter elementary schools that have limited educational resources or remedial training, academic progress can be severely limited. As children fall further behind, they are less likely to feel connected to school and are more likely to engage in disruptive and aggressive behavior. If parents do not monitor their child's progress or become involved in their child's schooling — or the school does not intervene appropriately — children are likely to fall even further behind.

Social Information-Processing Deficits and Antisocial Beliefs

During the ages of 6-12, children also learn how to interact with their peers and solve social problems. They learn cognitive and social information-processing skills, such as thinking about the consequences of behavior. They also develop their own ideas or beliefs about right and wrong, and these tend to stabilize between the ages of 10 and 12.[17] If their friends support aggressive behavior, they are more likely to see aggression as appropriate. Thus, patterns of thought begin to take shape prior to adolescence as children build on their internal working models from early attachment experiences and develop their own characteristic ways of thinking and acting. These ways of thinking and acting can have an influence on which peers accept them.

Peer Social Status, Including Being Rejected and Victimized by Peers

When children enter school, they spend a good deal of time with their peers. Aggressive children who are quick to fight, and slow to negotiate and solve problems, are more likely to be rejected by peers.[18] Rejection can then lead to increased aggression, and the cycle continues. This is also true with victimization — victimized children often fight back and take their anger out on others. Many bullies report having been victimized earlier by siblings or peers.[19]

Poor Parental Monitoring

As children become more involved in school, their focus shifts from the family to peers and school activities. This is also a time when parents become less involved in their children's daily activities, as the majority of youth's time is spent in school and with peers, making it more challenging to monitor children's activities (for example, who they are with, where they are going, what they are doing). Low levels of parental monitoring have been associated with risk for a range of delinquent behaviors.[20] Parental monitoring can reduce the risk of youth associating with deviant peers, such as gang members. Several factors influence the ability of parents to monitor their children effectively. Parents who are economically disadvantaged and/or working multiple jobs may have less time and resources to monitor their children's activities adequately or pay for their children to participate in supervised activities. Some schools and community organizations address this by providing safe places for youth after school, where they are monitored and have the opportunity to engage in positive activities.

Prevention During the Elementary School Years

As children get older, risk factors can accumulate. The evidence is clear that the more risk factors and the more developmental contexts in which they occur, the greater the likelihood that a youth may join a gang. For example, youth with seven or more risk factors are 13 times more likely to join a gang than youth with zero or one risk factor.[12]

Sometimes risk in one context can be offset or reduced by protective factors in another context. For example, children who have family problems but do well in school may be less affected by family risk. The most promising prevention programs reduce risk factors and enhance protective factors in multiple contexts, including family, school and community. As University of Washington professor Karl G. Hill said, "There is no single solution, no 'magic bullet' that will prevent youth from joining gangs."[12] Clearly, because families are a consistent influence on children's development over time, family-based programs should be a high priority. In addition, the best programs are those that are multicontext and are provided over an extended time.

Policy Issues: Next Steps and Future Directions

What have we learned about how best to prevent children from joining gangs while they are still young, between birth and age 12? Here are some of the most important issues to understand:

- Multicontext, multicomponent programs should be implemented in poor, urban neighborhoods with a large gang presence. These should begin from before children are born and continue throughout childhood because children between ages 0 and 12 are developing beliefs about right and wrong, trying on different behaviors, learning how to solve problems with others — and what they learn becomes "hard-wired" into their brain circuitry.

- An important first step is to identify at-risk mothers — poor, single mothers, especially those with a history of criminality or gang involvement — and ensure that they receive adequate prenatal and postnatal care. Evidence-based prevention programs, such as nurse-home family partnerships, should be extended to these families. These programs also should emphasize the importance of early learning and school readiness and provide parents with books and other resources to stimulate their children's development. Additional resources through enhanced preschool enrichment programs should be provided, as many programs have been shown to prevent antisocial behavior.

- Early school engagement is critical to healthy child development. Adequate resources should be directed at the early grades when children are learning important literacy and numeracy skills so that they do not fall behind or disengage from school. Early remediation is more cost-effective than the long-term costs of school dropout and lack of productivity.

- Social-emotional learning and social problem-solving skills should be emphasized in elementary curricula. These skills have been found to improve social information-processing deficits by promoting accurate assessment and interpretation of social interactions and prosocial problem-solving, and by addressing delinquent beliefs that accept antisocial behavior. These skills are critical for youth to establish healthy peer relationships and deter them from deviant peers.

- Even with the best early prevention programs in place, some youth may fall through the cracks and consider joining gangs. For these youth, it is important to intervene in the early teens, before they have made a firm decision to join a gang.

In conclusion, strategies and programs to prevent gang membership must start early and be developmentally appropriate to set children on a positive path. These strategies should be designed to improve family functioning and connections with schools, facilitate involvement with socially appropriate peers, and reduce bullying and victimization. Such programs have the potential not only to prevent gang membership but also to improve a range of health and social outcomes related to positive adjustment and well-being for children and youth. Although a child's developmental course begins to take shape very early in development, it is also possible to "redirect" youth who are lured by antisocial lifestyles through early identification programs for young teens such as the GIFT program described in this chapter. An important next step for programs like this is to augment home visits with more sustained preventive interventions to help youth and their families.

About the Authors

Nancy G. Guerra

Nancy G. Guerra is a Professor of Clinical/Developmental Psychology at the University of Delaware, and Associate Dean of Research in the College of Arts and Sciences. Prior to this, she was a Professor of Psychology at the University of California, Riverside, and Director of the Academic Center of Excellence on Youth Violence Prevention, funded by the Centers for Disease Control and Prevention (2000-2011). Dr. Guerra received her Ed.D. from Harvard University. She is an outgoing Associate Editor of the journal, *Child Development,* and the current editor of the *Journal of Research on Adolescence.*

Carly B. Dierkhising

Carly B. Dierkhising is a doctoral student in Developmental Psychology at the University of California, Riverside. Her research focuses on chronic violence exposure, adolescent delinquency and posttraumatic stress disorder. Previously, Ms. Dierkhising worked as a clinical intern at the Los Angeles County Probation Department, counseling incarcerated youth gang members. In addition to her studies, Ms. Dierkhising works for the National Center for Child Traumatic Stress, where she advocates for trauma-informed policies and services for youth involved in the juvenile justice system.

Pedro R. Payne

Pedro R. Payne manages a community-based nonprofit organization at Loma Linda University Medical Center in California. His expertise is in community-based research and outreach, specializing in building social capital through neighborhood mobilization. Dr. Payne has worked as Community Programs Director for the Southern California Academic Center for Excellence at the University of California, Riverside, and as the Executive Director of the Human Relations Commission for the city of Riverside. He received his Ph.D. from the University of California, Riverside, and he has written a number of publications on youth violence and community engagement.

Endnotes

1. Vigil JD. The established gangs. In: Cummings S, Monti DJ, eds., *Gangs: The Origins and Impact of Contemporary Youth Gangs in the United States.* Albany, NY: SUNY Press, State University of New York, Albany, 1993.

2. Wood J, Foy DW, Layne C, Pynoos R, James CB. An examination of the relationships between violence exposure, posttraumatic stress symptomatology, and delinquent activity: An "ecopathological" model of delinquent behavior among incarcerated adolescents. *J Aggress Maltreat Trauma* 2002; 6:127-147.

3. Taylor TJ. The boulevard ain't safe for your kids … youth gang membership and violent victimization. *J Contemp Crim Justice* 2008; 24:125-136.

4. Maxson C. Street gangs: How research can inform policy. In: Wilson JQ, Petersilia J, eds., *Public Policies for Crime Control.* New York, NY: Oxford University Press, 2010.

5. Shakur S. *Monster: Autobiography of an L.A. Gang Member.* New York, NY: Grove Press, 1993:4-5.

6. Fox S, Levitt P, Nelson CA. How the timing and quality of early experiences influence the development of brain architecture. *Child Dev.* 2010; 81:28-40.

7. Cicchetti D, Rogosch FA, Gunnar MR, Toth SL. The differential impacts of early physical and sexual abuse and internalizing problems on daytime cortisol rhythm in school-aged children. *Child Dev.* 2010; 81:252-269.

8. Decker SH. Collective and normative features of gang violence. *Justice Q.* 1996; 13:243-264.

9. Luntz BK, Widom CS. Antisocial personality disorders in abused and neglected children grown up. *Am J Psychiatry* 1994; 151:670-674.

10. Fearon RP, Bakermans-Kranenburg MJ, Van Ijzendoorn MH, Lapsley AM, Roisman GI. The significance of insecure attachment and disorganization in the development of children's externalizing behavior: A meta-analytic study. *Child Dev.* 2010; 81:435-456.

11. Bowlby J. *Attachment and Loss, Vol. 2: Separation.* New York, NY: Basic Books, 1973.

12. Hill KG, Lui C, Hawkins JD. *Early Precursors of Gang Membership: A Study of Seattle Youth.* Washington, DC: U.S. Department of Justice, Office of Justice Programs, Office of Juvenile Justice and Delinquency Prevention, 2001:4.

13. Lally JR, Mangione PL, Honig AS, Wittner DS. More pride, less delinquency: Findings from the ten-year follow-up study of the Syracuse University Family Development Research Program. *Zero Three* 1988; 8:13-18.

14. Karoly LA, Kilburn MR, Cannon JS. *Early Childhood Interventions: Proven Results, Future Promise.* Santa Monica, CA: RAND Corporation, 2005.

15. Bilukha O, Hahn RA, Crosby A, Fullilove MT, Liberman A, Moscicki E, et al. The effectiveness of early childhood home visitation in preventing violence: A systematic review. *Am J Prev Med.* 2005; 28:11-39.

16. Hill KG, Howell JC, Hawkins JD, Battin-Pearson SR. Childhood risk factors for adolescent gang membership: Results from the Seattle Social Development Project. *J Res Crime Delinq.* 1999; 36:300-322.

17. Huesmann LR, Guerra NG. Normative beliefs and the development of aggressive behavior. *J Pers Soc Psychol.* 1997; 72:1-12.

18. Fraser MW. Aggressive behavior in childhood and early adolescence: An ecological-developmental perspective on youth violence. *Soc Work* 1996; 41:347-361.

19. Guerra NG, Williams KR, Sadek S. Bullying and victimization from childhood to adolescence: Developmental changes and implications for prevention. *Child Dev.* 2011; 82:295-310.

20. Robertson AA, Baird-Thomas C, Stein JA. Child victimization and parental monitoring as mediators of youth problem behaviors. *Crim Justice Behav.* 2008; 35:755-771.

What Should Be Done in the Family to Prevent Gang Membership?

Deborah Gorman-Smith, Andrea Kampfner and Kimberly Bromann

- Aggressive and antisocial behavior during childhood is a risk factor for more serious crime, violence and gang involvement later in life: age of onset (earlier) is related to the severity of involvement.

- Effective parenting and strong family functioning that include warm affective bonds, high monitoring and consistent discipline are *protective* against a variety of antisocial and problem behaviors, including involvement with delinquent peers and subsequent likelihood of gang membership and violence.

- Family-focused strategies prevent gang involvement by targeting important underlying risks for gang membership.

- Particularly for families living in high-risk neighborhoods, programs that help to build networks of social support and foster family-community ties can provide an additional protective factor to support healthy development and prevent youth involvement in gang and other types of violence.

- Early-childhood prevention programs, including those focused on pregnant mothers and families of young children, are currently among the most promising evidence-based prevention approaches.

- Practitioners, policymakers, and prevention scientists need to coordinate efforts for "scaling up" and disseminating evidence-based, family-focused programs. Increasing both the science and the use of evidence-based interventions will have a significant impact on the lives of children, families and communities.

In Brief

The path toward gang involvement is complicated, with multiple determinants and no easy answers for prevention. It is clear, however, that family factors are central to youth risk. Parenting and family functioning early in development set the stage for children's experience and interaction in other contexts. Poor family functioning, broadly construed, is related to risk for a host of poor outcomes for youth, including aggression, violence and gang affiliation. Good family functioning has been identified as protective for youth but, even more important, promotes healthy development.

The overwhelming majority of adolescents in the U.S. never become involved with a gang. But, for those who do, the nature, extent and consequences of involvement vary. This variation in gang involvement, from minimal involvement to deep association, tends to be related to age of onset of co-occurring problem behaviors, where earlier onset is related to more serious forms of delinquent behavior. Age of onset, in turn, tends to be related to family functioning. Serious disruptions in parenting and family functioning are related to earlier onset of delinquent behavior, which tends to be more severe and more dangerous than when criminal activity begins later in adolescence.[1]

It is clear, from both research and the experiences of service providers, that strengthening the family can help protect an at-risk child. The questions for family-focused preventive interventions are, first, which specific aspects of parenting and family functioning are factors in youth risk for gang involvement, and second, how can service providers work with families to decrease those risks?

There are remarkably few high-quality evaluations of family-focused interventions that focus solely on gang membership; however, we can use principles developed from juvenile delinquency and youth-violence research to think about a continuum of approaches to gang-membership prevention. Such a continuum would move from *universal* strategies for all parents and families to *targeted* strategies for youth and families at greatest risk.

The popular conception of gang life and membership is largely a caricature that has remained static in the past decades: a young man of color, alienated from society, entering into a binding allegiance with a group he calls "family." The reality is that gang involvement is fluid and dynamic, with youth moving in and out of gang membership and sometimes even including overlapping gang affiliations.[2,3,4,5] This mythology of gang affiliation as definite and terminal can have detrimental effects on how stakeholders — including the justice system, communities and families — respond to a child who is at risk for or suspected of being gang-involved. The justice system may dole out harsher sentences for that child, communities may reject and isolate him or her and, most tragically, families may give up hope for their child. But parents must be told that the family is key. Research and most theories of child development and risk show that families are central to the prevention of gang involvement and violence.

There is nothing easy about being a parent. All parents struggle, some more than others, and all parents need support. All children are different and, even within the same family, different children may require different ways of parenting. Some children are "easy" to parent, whereas others (even at a very young age) may challenge even the most competent parents. The majority of parents and families can find the support and assistance they need through other families, friends or other informal sources of support.

Some, however, need more formal kinds of intervention. There is strong evidence that family-focused programs not only prevent negative behaviors but, in fact, also increase the likelihood of the kinds of positive outcomes that lead to a successful and productive future. The earlier that prevention programs are put into place in a child's development (even as early as prenatal care), the higher the likelihood of a positive developmental trajectory. The child is not only more likely to avoid gang involvement but is also more likely to succeed across areas of behavioral, social and emotional development. The evidence shows us that we can intervene before a negative cycle begins and help parents and families raise their children to become healthy and productive adults. (For more on developmental aspects of preventing gang-joining, see chapter 5.)

When discussing gang involvement in the context of prevention, it is important to consider the behavior, or set of behaviors, that is the target of prevention. The most effective way to prevent gang involvement and gang violence is to focus efforts on decreasing the risk for involvement in the kinds of behaviors that are related to youth getting involved in gangs. Aggression, delinquency and other types of violence tend to precede gang involvement, so programs that decrease these behaviors are likely effective in reducing gang involvement. The most successful prevention programs focus on empowering strong parenting practices and changing family functioning to support positive outcomes.

The Role of Child Development in Risks for Gang-Joining

Peer influences are among the strongest predictors of a youth joining a gang. However, the strongest predictor of kids associating with antisocial or delinquent peers in the first place is family. Effective parenting — consistent discipline, close parental monitoring and engagement, warmth and strong connection — are considered *protective* factors; they decrease the likelihood of involvement with delinquent peers. Poor family functioning — inconsistent and harsh discipline, low parental monitoring, poor communication, and low emotional engagement and attachment — is related to risk for aggression and increases the likelihood of involvement with delinquent peers. A lack of parental monitoring can lead to children associating with negative peers. This is compounded with neighborhood and community risk factors that make parenting skills even more important. Monitoring becomes critical in neighborhoods where gangs are more prevalent, there is easy access to drugs and alcohol, and community violence is pervasive.

Understanding the particular developmental and "ecological" (setting) influences on an individual provides a way to assess risk and prevent gang involvement before it begins. An individual child's development is influenced by the social settings in which the child lives or participates, and the extent and nature of the interaction between these settings. "Settings" refers to social systems such as family functioning, peer relationships, schools, communities, and larger societal influences such as policies and media. Looking specifically at the family setting, however, it is important to understand that the same level of family functioning (including parenting practices) may have different effects on a child's development, depending on the neighborhood in which the child lives.[6,7] For example, the level of monitoring that a parent provides when living in a relatively crime-free neighborhood may not be appropriate when living in a high-crime urban neighborhood.

As children grow, their needs and the demands of the environment change, and the nature and extent of exposure to developmental settings shift. For example, as children enter school and spend more time with peers, schools and peers become greater influences; as youth spend more time on their own, the impact of neighborhoods becomes greater. As these influences shift over time, the family must manage both the child's individual behavior and the influences of other social settings. This is why early establishment of effective parenting and a strong connection to family is so important to decreasing the likelihood of a child's involvement with delinquent peers, which can, in turn, decrease the risk of joining a gang.

Family Risk

Throughout this chapter, we refer to "family" and "parents," although it is important to note that what constitutes a family varies — and parenting may not necessarily be done by a biological parent or two parents. The additional stress of parenting alone brings a unique set of challenges, as single parents can be isolated and lack support and, therefore, be more affected by daily hassles. Combined with financial strain, this stress can impact parental mental health and lead to less than optimal parenting. Low-income parents, less educated parents, and parents with more children tend to display less warmth and harsher discipline than parents without these stresses.[8] These parenting behaviors, in turn, relate to increased risk for child behavior problems.

Early Childhood Risk

Youth who are at highest risk for serious gang-related violence show signs of aggression at a very early age, some as early as kindergarten. Youth who begin on the path toward aggression and violence very early — those who are defiant and aggressive in early childhood — tend to come from families with multiple problems that significantly disrupt the parent-child relationship. These families are often characterized by problems in parenting, including harsh and inconsistent discipline and low levels of parental warmth and support, sometimes so severe as to constitute abuse or neglect.[9,10] Over time, the parent-child relationship can continue to deteriorate, increasing levels of hostility and discord. As the relationship is disrupted, less supervision and monitoring occur, increasing hostile and problem behavior as well as opportunities for involvement with delinquent or otherwise antisocial peers.

Often, youth who demonstrate aggression early also stand apart from their peers because of other identifiable problems, such as impulsivity, problems with self-regulation and poor social skills. These are children who can be very difficult to parent under the best of circumstances, but a lack of effective parenting skills, compounded with environmental risks, causes these antisocial behaviors to escalate even more.

This can sometimes be seen most vividly at school. Children with serious behavior problems tend to also have academic problems. Success requires schools and families to work together to address the additional educational and disciplinary needs of these children. This can be quite complicated, however, as beliefs and experiences of both schools and families can compromise the ability to work well together. Parents may feel blamed or unwelcome, or may simply be struggling to navigate the school requirements. Prior experience with teachers or school staff can make parents more or less motivated to get and stay involved. Despite that fact that at-risk children require the most family-school collaboration and consistency, often these relationships become highly conflictual and unproductive. As a wedge is driven between the school and parents, the child's outcomes decline. In these situations, parents may need help and support with respect to the organization of curricula and school personnel, or skills training for interacting with the teacher and other personnel, or how better to promote their child's academic achievement.

Adolescent Risk

Pervasive problems in multiple aspects of parenting (discipline and monitoring) and family functioning (support, communication, emotional warmth and connection) often characterize families of young children who have serious problems with aggression. Youth whose aggressive, violent or delinquent behaviors emerge during adolescence tend to come from families that are different in significant ways and have different intervention needs than those who develop these behaviors earlier in life.

Most teens are at risk for some form of delinquent activity. However, the majority are involved in relatively minor transgressions and only for a short period of time. Typically, when delinquent behaviors do not develop until adolescence, it indicates that the youth's family has, for the most part, functioned well across areas of parenting and family interaction. The families' needs might be limited to additional support during the difficult developmental period of adolescence, particularly around issues of monitoring (that is, knowing where children are and knowing their children's friends and peer groups and the parents of their friends). Family-focused prevention strategies may be more in the form of helping families manage and adjust to developmental shifts, providing new strategies, and building networks of social support for parenting and for keeping youth out of trouble.

The Interaction Between Neighborhoods and Families

During this period of development, context — particularly neighborhood context — matters in regard to individual risk. In some communities, particularly impoverished urban neighborhoods where gang activity is prevalent, most children are at risk for becoming involved in gangs in some form or another. Yet these at-risk youth follow different patterns and are involved in different ways. Many avoid gang involvement altogether, whereas some become deeply affiliated and quickly escalate to participate in serious and violent offending. There are still others who may be marginally involved, associate with some negative peers, and engage in some delinquent behaviors but who, by and large, avoid violence. For practitioners, it can be difficult to assess the likelihood that an adolescent will follow one path or another. The structural characteristics of the neighborhood or community where the family resides must be considered in order to design appropriate family strategies; this is especially important in high-risk neighborhoods.

The neighborhood in which one lives appears to affect both the type of parenting that is needed for healthy child development and the way a given parenting practice affects a child's behavior. In the inner city, the environmental demands are such that all children and families are at greater risk for problem behaviors than children and families living in other types of neighborhoods, even if there is good parenting. The structural characteristics of a neighborhood (poverty and residential instability, for example) and the social organization of the neighborhood, including the level of cohesion and support, affect family functioning and its relation to youth risk.[8,11,12] Across communities that are similar in regard to structural dimensions such as poverty and single parenthood, there are significant differences in neighborhood social organization and networks that relate to differences in how families function and how parents manage their children. For example, in a study of parenting among single mothers in poor, urban neighborhoods, researchers found that those residing in the most dangerous neighborhood adapted to this environment by isolating themselves and their families from those around them.[13] Although this served to increase the mother's sense of safety, it also cut her off from potential social supports. Similarly, others have found that parents in poor neighborhoods often use "bounding" techniques that restrict children to their homes and limit access to neighborhood influences, particularly peers.

Other research has pointed to the importance of "precision parenting" in poor, urban neighborhoods.[14,15] That is, in some urban neighborhoods, the relationship between parental monitoring and involvement is such that both too little and too much are associated with increased behavior problems among youth. This challenging balance, requiring almost "perfect parenting," is not found in studies of families residing in other types of neighborhoods. This means that the least well-resourced and highest stressed families are faced with having to provide the highest quality parenting.

Neighborhoods with an extremely high presence of gangs and community violence necessitate additional attention from practitioners and policymakers. Families living in these neighborhoods are in need of additional services to reduce isolation and provide services and support, not just for youth but also for parents. Unfortunately, these neighborhoods tend to be the most under-resourced. Given the lack of available resources, it is critical that resources be targeted to programs with evidence that those receiving the program or intervention actually benefit. Too often, programs are implemented because they are politically popular or are "believed" to be effective, despite a lack of evidence supporting that claim.

Family-Focused Prevention Programs and Strategies

Effective prevention connects outcomes to underlying causes. Although no family-focused programs specifically designed to prevent gang involvement have been evaluated to demonstrate effectiveness, there are programs that prevent the underlying risk behaviors. By focusing on strategies that strengthen families at the outset, mitigate the harm of adolescent delinquency, and bolster community ties, we believe that gang involvement and the related community violence can be effectively neutralized.

We focus here on examples of prevention strategies that address the risk factors and early behavior problems that relate to youth joining gangs. These risk factors include aggression, poor academic functioning, deficits in parenting, low family cohesion and support, and exposure to early childhood violence and trauma.

Generally speaking, there are two types of prevention strategies: "universal," which means that the strategy is directed toward a population regardless of risk (this could be an entire school, neighborhood or community, for example), and "selected," which means that the strategy is directed toward a specific risk group.

In the following discussion (intended to be illustrative, not comprehensive), we present examples of both types of strategies, all of which have been demonstrated through rigorous evaluation — typically, randomized controlled trials — to reduce delinquency, violence, or criminal or gang involvement. For a more complete review of prevention strategies that have been desig-nated as effective or "promising," see, for example, Social Programs That Work (http://www.evidencebasedprograms.org/), produced by the Coalition for Evidence-Based Policy, and Blueprints for Healthy Youth Development (http://www.blueprintsprograms.com), a national violence-prevention initiative to identify strategies — evaluated through randomized controlled trials — that reduce adolescent violent crime, aggression, delinquency and substance abuse.

Early Childhood Programs

A broad body of research highlights the first three years of life as an important period for influencing a child's trajectory and the nature of the parent-child relationship.[16] Unfortunately, exposure to trauma in this fragile period (exposure to violence, neglect and out-of-home placement) greatly increases the likelihood of disrupted development and increases risk for involvement in antisocial behaviors in adolescence. Conversely, consistent and nurturing caregiving during the early years of life relates to better outcomes as adults. The positive results of healthy early childhood development are far-reaching and include improved physical and emotional health, higher education, improved employability, and greater engagement in positive social exchanges and civic life.[17, 18, 19, 20]

One model — early home-visitation services to high-risk parents and their children — has received a great deal of attention and has been at the forefront of recent federal efforts. The U.S. Advisory Board on Child Abuse and Neglect concluded that "no other single intervention has the promise of home visitation."[21] Research demonstrating initial and long-term benefits from regular nurse visits during pregnancy and a child's first two years of life has provided some of the strongest evidence to support a home visitation model and has led to its inclusion in recent health-care reform legislation.[22]

Over the past 15 years, numerous researchers have examined the effects of home visitation programs on parent-child relationships, maternal functioning and child development. These evaluations also have addressed such issues as cost, program intensity, staff requirements, training and supervision, and the variation in design necessary to meet the different needs of the nation's very diverse new-parent population. One program in particular, the Nurse-Family Partnership, stands out as having the strongest evidence.

The Nurse-Family Partnership

The Nurse-Family Partnership provides monthly in-home visits by nurses to low-income women during the first pregnancy and for the first two years of the child's life.[23] This preventive pro-gram is offered at no cost and on a voluntary ba-sis to first-time mothers meeting the low-income criteria. The nurses teach the mothers general health-related behaviors and how to care for their child, and provide assistance for the mother's personal development, such as family planning and educational or career development. The program's objective is to improve outcomes for mothers and their children, such as reducing child abuse and neglect, behavior problems and criminal behavior, and increasing educational achievement.

Three well-designed, randomized controlled trials, conducted in both urban and semirural settings with differing populations — which varied by race or ethnicity, marital status, age and income — have demonstrated the effectiveness of the Nurse-Family Partnership, providing evidence of positive effects for both mothers and their children. Although specific outcomes varied by study, patterns of meaningful, sustained effects were found across sites. This family-focused prevention strategy achieved long-term, meaningful reductions in delinquency and criminality for the targeted children. At age 19, the children of these relatively high-risk mothers were 43 percent less likely to be arrested, had 57 percent fewer arrests, were 58 percent less likely to have been convicted, and had 66 percent fewer convictions than children of mothers in a control group who did not receive the program. Thus, services provided for mothers by the Nurse-Family Partnership have proven to transcend mothers' experiences and act as early prevention strategies for their children, resulting in better outcomes.

Practitioners and policymakers who are not familiar with the effectiveness of focusing on pre- and postnatal care may not immediately understand how programs like the Nurse-Family Partnership can actually help reduce risks associated with gang-joining. However, data suggest that early prevention programs are the most cost-effective forms of prevention because the benefits to child and parent cut across behaviors and risks — from mental health and behavior to physical health and nutrition to academic and employment success to community safety.[24,25]

Triple P: The Positive Parenting Program

Triple P is an example of a multilevel prevention strategy that includes targeted components designed to strengthen parenting skills in families that have demonstrated problems in parenting.[26] The program is designed to prevent child maltreatment and emotional, behavioral and developmental problems. Again, prevention of these early risk behaviors can decrease risk for later involvement in delinquent and violent behavior and set children on a healthy and productive developmental trajectory.

The program emphasizes five core principles of positive parenting:

1. Ensuring a safe, engaging environment.

2. Promoting a positive learning environment.

3. Using assertive discipline.

4. Maintaining reasonable expectations.

5. Taking care of oneself as a parent.

In the most ambitious evaluation of Triple P — performed by University of South Carolina researcher Dr. Ron Prinz and colleagues — the program trained approximately 650 existing service providers in nine counties to deliver Triple P countywide for families with children ages 0-8. Investigators found county-level effects on multiple outcomes, including a 25-percent reduction in the rate of substantiated child maltreatment (11.6 cases of substantiated child maltreatment each year per 1,000 children ages 0-8 in Triple P counties vs. 15.5 cases in control-group counties); a 33-percent reduction in the rate of out-of-home placements, for example, in foster homes (3.4 out-of-home placements each year per 1,000 children ages 0-8 in Triple P counties vs. 5.1 in control counties); and a 35-percent reduction in the rate of hospitalizations or emergency room visits for child maltreatment injuries (1.3 each year per 1,000 children age 0-8 in Triple P counties vs. 2.0 in control-group counties).

Although the Prinz evaluation was the only randomized controlled trial of the multilevel Triple P system as implemented communitywide, 25 other randomized controlled trials have been carried out to evaluate component-level interventions — such as skills-training sessions tailored to parents of children with detectable behavior problems — within the Triple P system. Their findings are generally consistent with those of the study described above. By significantly reducing the level of childhood trauma and strengthening parenting skills, programs such as Triple P have great potential to reduce the likelihood that these children will become involved in antisocial and other problem behaviors, including gang membership.

Family-Focused Prevention Programs and Strategies: Adolescence

Multisystemic Therapy (MST) is one of the more widely implemented and empirically supported family-focused intervention strategies, targeting youth at highest risk for gang involvement. MST, a community-based alternative to incarceration for juvenile offenders, uses a combination of empirically based treatments (such as cognitive-behavioral therapy, parent behavioral training or home-based contingency-drug treatment) to address multiple factors — family, school or peer groups, for example — that are related to delinquent and violent behavior as well as gang involvement. The primary goal of the intervention is to prevent rearrest and incarceration.

At the state level, MST is a cost-effective alternative to mass incarceration of delinquent youth. Incarcerating a youth for one year can cost a state $40,000 to $80,000, not including the sizable legal costs.[27] MST treatment costs approximately $20,000 per child. Although the savings are immediately recouped, the most important saving is the accumulated justice costs over the lifetime of the child. Once a youth has been incarcerated, the likelihood of subsequent and more serious offenses increases. Preventing the child from becoming more deeply entrenched in criminal behavior will save hundreds of thousands of dollars in the long term.

As a gang-prevention strategy, MST works in three ways. First, by allowing a youth to avoid incarceration, the likelihood of gang affiliation is immediately reduced. Incarceration causes gang activity to proliferate. In Texas, for example, 40 percent of incoming juvenile offenders claim gang affiliation; however, the estimated rate of gang affiliation at the time of release is 70 to 80 percent of the population.[28] A youth could enter detention for something as minor as school truancy, become initiated in a gang, and return to the community as a gang member. Keeping youth out of detention or prison in the first place is critical to stopping the proliferation of gangs. Second, MST

81

▶ INTERVIEW WITH JAN HASSAN-BUTERA AND RHONDA JACKSON

SCO Family of Services is a New York City-based agency that provides Multisystemic Therapy (MST) for adjudicated youth through the Juvenile Justice Initiative program. MST has been demonstrated — through several high-quality randomized controlled trials —to significantly reduce a host of negative behaviors that place a youth at high risk for gang involvement, including delinquency, aggression, drug use, truancy and negative peer association. We interviewed Queens Program Director Jan Hassan-Butera, M.S., C.A.S.A.C., and clinical supervisor Rhonda Jackson, from the Juvenile Justice Initiative at SCO Family of Services.

We know that a juvenile's involvement in the court system disrupts family cohesion. So, what is the role of a program like MST in diminishing a youth's high-risk behaviors through strengthening the family?

Rhonda Jackson: MST helps reduce the risk that a child will become involved in gangs by strengthening that family as a unit. We focus on things that may seem small but are essential, like being the person the child can go to talk and know that they are being listened to — sometimes starting with little things, like having parents ask the child about their day and what interests them — just talking openly with their child. It can help the child feel like they have a place to belong. We also make goals for the family — not just the child — but goals that are focused on making the family function better as a whole. We talk to everyone, find out what goals they have, what strengths they offer. We take a very strengths-based perspective of the family. All families have positive qualities — just as all families have their problems and weaknesses — but we work to turn those weaknesses into strengths.

Jan Hassan-Butera: We talk to our parents about the restorative power of emotional attachment. We talk about how hungry their child is to hear from them, 'I'm proud of you.' Underneath it all, [they are children] eager for attention, eager to learn, eager to have success at something. But we don't only focus on the immediate family unit; we look to con-nect that family to broader social supports. Court-involved families are isolated; they have been cut off from their larger extended family networks. These parents actually need a lot of help, more help, to monitor their kids and keep up their motivation. The therapists help parents and youth rebuild those 'burnt bridges.'

What is the importance of working with families to help prevent youth from gang-joining?

Hassan-Butera: If the child wants to be with the family — if they feel that they are wanted, they feel that they belong, and they have hope that they can be successful in school and jobs — they are much less likely to be interested in gangs. The kids who join gangs feel estranged from their families. There are a lot of kids who are on the fence with gangs, but there is such a stigma around gang affiliation that people give up on these kids. [Service providers] need to help parents understand that you may look at that 'Gangland' television show and think, 'Oh my god, that's my son's life; there is nothing I can do about it!' But for the majority of kids — especially those who are just thinking about gang life — parents can actively intervene in those negative peer groups and be successful. Parents need to be made aware of what they can do to help their child where gangs are concerned. There are things parents can do; we say, 'Parents are the key factors in their child breaking away from a gang, not anybody else.'

Jackson: Parents, if they pay attention, can really be the best ones to identify if their child is at risk for gang involvement. If a child is a victim of attack or bullying, they are at risk for gang involvement, so parents can look out for physical signs. They should be aware of abrupt changes in friends, clothing, behavior or interests. Parents can look out for unusually strong reactions: neighborhoods they won't go to, colors they won't wear, clothing items they won't go without. If a parent is in tune with their child, they can intervene before the child becomes too involved. Unfortunately, many parents we work with ignored these signs. Parents may be unwilling because they might have the misconception that it is safer

diverts youth who are not yet involved in a gang (or perhaps minimally involved) into prosocial activities while making parents more aware of the risks for gang involvement and providing the tools to prevent their child from becoming affiliated. Last, and most challenging, MST can decrease the risky behaviors of actively involved gang members.

The success rate for intervening with "deep-end" youth is lower with every passing year. As economist James Heckman has shown, the returns for social intervention also diminish over time, making it more difficult and less cost-efficient to wait until youth have arrived at the point of gang involvement.[25]

Implementation Challenges

Engaging Families

One of the greatest challenges in implementing a program that may help prevent kids from later joining a gang is engaging families and keeping them involved. This is particularly true for universal and early childhood programs when the family may not seem in need of help. Participation rates of 20 to 50 percent of families in these types of programs are not uncommon. The reasons for low participation, however, are not necessarily easy to discern. It is not simply the case that families either attend or do not attend. Some not to confront the issue, or they may have ulterior motives such as the child is providing money and paying bills, so service providers can help families work on these cognitions and concrete barriers.

We know that a lack of parental monitoring can lead to children associating with negative peers. Can you address this?

Hassan-Butera: A lot of parents don't know anything about where their child is hanging out, who their child is hanging out with. Basically the child is given free rein to determine his own social interactions without any approval or oversight of the parent. Gangs seek out and target vulnerable kids: the young ones, the ones who are bullied, the newly immigrated, so parents need to know who their child is talking to and where they are going, especially in those hours after school before the parent gets home. In MST, we help parents take an active role in helping kids avoid negative peers. We do this, first, by getting kids to associate with more positive peers — usually by getting the kids into positive after-school programming, but when there isn't programming available, we get creative. For example, we've found positive neighborhood kids to tutor them and take them to the movies after school. The second thing we do is confront the negative peers directly. We've had parents walk up to gang members and say, 'You know what, you don't want to be

hanging out with my kid because he's on probation and that means that the police might be looking at you.' The gang might say, 'Yeah, we don't want this kid hanging around us ... .' Or, for example, an uncle confronted the local gang saying, 'If you know my kid is hanging out with you or other gang members, you call me.' And they did! They would call him on his cell and he would come and pick up his kid. Those things are getting the parent actively involved — supervising, monitoring, knowing the child's whereabouts, and approving or not approving of their friends. All of that significantly reduces the likelihood that that child is going to engage or remain in a gang.

What is the role of practitioners in helping families create organization and support within the networks available to them?

Hassan-Butera: Gangs have a huge negative impact on the community. They put communities in a stronghold. Residents want them out. Whether it is churches, houses of worship, police precincts or community centers, they need to band together. The problem is that there are barriers for families to connect with these resources. For example, I know that the police have a gang-prevention component, but parents may think that if they go there, the police will get their child in more trouble. Practitioners can help break down the fear of stigma by building relationships with these resources so that parents can know they

won't be penalized for reaching out. Another thing practitioners can do is help give youth opportunities to make up for their prior behavior. The community service they have them do — sweeping up stuff in the park — that's not something you really feel good about. When we have kids do stuff like work in food kitchens or working at a home for the elderly, they feel good about it and the staff appreciates having them. Then the community can visibly see what a benefit these children are.

Jackson: Community formation — families coming together to help each other with their children — will help reduce the impact of gangs in the long term. If a neighbor is struggling with their children, they can ask them, 'Is there anything I can do to help? Do you want me to call you when I see Johnny on the corner talking to people he has no business talking to?' Churches can play a big role in this, too. For bigger concerns, sometimes families might feel more comfortable going to a church to talk about what they see and then the church can go to the police and schools on behalf of the neighborhood. The best role for service providers in this process is to serve as a temporary link between families and community resources. They can help set up meetings, role-play with parents who have difficulty reaching out, problem-solve barriers, and then make sure that families feel comfortable taking over from there.

participate immediately and engage fully; others are initially reticent but actively participate over time; some may attend irregularly or never become fully engaged.

Studies have shown three factors that influence family participation:[29, 30, 31, 32]

- Perceived or anticipated benefits from the program (for example, improving child behavior or parenting skills).

- Logistical barriers (for example, access to transportation and child care, time commitments, and cost).

- Past use of resources (for example, the inclination to seek out help).

Engagement will likely require intensive and extensive outreach. Families are more likely to stay engaged when providers:

- Make themselves available or establish a positive affective bond with the family.

- Directly address the barriers to participation.

- Expect families to behave responsibly toward the program expectations but also be willing to acknowledge difficulties in committing to attendance.

- Stay focused on the practical aspects of the intervention; in addition to offering emotional support, providers must maintain an action-oriented approach and provide concrete, pragmatic and useful aid to families.

- Foster a collaborative, mutually respectful atmosphere between the provider and the family.

Workforce and Training

From a practitioner's perspective, there are a host of advantages to implementing evidence-based, family-focused prevention programs and strategies. However, without careful attention to implementation — such as evidence-based content and appropriate training for those delivering the content or implementing the strategy — outcomes may not be as consistent as the evidence predicts. In general, these tools improve fidelity in the implementation of prevention strategies and programs:

A manual or other written description of the content of the prevention strategy to be delivered. For example, a manual documenting the material to be covered during each session, and copies of handouts or any other program material.

Resources to help train those who will carry out the program. These resources might include written training manuals and/or workshops, discussing the philosophy behind the prevention strategy, and providing a clear, concrete description of the training curriculum and process.

Ongoing technical assistance. Some program developers provide ongoing support during program implementation, for example, through on-site supervision, "booster" training sessions, or consultations regarding implementation problems as they arise.

Because of the complexity of family-focused prevention strategies in particular, it is important to focus attention on strong workforce buy-in and thorough interventionist training. Interventionists need a full range of training, including an understanding of the theory and research behind the program, training and specialized workshops, and ongoing supervision and support. For many programs, successful implementation requires that program-delivery staff possess specific qualifications and experience. For example, evaluators of the Nurse-Family Partnership found that the program had much larger effects on key outcomes for the women and their children when the home visits were conducted by well-trained nurses as opposed to paraprofessionals.[33]

The prevention-program developers can be a helpful resource to guide staffing and training. It is a good idea to ask the developer about staffing concerns — for example, how many program-delivery staff are needed to successfully deliver the prevention program, how many program recipients can one staff member serve effectively, or what degrees or previous experience do program-delivery staff need?

Workforce consistency is a large part of successful implementation of evidence-based strategies.

Working in Highly Gang-Affiliated Territory

In neighborhoods that have very high gang presence and community violence, it is necessary for an even greater level of coordination across resources and service providers. In part, this is because the impact that a single family can have is somewhat diminished because of high levels of external pressures on a child. In Chicago, we found that parenting was able to buffer the effects of stress on youth delinquency in poor — but not in seriously impoverished or devastated — urban communities.[11] This was the case even though parenting skills were similar in the two types of neighborhoods. It is simply much harder to parent in these communities.

Although interest has been primarily in the stressful impact of these communities, there are also aspects of the fabric, or quality, of social life in such neighborhoods that might serve to buffer or mitigate the risks for youth and families, even in greatly impoverished communities. For example, we found extremely impoverished neighborhoods in Chicago where families reported feeling connected and supported and had a sense of belonging. Moreover, these social processes served a distinct protective role for families and youth. The perspective that neighborhood contexts are multidimensional points to the value in understanding how these protective factors might be leveraged and used to protect and promote healthy child development. It may be the case that when the neighborhood meets emotional needs, such as a sense of belonging, family risk is minimized. For this reason, practitioners can be the key to initiating and fostering this connection.

Policy Challenges

Gang-joining has real risks for violence and the costly consequences of violent victimization and perpetration. In addition to the unquantifiable toll it takes on families and communities, youth violence costs taxpayers billions in police surveillance, hospital bills, more detention centers and, ultimately, the loss of productive human capital. Although high-quality programs demonstrated to prevent these outcomes exist, often they are not implemented because the cost seems prohibitive. However, a cost-benefit analysis of the prevention programs suggests that the initial investment is returned.[34] For example, although Nurse-Family Partnership (NFP) may cost $4,500 per family per year, the Pacific Institute for Research and Evaluation[35] found that NFP (a) significantly reduced the number of families enrolled in Medicaid and food stamp programs, (b) decreased costly health complications, and (c) improved parental employment and educational achievement. These qualitative outcomes all lead to net gains for taxpayers, realizing more than $5.00 for every $1.00 spent on nurse-family partnerships. Our system of delaying action until the consequences are criminal or fatal is detrimental to our communities and is ultimately fiscally unsustainable.

Based on the scholarship of prevention scientists and the experience of practitioners, family-focused interventions are among the most successful and cost-effective approaches to preventing youth involvement in risky, antisocial behaviors. We must promote evidence-supported, family-focused preventive strategies that view gang involvement as the symptom rather than the cause of systemic failure.

Policymakers can play a role in connecting rigorous research to practice, which will increase the dissemination and widespread use of effective programming. Likewise, additional research on how practitioners can implement evidence-based strategies in the context of their population needs is sorely needed and can be advanced by policymakers. By promoting family-centered, evidence-based programming, policymakers can ensure that the need to continue developing and evaluating family-focused interventions will be met. Future research efforts for gang-membership prevention should center on interventions that target families of children at different developmental ages and youth at varying levels of associated risk and involvement with gangs and delinquency. It is critical that efforts should be coordinated with implementation of evidence-based prevention strategies and policies in other social systems such as schools, community agencies and the justice system.

Conclusion

Jan Hassan-Butera and her team of MST therapists are fighting an uphill battle. By the time they become involved with a family, the adolescent is already deeply involved in criminal behavior; destructive patterns of family functioning have been crystallized into somewhat rigid systems and, developmentally, the influence of peers may be greater than that of parents and other adults. The high success rate of the Juvenile Justice Initiative program (see the sidebar "In the Spotlight: SCO Family of Services") is a testament to the staff's personal dedication; however, as a national policy, waiting until a youth is already involved in the criminal justice system is not advised. The best possible prevention of criminal and gang involvement begins early in life, working with parents and families to provide support, establish strong parenting practices and emotional connection, and increase parents' connection to schools and their communities.

As a nation, we cannot move forward with gang-membership prevention until we think differently about risk and build systems that support all families.

About the Authors

Deborah Gorman-Smith

Deborah Gorman-Smith has been working in the area of youth-violence prevention for 20 years. Her work has focused largely on understanding the influence of family and neighborhood context on children's development, particularly with respect to minority families that live in poor urban neighborhoods. Dr. Gorman-Smith and her colleagues have developed and tested several family-focused preventive interventions designed to support families and deter children from later involvement in youth violence. She received her Ph.D. from the University of Illinois at Chicago and currently teaches at the School of Social Service Administration at the University of Chicago.

Kimberly Bromann

Kimberley Bromann has conducted evidence reviews on "what works" in social policy for a wide range of audiences — including federal officials, foundation leaders and social-service providers — through her work with the nonpartisan, nonprofit Coalition for Evidence-Based Policy. Before joining the Coalition, Ms. Bromann coordinated data operations for research studies focused on youth-violence prevention among inner-city youth.

Andrea Kampfner

Andrea Kampfner is pursuing her master's degree in clinical social work at the University of Chicago School for Social Service Administration. She has worked on violence-prevention issues as a multisystemic family therapist and as a research associate at the Chicago Center for Youth Violence Prevention, at the University of Chicago, where she is involved in implementing and evaluating the effects of family-focused violence-prevention programs for youth and families living in inner-city neighborhoods. Ms. Kampfner's primary interest is working with community agencies to implement evidence-based preventive interventions.

Endnotes

1. Steinberg L. Familial factors in delinquency: A developmental perspective. *J Adolesc Res.* 1987; 2:255-268.

2. Gatti U, Tremblay RE, Vitaro F, McDuff P. Youth gangs, delinquency and drug use: A test of the selection, facilitation, and enhancement hypotheses. *J Child Psychol Psychiatry* 2005; 46:1178-1190.

3. Gordon RA, Lahey BB, Kawai E, Loeber R, Stouthamer-Loeber M, Farrington DP. Antisocial behavior and youth gang membership: Selection and socialization. *Criminology* 2004; 42:55-88.

4. Thornberry TP. Membership in youth gangs and involvement in serious and violent offending. In: Loeber R, Farrington D, eds., *Serious and Violent Juvenile Offenders: Risk Factors and Successful Interventions.* Thousand Oaks, CA: Sage Publications, 1998:147-166.

5. Thornberry TP, Freeman-Gallant A, Lizotte AJ, Krohn MD, Smith CA. Linked lives: The intergenerational transmission of antisocial behavior. *J Abnorm Child Psychol.* 2003; 31:171-184.

6. Gorman-Smith D, Tolan PH, Henry D. A developmental-ecological model of the relation of family functioning to patterns of delinquency. *J Quant Criminol.* 2000; 16:169-198.

7. Sampson RJ, Raudenbush SW, Earls F. Neighborhoods and violent crime: A multilevel study of collective efficacy. *Science* 1997; 277:918-927.

8. Brooks-Gunn J, Duncan GJ, Leventhal T, Aber JL. Lessons learned and future directions for research on neighborhoods in which children live. In: Brooks-Gunn J, Duncan GJ, Aber JL, eds., *Neighborhood Poverty: Context and Consequenc-for Children.* New York, NY: Sage Publications, 1997:279-297.

9. Patterson GR. *Coercive Family Process.* Eugene, OR: Castalia, 1982.

10. Loeber R, Stouthamer-Loeber M. Family factors as correlates and predictors of juvenile conduct problems and delinquency. In: Tonry MH, Morris N, eds., *Crime and Justice: An Annual Review of Research,* Vol. 7. Chicago, IL: University of Chicago Press, 1986:29-149.

11. Gorman-Smith D, Tolan PH, Henry D. The relation of community and family to risk among urban poor adolescents. In: Cohen P, Robins L, Slomkowski C, eds., *Where and When: Influence of Historical Time and Place on Aspects of Psychopathology.* Hillsdale, NJ: Lawrence Erlbaum Associates, 1999:349-367.

12. Ingoldsby EM, Kohl GO, McMahon RJ, Lengua L. Conduct problems, depressive symptomatology and their co-occurring presentation in childhood as predictors of adjustment in early adolescence. *J Abnorm Child Psychol.* 2006; 34:603-621.

13. Furstenberg FF Jr. How families manage risk and opportunity in dangerous neighborhoods. In: Wilson WJ, ed., *Sociology and the Public Agenda.* Newbury Park, CA: Sage Publications, 1993:231-258.

14. Gonzales N, Cauce AM, Friedman RJ, Mason CA. Family, peer and neighborhood influences on academic achievement among African-American adolescents: One year prospective effects. *Am J Community Psychol.* 1996; 24:365-387.

15. Mason CA, Cauce AM, Gonzales N, Hiraga Y. Neither too sweet nor too sour: Problem peers, maternal control, and problem behavior in African American adolescents. *Child Dev.* 1996; 67:2115-2130.

16. Shonkoff J, Phillips D. *From Neurons to Neighborhoods: The Science of Early Childhood Development.* Washington, DC: National Academy Press, 2000.

17. Campbell FA, Ramey CT, Pungello E, Sparling J, Miller-Johnson S. Early childhood education: *es* Young adult outcomes from the Abecedarian Project. *Appl Develop Sci.* 2002; 6:42-57.

18. McCormick MC, Brooks-Gunn J, Buka SL, Goldman J, Yu J, Salganik M, Scott DT, Bennett FC, Kay LL, Bernbaum JC, Bauer CR, Martin C, Woods ER, Martin A, Casey PH. Early intervention in low birth weight premature infants: Results at 18 years of age for the Infant Health and Development program. *Pediatrics* 2006; 117:771-780.

19. Reynolds AJ, Temple JA, Robertson D, Mann E. Long-term effects of an early childhood intervention on educational attainment and juvenile arrest. *JAMA* 2001; 285:2339-2346.

20. Schweinhart LJ. The High/Scope Perry Preschool Study Through Age 40: Summary, Conclusions, and Frequently Asked Questions. Ypsilanti, MI: High/Scope Educational Research Foundation, 2004.

21. U.S. Department of Health and Human Services, U.S. Advisory Board on Child Abuse and Neglect. *Creating Caring Communities: Blueprint for an Effective Federal Policy for Child Abuse and Neglect.* Washington, DC: U.S. Department of Health and Human Services, U.S. Advisory Board on Child Abuse and Neglect, 1991:145.

22. Olds DL, Sadler L, Kitzman H. Programs for parents of infants and toddlers: Recent evidence from randomized trials. *J Child Psychol Psychiatry* 2007; 48:355-391.

23. Olds DL, Eckenrode J, Henderson CR Jr, Kitzman H, Powers J, Cole R, Sidora K, Morris P, Pettitt LM, Luckey D. Long-term effects of home visitation on maternal life course and child abuse and neglect: Fifteen-year follow-up of a randomized trial. *JAMA* 1997; 278:637-643.

24. Duncan GD, Ludwig J, Magnuson KA. Reducing poverty through preschool interventions. *Future Child* 2007; 17:143-160.

25. Heckman, J. Skill formation and the economics of investing in disadvantaged children. *Science* 2006; 312:1900-1902.

26. Prinz RJ, Sanders MR, Shapiro CJ, Whitaker DJ, Lutzker JR. Population-based prevention of child maltreatment: The U.S. Triple P System population trial. *Prev Sci.* 2009; 10:1-10.

27. Illinois Department of Corrections. IDOC Facilities. Available at http://www.idoc.state.il.us/subsections/facilities/default.shtml. Accessed on January 10, 2012.

28. Noles D, Haider K, Rangel G, Youth Ombudsman SM. Interview by the Office of the Independent Ombudsman for the Texas Youth Commission. In: *Special Report from the Office of the Independent Ombudsman for the Texas Youth Commission,* 2009.

29. Gorman-Smith D, Tolan PH, Henry DB, Leventhal A, Schoeny M, Lutovsky K, et al. Predictors of participation in a family-focused preventive intervention for substance use. *Psychol Addict Behav.* 2002; 16:S55-S64.

30. Kazdin AE, Holland L, Crowley M, Breton S. Barriers to Treatment Participation Scale: Evaluation and validation in the context of child outpatient treatment. *J Child Psychol Psychiatry* 1997; 38:1051-1062.

31. Spoth R, Redmond C. Parent motivation to enroll in parenting skills programs: A model of family context and health belief predictors. *J Fam Psychol.* 1995; 9:294-310.

32. Spoth R, Redmond C, Kahn J, Shin C. A prospective validation study of inclination, belief, and context predictors of family-focused prevention involvement. *Fam Process* 1997; 36:403-429.

33. Olds DL, Robinson JA, Pettitt L, Luckey DW, Holmberg J, Ng RK, Isacks K, Sheff K, Henderson CR Jr. Effects of home visits by paraprofessionals and by nurses: Age 4 follow-up results of a randomized trial. *Pediatrics* 2004; 114:1560-1568.

34. Foster EM, Prinz RJ, Sanders MR, Shapiro CJ. The costs of public health infrastructure for delivering parenting and family support. *Child Youth Serv Rev.* 2008; 30:493-501.

35. Miller TR. *Estimated Medicaid Costs and Offsetting Federal Cost-Savings of Nurse-Family Partnership.* Calverton, MD: Pacific Institute for Research & Evaluation, 2009.

What Can Schools Do to Help Prevent Gang-Joining?

Gary D. Gottfredson

- Providing a safe environment so that students are not fearful may be the single most important thing schools can do to prevent gang involvement; we need to test this proposition rigorously.

- Many principals in schools with gang problems do not recognize or admit a problem: In a large sample of secondary schools with gang problems (defined as more than 15 percent of students reporting that they belonged to a gang), only one-fifth of principals said their school had a problem.

- Data show that youths at the greatest risk of gang participation are not reached by traditional, school-based prevention programs; youths who have left school require alternative learning environments to engage them in learning and prevention programs.

- School activities intended to prevent gang involvement are likely to be ineffective if they fail to incorporate elements of demonstrated efficacy or are poorly implemented; therefore, educational leaders should carefully consider whether programs (1) make efficient use of educational time, (2) use state-of-the-art methods, (3) have been shown to be effective in preventing problem behavior or gang involvement, and (4) are implemented as designed.

- Assessments of gang risks, as well as the reach and usefulness of current prevention activities, are necessary to guide future action. Systematic self-report gang-involvement and victimization surveys should be used to supplement existing, inadequate mechanisms — such as school- or principal-reported incident or suspension rates — which do a poor job of surfacing emerging problems, including school safety problems.

In Brief

Schools that provide safe and rewarding educational environments capable of engaging youths in learning, attracting high student attendance, and producing high levels of student achievement are an important part of the infrastructure of well-functioning communities. Schools are not only charged with the socialization of young people but they also drive the economic and social development of the communities in which they are located.

If a community's schools are weak — characterized by low achievement, poor attendance, high dropout rates, disruptive classroom behavior and a climate of incivility — the community becomes an undesirable place to live. In contrast, schools that engage students in learning so that they produce expected levels of achievement contribute to the community's capacity to regulate the behavior of youths and to make it a desirable place to live. Put simply, safe schools may prevent the establishment of gangs in communities.

Research on schools, delinquency and gangs has found that (a) administrators often overlook or minimize problems; (b) unsafe schools and gang problems go hand-in-hand; (c) evidence-based prevention strategies can be put in place in schools, implying that (d) schools continually assess themselves for potential gang or safety problems to identify specific needs for improvement; and (e) educators should carefully monitor the implementation strength of their gang-membership prevention activities and attend to whether the prevention programs reach those young people who are at highest risk of gang involvement.

Gang problems are more likely in schools that serve areas of concentrated poverty and disorganization. This means that schools in communities with relatively many people receiving public assistance income, many children living in female-headed families, high unemployment rates, and most residents occupying dwellings they do not own are more likely to experience gang problems. In essence, fear is likely both a product of and a cause of gang problems in schools and communities.

Despite the large number of prevention programs in schools, school-based gang-membership prevention programs are seldom based on a careful consideration of specific needs. Universal prevention programs can be helpful generally, but strategies that are more directly focused on gang participation and school safety are also indicated in some schools. Yet, school administrators usually fail to recognize gang problems, even in schools where large numbers of students are involved in gangs.

Communities must prevent gang problems and provide safe school environments not only to protect students and improve their educational outcomes but also to forestall a cycle in which school disorder and community disorganization perpetuate each other.

Communities with concentrations of disadvantaged populations tend to have difficult-to-manage schools, making both education and prevention programs hard to conduct and leading to a continuing cycle of disadvantage and high rates of delinquent behavior in school and the community. Therefore, policymakers must understand that gang prevention may be most needed where it is most difficult to implement.

Unfortunately, many school principals are pecu- unaware of — or unwilling to admit to — problems in their schools. In a large na- sample of secondary schools, student reports of gang participation were used to schools as having a gang problem if more about 15 percent of students reported being participants. These self-reports revealed about 10 percent of all schools had a gang problem. However, only one-fifth of the principals of these problem schools indicated that their schools had a gang problem.[1]

Just as effective supervision and control by families are important in regulating the behavior of youths,[2,3,4,5] effective supervision and control of behavior in schools are required to provide safety. Supervision and control require identifying problem behaviors — including risks for gang-joining — when they occur, signaling desired and undesired behavior, tracking behavior and responding to it.

Excluding weapons from the school, being vigilant for signs of harassment or intimidation and responding to stop them whenever they liarly occur, and providing a social environment where gang all students feel they can count on teachers and tional administrators for safety and for emotional and self- social support may help regulate youth behav-classify ior in schools. For instance, schools that create than schoolwide practices for managing discipline gang that incorporate behavioral principles, have clear that expectations for conduct, and enforce rules firmly and fairly have repeatedly been found to experi- ence less disorder.[6,7] One salient feature of an efficacious anti-bullying program involves clarifying proscribed behavior to adults and students who watch for that behavior where it is likely to occur.[8]

Research on the steps that schools can take to reduce problem behavior provides guidance by identifying efficacious programs and arrangements.[9,10] For example, if weapons *could* be excluded from schools, schools would obviously be safer. Ways of achieving this have not been well-studied, however. Many schools employ metal detectors, but even casual observation indicates that this equipment is not at all consistently well-implemented in many schools. Some evidence suggests that metal detectors *could* be helpful,[11] but more and better research on this is required.[12]

Risk Factors for Gang-Joining

The predictors of individual adolescent participation in gangs are, in most respects, similar to the predictors of serious or violent delinquency.[1] We know, of course, that delinquent behavior increases when individuals are affiliated with a gang.[13,14,15,16] Other risk factors for gang participation are the presence of gangs in the school or community and fear for one's safety.

Gang problems disproportionately occur in schools that serve areas of concentrated poverty and social disorganization, where many families experience economic hardship, the unemployment rate is high, and many children live in families headed by a single woman.[1]

Fear for One's Safety

A nationwide sampling of schools found that, even after controlling for other predictors of delinquent behavior, students who felt that the school was safe were much less likely to participate in a gang.[1] This does not necessarily imply that fear causes gang involvement, because the presence of gangs no doubt also produces fear. But the findings of this study are consistent with evidence suggesting that youths join gangs, in part, because of a perceived threat from rivals — and that being part of a gang may reduce anxiety about the threat of victimization.[17,18]

Indeed, student perceptions about their personal safety are powerful predictors of gang-participation rates, even when community characteristics such as concentrated poverty and community social disorganization are taken into account.

Schools in which students do not feel safe are much more likely to have many students involved with gangs, even when these other community features are adjusted statistically.[1]

Gang-participation rates are higher in schools in communities characterized by concentrated disadvantage, concentrations of immigrants and residential crowding, and urbanicity. Beyond this, the most impressive *school* correlate of gang-participation rates is school climate: Gang participation is much greater in schools perceived by students to be unsafe.

No rigorous research has tested whether programs that enhance feelings of safety or make schools safer have an effect on youth gang participation. This plausible theory should be tested.

Gangs as "Social Malignancy"

Gang involvement can be viewed as a social process involving contagion, akin to the transmission or spread of a disease. One of the mechanisms through which contagion operates may involve an erroneous perception by adolescents that joining a gang will protect them from harm by others. We know that some youths join a gang as a way of coping with the threat of harm in unsafe environments, despite clear evidence that the victimization rate of individuals affiliated with a gang is much higher than that of unaffiliated individuals.[1,18,19]

Gang problems vary by *place* (tending to be greater in urban areas of concentrated poverty and social disorganization) and *time* (an area that would seem, on the basis of community characteristics, to be at risk of gang problems may not initially have a problem but may develop one later). The development of gang problems may involve a cyclical process of "social malignancy" in which real or perceived threat, intimidation, social contagion and retaliation feed on each other to exacerbate a gang problem.

Because gang participation is greater in unsafe schools, educational leaders should be vigilant for the emergence of problems. They should focus attention on specific identifiable problems to provide safe schools and intervene when the escalation of a problem appears likely.

Prevention Principles for School-Based Strategies

Because individual, family, school and community risk factors for gang participation are, in most respects, similar to those for delinquency, violent offending and problem behavior in general, there is reason to believe that prevention initiatives directed at general problem behaviors — such as impulse control, lack of attachment to school, and rejection of conventional rules — may be universally helpful.[1, 2, 14, 20, 21, 22] Such prevention pro-grams include school experiences that foster expectations of rewards for engagement and that develop skills in resisting negative peer influence.

Indeed, systematic reviews of multiple studies conclude that school-based prevention programs generally reduce problem behavior, including aggression and other delinquency.[23, 24, 25] Generally, these reviews show that more intensive prevention strategies directed at selected groups of higher risk students have larger effects than universal strategies directed at the population more diffusely. In short, targeting youths at high risk of gang involvement is likely to have larger effects on this group, even though universal interventions may provide modest benefits for the entire population of students.

Prevention programs or strategies that are implemented well (or are implemented by the research teams evaluating them) also generally have larger effects. Nevertheless, prevention activities implemented as part of routine practice in schools (without researcher involvement in implementation) have also been found to have modest beneficial effects.[24] Unfortunately, the efficacy of these practices is not fully understood because credible evaluations of routine prevention practices in schools are rare. (For more information on the importance of evaluations, see chapter 11.)

In addition to the importance of careful program implementation, we know that behavioral and social-cognitive programs are more effective than noncognitive or nonbehavioral counseling interventions.[25] Behavioral programs support desired behavior by arranging the cues in the social environment and by managing the reward properties of environments so that desired rather than undesired behaviors are reinforced. Cognitive-behavioral approaches — based on the theory that thoughts are related to feelings and behav-ior — assist young people in managing their thoughts and feelings in ways that reduce the likelihood of problem behavior.

Social-cognitive strategies or programs are based on the way people learn, in part by observing what others do and what happens, and how this kind of learning affects how people think, feel and believe about the consequences of their actions. In general, prevention strategies and programs based on cognitive-behavioral principles are more efficacious than counseling or instructional programs that are not based on them.

Universal and Selective Programs

One example of a promising *universal* prevention program is the classroom-based social skills instructional program that uses the **P**romoting **A**lternative **TH**inking **S**trategies (PATHS) curriculum.[26] PATHS develops the social competencies of students and addresses the classroom management practices of teachers. A study of PATHS as part of a multicomponent program found that it resulted in less problem behavior in elementary school, with some evidence of effects — such as lower rates of diagnosed conduct disorder and fewer juvenile arrests, according to court records — that persisted to the end of high school.[27,28] These outcomes of a universal prevention program are important because general problem behavior and delinquency are signs of elevated risk for gang involvement. PATHS is an example of a well-documented prevention program with clear guidance available for those who wish to implement it in schools.[29]

The evidence about the efficacy of such school-based programs is stronger for general problem behavior than it is specifically for gang involvement. With the exception of the G.R.E.A.T. program (which is discussed at greater length in chapter 11), research has rarely focused specifically on gang involvement; rather, it has focused on other outcomes, such as delinquent behavior, that are known to be risk factors for gang involvement. For example, universal programs in kindergarten through secondary school, which are directed at providing a predictable, engaging and rewarding educational environment (so that students will have something to lose by engaging in delinquent behavior), and improving students' social competencies (helpful for avoiding problem behavior) can, if well-implemented, be beneficial in a variety of ways, including the prevention of violent behavior.[27] For instance, the PATHS program has been shown, in one long-term follow-up of a school-randomized trial, to lower rates of use of health and mental health services.[30] (See the sidebar, "Reaching Youths Who Are Not in School.")

Selective prevention programs are aimed at individuals who are at elevated risk. An example of a useful selective strategy is home-based backup reinforcement (HBR) for school behavior or attendance.[31, 32, 33] HBR involves collaboration between one or more educators in the school and a parent in the home. HBR may be appropriate when problem behavior is unresponsive to reinforcers available in the school, because parents usually have access to a broader range of reinforcers and can reinforce behavior in multiple settings. Specific problem behaviors in the school setting are targeted and monitored. Through a daily report card, example, information about performance with

respect to these behavioral targets is communicated to the home, and specified consequences are applied in the home for the in-school behavior. When desired behavior changes are achieved, the reinforcement for the target behavior is "faded," and a new behavior may be targeted. Although HBR-type strategies have repeatedly been shown to reduce problem behavior in school, the consequences for delinquent behavior and gang involvement have generally not been studied.

One extension of in-school behavior monitoring and home notification, which has been used in combination with other in-school interventions, is a Behavioral Monitoring and Reinforcement Program, which was the subject of a randomized trial involving junior high school youths. Those who were involved in the program showed less problem behavior, absenteeism and poor school performance; more employment at a one-year follow-up; and fewer court records at a five-year follow-up.[37, 38] This example is worthy of further for application and more randomized trials that

Reaching Youths Who Are Not in School

Despite their value in reducing the general risk for problem behavior, school-based programs and strategies are unlikely to reach youths who may be at greatest risk of joining a gang: those who have dropped out of school.

The link between delinquent behavior and poor school performance and school dropout has long been established.[34, 35, 36] Accordingly, delinquency-prone youths — including those prone to joining a gang — are less likely to be exposed to school-based preventive programs or gang interventions. Survey data on exposure to prevention programs are in line with this expectation, showing that gang members are less frequently exposed to a wide variety of school-based prevention activities.[1]

Among some populations in some locations, the school dropout rate is so high that it is unrealistic to expect gang-intervention programs to reach youths at risk for gang-joining with school-based programs. It is even unrealistic to expect "universal" prevention programs in high schools to reach those most at-risk. Urban, central-city dropout

rates are staggering in many metropolitan areas, for example: [39]

Baltimore City	41 percent
Philadelphia	61 percent
Albuquerque	49 percent

Much of the dropout occurs in the ninth grade, which means that youths at risk of dropout — who are typically poor school attendees while they remain enrolled — have little chance of exposure to programs in high school.[40]

Because these high-risk youths are less likely to regularly attend school, in-school and after-school programs are less likely to reach them. Therefore, strategies must be designed to appeal to them and meet their needs. Alternatives such as evening programs or other alternatives may help reach a fraction of this population that is willing to engage in education. Unfortunately, however, rigorous research on the efficacy of such approaches remains lacking.

▸ *INTERVIEW WITH THOMAS GORE*

The Associates for Renewal in Education (ARE) Public Charter School was one of the first charter schools authorized by the Public Charter School Board (CSB) when it began to operate in 1997 in the District of Columbia. It aimed to get youth who had been involved with the juvenile justice system back into a school. I interviewed the ARE president and executive director, Thomas W. Gore, M.S.W.

Why was the school created?

ARE and several other not-for-profit organizations began operating group homes for youth involved in the juvenile justice system in the early 1980s. These homes served adolescents who were coming out of detention in the Oak Hill Youth Center, youths who hadn't been in a regular school for two or three years. The Charter school was started because of the difficulty of getting these youths enrolled in regular schools.

Tell me about the school.

We used an approach based on William Glasser's *choice theory*. We wanted the students to realize that their behavior — their choices — have consequences. Our initial enrollment was 27 youths. The classes were small (no more than 8 to 10 students), each about 90 minutes long.

Can you describe a typical student?

The typical student had little involvement in education; some were parents, some had criminal charges, some were homeless, and others had little supervision in the home — which meant that they had probation officers and social workers. The students were not accustomed to regular school attendance. Students would miss school because they had to care for a younger sibling or child, see a lawyer, or had been arrested. Some youth were afraid to venture out to school because someone might hurt them. For example, a young man might get into a misunderstanding with someone on the weekend and then be afraid to come to school. Youths who often got into pickles with other people were our typical population. But the students *wanted* to be in the safe environment that the school afforded. What prevented violence *in the school* was that it was small. There was a caring atmosphere. The youths knew that if they became homeless, the school staff would find them a place to stay. If they came to school hungry, the school would have food.

What were some components of the program?

The students were assessed academically, and an educator developed individual learning packages. Each student worked at an individual pace. What helped get these youths back into school was the presence of experienced educators, behavioral counselors and the availability of child care. Although we had a standard curriculum in reading, math and history, we also had job-readiness education. A lot of the education was done outside of the walls of the school. Out-of-classroom instruction engaged youth in the school. In the job-readiness component, we focused on finding evening jobs. Some of the students were literally on their own.

Is there any downside to youths' employment when they are in school?

We saw it as meeting a need. If a young person doesn't have a regular place to live and doesn't have resources, providing that youth with part-time employment allows him or her to avoid getting into stealing or selling drugs. It cuts down the youth's need to be dependent on others, for example, a drug dealer. Employment is not for everyone. One

examine delinquent behavior and gang participation as outcomes.

Implementation Challenges

Although gang-prevention activities in schools are common, these programs are generally far from optimal and are therefore often unlikely to be efficacious. This section describes challenges related to implementation and leadership deficits in recognizing and acting on gang problems. It also describes a vicious cycle leading to a downward spiral of social control in some communities and schools. It also addresses one of the major challenges in implementing a successful gang-membership prevention program: the complex nature of multiple, interdependent processes that underlie delinquency and gangs in social areas. This section concludes that multiple, parallel efforts — rather than a single program — will be required to prevent gang problems in schools and communities and that development of alternatives to traditional schooling may be one helpful part of the mix of approaches to prevention.

Weaknesses of Existing Prevention Activity

School-based gang-prevention programs often fail to use best practices. According to the findings of a study that assessed the prevention activities of a large national sample of schools, these weaknesses included adopting programs without doing careful planning to match needs, poorly implementing programs with little supervision, and failing to engage youths who are at highest risk of gang involvement.[1]

of the objectives of the job-readiness activity was to get a good measure of whom we were dealing with.

Nearly half of the residents of the ARE group homes had histories of substance abuse at intake, and 29 percent had been convicted of possession with intent to distribute. Some of these youths may have been coming out of Oak Hill owing money to drug dealers. That must have created problems in getting these youths reintegrated with schooling.

Sometimes, a youth came out of Oak Hill owing someone money. Or you may learn that a youth is being used by a dealer as a "runner." Staff may have to utilize informal community contacts to negotiate with the dealer not to utilize this particular youth in this way. Being able to do this requires knowing the people in the community and having a sense of how to reach them.

What were the biggest challenges for the Charter School?

Our new school was part of a new charter school *system* that was trying to prove its

value. With the aim of reconnecting youths who had not been in school, we weren't able to produce high enough test scores to meet the CSB's expectations. We had to spend time educating the youths about the behavior expected in a school and about handling the stressors they faced in their lives. These outcomes are not measured by standardized achievement tests.

High attendance and test scores are not bad things; what was bad for us was being compared to schools serving traditional students. If it is a success to get a disconnected youth to go to school at all, a school should get credit for doing that. The initial focus of the CSB was to establish a viable alternative to the traditional public schools. Serving students who had a history of difficulties in education is not likely to provide the kind of quick wins that are needed in this situation. The school closed after five years because (a) our students were not meeting the CSB's academic achievement expectations, and (b) we couldn't increase enrollment enough to generate the revenue required to run the school. Funding is based on capitation.

What is your advice to someone who is contemplating starting a school to serve youth who have become disconnected from school?

Six things:

- Those who control funding must understand that the initial achievement and attendance of re-entry students will not compare well with students in regular schools.
- Keep the school small: no larger than about 50 students, no more than eight youth to one instructor.
- Have clear expectations for behavior, and clear policies and procedures with consequences built in.
- Be nontraditional in the way you conduct instruction.
- Have supportive services to help youth cope with having to see probation agents, deal with homelessness, being hungry and being arrested.
- Individualize learning strategies.

In this study, principals and program coordinators in schools were asked to describe the nature and extent of activities to prevent or reduce gang involvement, delinquency, drug use or other problem behavior and to promote a safe and orderly school environment. The researchers defined a gang-membership prevention activity as one that aims to reduce or prevent gang involvement, and they defined a gang-intervention activity as a program in which component activities are directed at youths who are gang members.

The researchers estimated that there were 781,800 gang-membership prevention activities and 159,700 gang-intervention activities under way in the nation's schools at the time of the survey.[1] It is important to note that most of the activities did not focus exclusively on gang-membership prevention but also targeted other forms of problem behavior, such as drug use.

The most common *prevention* activities — about 15 percent — were curriculum, instruction or training. About 11 percent of school-based gang-membership prevention programs involved efforts to create or maintain a distinctive school culture or climate for interpersonal exchanges, and about 8 percent involved recreation, enrichment or leisure activities.

Other types of prevention activities were less common. For example, fewer than 3 percent of gang-membership prevention programs provided a role for youths in regulating or responding to student conduct through conflict resolution, mediation or youth courts, for example.

The most common gang-*intervention* activities in schools — constituting 20 percent — were counseling, social work, and psychological or therapeutic intervention. About 10 percent of gang-intervention activities involved activities to improve intergroup relations, including activities to improve relations or resolve conflict and to promote school-community relations, including with the police or court, as well as multicultural activities.

But what about the quality of these gang-membership prevention programs? See the sidebar "Judging the Quality of a Gang-Membership Prevention Program." Also, for more information on program and outcome evaluation, see chapter 11.

Two recent reviews that summarize what is known about effective prevention programs in schools can provide some guidance in selecting best practices in schools.[9, 10] For example, programs that employ cognitive-behavioral principles have been shown to be effective in preventing problem behavior, according to a variety of measures; such programs usually involve instruction

and rehearsal of skills that help youths identify signs of impending problem situations, learn to stop before engaging in impulsive behavior, and improve competencies for redirecting or refusing peer pressure to engage in problem behavior.

Other strategies are designed to improve the school environment. Schoolwide strategies to promote a safe climate via clear and consistently enforced rules show promise.[7,41,42] Such programs clarify expectations for student behavior and disciplinary action, and they communicate rules and consequences. Monitoring the consistency of the application of disciplinary responses (which is a component of some programs) may be essential because it is otherwise difficult for teachers and administrators to know how consistent disciplinary action actually is. Planning teams involving teachers and administrators can be used to assess needs and to devise and monitor schoolwide activities in such programs.

Judging the Quality of a Gang-Membership Prevention Program

In some areas of human endeavor, "quality" is a concept that is reasonably well-understood. For instance, refrigerators are rated by *Consumer Reports* on features such as temperature control, energy efficiency, noise and capacity; and most people regard appliances that regulate temperature, use relatively little electricity, are quiet, and hold a lot of food as higher quality than those that let the ice cream melt, drive up the electricity bill, are noisy, and don't have room for a half-gallon carton of milk.

Popular magazine ratings of energy consumption and other features of refrigerators compare a particular model to other appliances on the market, and reviewers offer sensible advice on the suitability of the product for household use. But, in education — and particularly in the areas of delinquency and gang-membership prevention — information regarding program quality is not so clear. For instance, some schools adopt programs that are offered by vendors or technical assistance providers without careful consideration of

whether they make efficient use of educational time, use state-of-the-art methods, or are suited to the task of preventing gang involvement. A typical gang-membership prevention program involving curriculum or instruction in schools involves about 28 sessions or lessons over a 25-week period, with slightly less than half of the students participating approximately weekly. But there are also prevention programs in schools that involve five or fewer lessons — or that may be over in a week — or that involve very few students.

There also are programs that use methods or content that is unlikely to prevent gang involvement at all. For instance, recreational activities are sometimes employed with the stated purpose of preventing gang participation. Yet, we lack convincing evidence that school-based recreational programs reduce any form of problem behavior, and youth involvement in extracurricular activities is not strongly associated with the prevention of violence or gang membership.[14, 43]

To improve the usefulness of a school-based prevention program, program planners should:

- Select strategies based on recent scientific reviews, and other sources about prevention strategies and programs, that have been found to be efficacious when well-implemented.[9, 10, 44]

- Eschew programs (except when conducting rigorous efficacy research) that may seem appealing or to be good ideas but have not shown evidence of efficacy.[45]

- Attend carefully to measuring the extent and quality of implementation as the program is put in place.

The Importance of a Needs Assessment

Prevention activities in schools should be based on an assessment of the specific nature of the problems that gangs present in the school and the locality. A universal prevention program may be appropriate in a wide variety of schools. But, in a location where gangs are already active, more targeted and responsive intervention will be required to promote feelings of safety and to reduce conflict and further gang-joining.[46] Furthermore, there is evidence that existing programs are often weakly implemented and fail to engage the highest risk individuals. Therefore, the school assessment should go beyond looking at existing gang activity and indicators of risk for problem behavior to determine whether existing activities and programs have evidence of effectiveness, are being well-implemented, and are reaching those most at risk of gang involvement.

In a nationwide survey of more than 16,000 students in secondary schools, my colleagues and I found that significantly smaller percentages of current students who reported involvement with gangs during the past year were exposed to gang-membership prevention activities in the current school year than were nongang students.[1] In retrospect, this is unsurprising because among the risk factors for delinquency and gang involvement are poor attendance and low commitment to school, and because youths who display problem behavior are generally more difficult to engage in school activities.

This survey also showed that:

- Fewer gang-involved (vs. non-gang-involved) boys received instruction about ways to avoid getting involved in fighting, drug use and/or risky behavior.

- The percentage of youths participating in activities outside school was much lower for those involved in a gang than not involved in a gang.

- A much smaller percentage of gang-involved (vs. non-gang-involved) youths were in classrooms characterized by clear rules, good use of time, and other sound classroom management practices.

- Youths in gangs were much less likely to be involved in school activities with people or groups from the community.

Such findings in schools where prevention and intervention programs were being implemented imply that needs assessments should consider the strength and fidelity of *existing* prevention and intervention programs. In addition, the findings imply that a needs assessment should focus particularly on the extent to which prevention and intervention activities reach those youths who are involved in delinquent behavior and are at elevated risk for delinquency and gang involvement.

The same study also assessed the quality of school programs directed at gang problems. We found that prevention or intervention programs that were developed *after* a needs assessment:

- Were of higher quality.

- Were of longer duration.

- Made more use of best practices.

- Involved a larger proportion of students.

- Engaged more school personnel.

School Leader Recognition of Gang Problems

The degree to which school principals deny the presence of gang problems in their schools is astonishing. Although 36 percent of school principals report gang problems in their *communities*, only about 5 percent report problems in their *schools*.[47]

In about 1 in 10 schools, 15 percent or more of the students self-reported that they were involved in a gang; but only 20 percent of the principals in these same schools said that there was a gang problem in their school. Evidently, principals' reports are of questionable validity in assessing the extent of gang problems in schools.

Principals' failure to recognize gang problems may often be an obstacle to the development of effective prevention and intervention programs. In all likelihood, it will be necessary to develop plans to cope with the reluctance of many school administrators to recognize gang problems. For instance, educational systems might *require* schools to conduct periodic surveys to measure student and teacher perceptions of safety and student involvement in problem behavior and gangs.

Getting Programs to Reach Those Who Need Them Most

Earlier in this chapter, I discussed some of the challenges of reaching youths who have dropped out of school with any kind of gang-membership prevention strategies or programs (see the sidebar, "Reaching Youths Who Are Not in School").

Another challenge is that the greatest need may be in areas of concentrated poverty with large numbers of language-minority immigrants.[1,48] In these areas, schools serve large numbers of youths who are vulnerable to dropping out or becoming involved in delinquent behavior and gangs. A destructive cycle may operate in such schools and school districts, where the schools have difficulty recruiting and retaining quality staff. In addition, weaknesses in school administration contribute to disorderly schools and weak social control, which lead to perceptions of the unattractiveness of the schools and neighborhoods, which in turn perpetuate a cycle of concentrated disadvantage in the area.[49] The figure below depicts the cycle of concentrated disadvantage.

Policy Implications

Achieving the successful implementation of effective interventions specifically aimed at gang problems (as well as those directed at delinquent behavior generally) will require simultaneous attention to all of the issues described in this chapter: assessment of needs, open recognition of problems, selection of strategies that have been shown to be effective, assessment of and resolution of obstacles to program implementation, and breaking the cycle of community disadvantage and school ineffectiveness.

This is a tall order. Multiple, parallel efforts — rather than single programs — are required to prevent gang problems in schools and communities. A broad multifaceted approach is necessary not only to cope with delinquency and gang problems but also to address other problems of systematic inequity in education and society.

Because resolution of all of these problems is unlikely in the short run, and because so many gang-prone or gang-involved youths will be school dropouts, the development of effective alternative education programs suitable for youths who have not succeeded in school will likely also be required. Despite interest for many years in such alternative education programs for youths who do not engage successfully in traditional schools, there is little trustworthy evidence from evaluations of the efficacy of such programs. Small alternative programs suitable for dropouts who may have experienced difficulties and few rewards in traditional educational settings — and which allow dropouts simultaneously to cope with employment and child care — should be developed and carefully evaluated.

Here are some principles that should guide gang-membership prevention efforts in schools:

Target Efforts Where Needed

Gang problems are greater in some places than in others, and problems may emerge in locations where few problems existed in the past. Therefore, efforts should be directed where and when they are most needed to cope with evident or emerging gang problems. In some respects, the presence of gangs in a community or a school seems like the presence of an infectious agent: The problem tends to spread, involving more people than those initially "infected." When youths become involved with a gang, their levels of delinquent behavior accelerate beyond the levels that would otherwise be expected based on their other personal characteristics. Gangs appear to generate and feed on fear, and they are stimulated by and generate the higher levels of delinquent behavior in places where they are present. Therefore, gang problems should be openly recognized when they occur, and they should be confronted directly.

Intervene to Make Environments Safer

Fear for one's safety appears to be a key factor in an individual youth's decision to join a gang. Therefore, helping vulnerable persons feel safe in their schools and neighborhoods may be useful in stemming gang involvement. This means intervening in school *environments* to make them safer and to make the people in them *feel* safer. Efforts to alter school environments will generally be fundamentally different from working with *individual youth* to decrease their propensity for gang involvement. For example, the school interventions will likely involve interventions that firmly and clearly enforce rules related to safety; target efforts at crime control at locations where and at times when evidence shows that safety problems exist; and reduce the tolerance for threats or threatening symbols in the environment.[41, 42, 50, 51, 52]

Transforming environments to make them safer is a complex task. Gangs and other crime problems disproportionately occur in areas of concentrated disadvantage, where there is concentrated poverty and a high proportion of speakers of languages other than English. These are loca-tions where schools often do not function well. Schools in these areas may have high dropout rates, high rates of teacher turnover, and difficulty attracting and retaining good teachers. Teacher turnover is high in schools where teachers perceive student incivilities and little commitment to education — and where teachers do not get the administrative support they need. Addressing this issue will require attention to staffing and administration of schools as well as to the nuts and bolts of providing safe, engaging educational environments.[49]

Monitor Schools for Safety

Our nation's schools should have more explicit and more valid mechanisms for monitoring safety so that interventions can be targeted where they are required. Existing methods (such as those required in the No Child Left Behind Act) are inadequate and should be improved upon.[53]

Principals are reluctant to recognize safety or gang problems in their schools, and state and local educational agencies also tend to avoid pinpointing schools with gang or safety problems. Indeed, rather than encouraging school principals and administrators to identify and plan to ameliorate safety problems, system administrators unfortunately may punish principals who bring problems to their attention and seek to address them. This should stop; problem identification and planning should be understood to be and be treated as professional leadership. Because we can expect some persons occupying leadership positions to fear bringing problems out into the open, formal mechanisms such as systematic self-report victimization surveys should be required of schools to supplement the existing inadequate mechanisms, including school- or principal-reported incident or suspension rates.

Pay Attention to Implementation

Achieving full implementation of interventions in the forms intended has always been a problem in education (as in other human services), and policymakers should assume that implementation strength and fidelity will be problematic for gang-membership prevention programs as well. It has become commonplace to say that program evaluation is needed — however, too often this is interpreted to mean that *outcome* evaluations are required. But the first need is for evaluation focused on the extent to which program implementation is being achieved. Programs must be delivered to the populations intended for the planned durations and must include the key features found to be associated with efficacy in research. For more on the importance of program evaluation, see chapter 11.

Conclusion

Maintaining an environment in which young people feel safe may be one of the most important things to do to prevent youths from joining a gang. Although this proposition has not been subjected to rigorous scientific testing, what we know about risk and preventive factors points to the promise of this approach.

Achieving safe schools and implementing effective prevention programs will be most difficult in the schools and communities most in need of gang-membership prevention but, of course, this is precisely where increased prevention measures are needed. Furthermore, youths who are at greatest risk of gang involvement will be particularly difficult to reach in schools.

The task of increasing the effectiveness of school programs is daunting, in part, because schools are already engaged in so much prevention activity that cannot be expected to be efficacious. Improving gang-membership prevention will have to involve the assessment of the specific needs of specific schools, as well as an assessment of how well current activities are being implemented and whether they can be expected to be efficacious. The creation of formal mechanisms to assess gang problems and the quality of program implementation is likely to be required to provide the impetus for the improvement of gang-membership prevention activity in schools.

Fortunately, there are school-based programs — including those focused on substance abuse, delinquency and violence prevention — that have been shown to be efficacious in addressing some of the risk factors for gang-joining. Schools should select one, or a few, such programs, based on their match to the individual school's specific needs, and take care to implement them fully.

About the Author

Gary D. Gottfredson

Gary D. Gottfredson has conducted research on school safety and delinquency prevention for more than three decades. His research on the efficacy of school-based prevention programs led to a model for evaluating programs that has guided numerous prevention research projects. An applied psychologist who has published extensively, Dr. Gottfredson was elected a Fellow of the Academy for Experimental Criminology for his research on program efficacy. He earned his Ph.D. from Johns Hopkins University and now teaches at the University of Maryland, College Park.

Endnotes

1. Gottfredson GD, Gottfredson DC. *Gang Problems and Gang Programs in a National Sample of Schools.* Ellicott City, MD: Gottfredson Associates, 2001.

2. Hawkins JD, Catalano RF, Miller JY. Risk and protective factors for alcohol and other drug problems in adolescence and early adulthood: Implications for substance abuse prevention. *Psychol Bull.* 1992; 112:64-105.

3. Forgatch MS, Patterson GR, Degarmo DS, Beldavs ZG. Testing the Oregon delinquency model with 9-year follow-up of the Oregon Divorce Study. *Dev Psychopathol.* 2009; 21:637-660.

4. Granic I, Patterson GR. Toward a comprehensive model of antisocial development: A dynamic systems approach. *Psychol Rev.* 2006; 113:101-131.

5. Loeber R, Farrington DP, Stouthamer-Loeber M, White HR, eds., *Violence and Serious Theft: Development and Prediction From Childhood to Adulthood.* New York, NY: Routledge/Taylor & Francis Group, 2008.

6. Gottfredson GD, Gottfredson DC. *Victimization in Schools.* New York, NY: Plenum, 1985.

7. Gottfredson DC, Wilson DB, Najaka SS. School-based crime prevention. In: Sherman LW, Farrington DP, Welsh B, Mackenzie DL, eds., *Evidence-Based Crime Prevention.* London, England: Routledge, 2002.

8. Olweus D, Limber S, Mihalic S. *Blueprints for Violence Prevention: Bullying Prevention Program.* Boulder, CO: Center for the Study and Prevention of Violence, 1999.

9. Gottfredson GD, Gottfredson DC. School violence. In: Flannery D, Vazonsyi A, Waldman I, eds., *The Cambridge Handbook of Violent Behavior and Aggression.* New York, NY: Cambridge University Press, 2007:344-358.

10. Cook PJ, Gottfredson DC, Na C. School crime control and prevention. In: Tonry M, ed., *Crime and Justice: A Review of Research,* Vol. 39. Chicago, IL: University of Chicago Press, 2010:313-440.

11. Correlational studies are of little use because metal detectors tend to be used only in schools where school safety problems already exist. One study of secondary students in 115 New York schools found that students in schools with metal detectors (19 schools) less often carried weapons in school than did those in schools without metal detectors (96 schools) but that students were about equally likely to carry weapons outside of school (Ginsberg C, Loffredo L, Violence-related attitudes and behaviors of high school students — New York City, 1992. *MMWR Morb Mortal Wkly Rep.* 1993; 42(40):773-777). Because of the extent of use of metal detectors, their intrusiveness and their unknown efficacy, more rigorous research on their efficacy and on factors that influence efficacy (notably, consistency of use) is required.

12. Hankin A, Hertz M, Simon TR. Impacts of metal detector use in schools: Insights from 15 years of research. *J Sch Health* 2011; 81(2): 100-106.

13. Hill KG, Howell JC, Hawkins JD, Battin-Pearson SR. Childhood risk factors for adolescent gang membership: Results from the Seattle Social Development Project. *J Res Crime Delinq.* 1999; 36:300-322.

14. Thornberry TP. Membership in youth gangs and involvement in serious and violent offending. In: Loeber R, Farrington D, eds., *Serious and Violent Juvenile Offenders: Risk Factors and Successful Interventions.* Thousand Oaks, CA: Sage Publications, 1998.

15. Gordon RA, Lahey BB, Kawai E, Loeber R, Stouthamer-Loeber M, Farrington DP. Antisocial behavior and youth gang membership. *Criminology* 2004; 42:55-88.

16. Thornberry TP, Krohn MD, Lizotte AJ, Chard-Wierschem D. The role of juvenile gangs in facilitating delinquent behavior. *J Res Crime Delinq.* 1993; 30:55-87.

17. Decker SH. Collective and normative features of gang violence. *Justice Q.* 1996; 13:243-264.

18. Melde C, Taylor TJ, Esbensen F-A. "I got your back:" An examination of the protective function of gang membership in adolescence. *Criminology* 2009; 47:565-594.

19. Padilla F. *The Gang as an American Enterprise.* New Brunswick, NJ: Rutgers University Press, 1992.

20. Klein M, Maxson CL. *Street Gang Patterns and Policies.* New York, NY: Oxford University Press, 2006.

21. Esbensen F-A, Peterson D, Taylor TJ, Freng A. Similarities and differences in risk factors for violent offending and gang membership. *Aust NZ J Criminol.* 2009; 42:310-335.

22. Lipsey MW, Derzon JH. Predictors of violent or serious delinquency in adolescence and early adulthood: a synthesis of longitudinal research. In: Loeber R, Farrington DP, eds., *Serious and Violent Juvenile Offenders: Risk Factors and Successful Interventions.* Thousand Oaks, CA: Sage Publications, 1998:86-105.

23. Hahn R, Fuqua-Whitley D, Wetherington H, Lowy J, Crosby A, Fullilove M, Johnson R, Liberman A, Moscicki E, Price L, Snyder S, Tuma F, Corey S, Stone G, Mukhopadhaya K, Chattopadhyay S, Dahlberg L. Effectiveness of universal school-based programs to prevent violent and aggressive behavior: A systematic review. *Am J Prev Med.* 2007; 33(2S):S114-S129.

24. Wilson SJ, Lipsey MW. School-based interventions for aggressive and disruptive behavior: Update of a meta-analysis. *Am J Prev Med.* 2007; 33(2S):S130-S143.

25. Wilson DB, Gottfredson DC, Najaka SS. School-based prevention of problem behaviors: A meta-analysis. *J Quant Criminol.* 2001; 17:247-272.

26. Greenberg MT, Kushé CA, Cook ET, Quamma JP. Promoting emotional competence in school-aged children: The effects of the PATHS curriculum. *Dev Psychopathol.* 1995; 7:117-136.

27. Conduct Problems Prevention Research Group. The Fast Track randomized controlled trial to prevent externalizing psychiatric disorders: Findings from grades 3 to 9. *J Am Acad Child Adolesc Psychiatry* 2007; 46:1250-1262.

28. Conduct Problems Prevention Research Group. Fast Track intervention effects on youth arrests and delinquency. *J Exp Criminol.* 2010; 6:131-157.

29. Greenberg MT, Kusché C, Mihalic SF. *Blueprints for Violence Prevention, Book Ten: Promoting Alternative Thinking Strategies (PATHS).* Boulder, CO: Center for the Study and Prevention of Violence, Institute of Behavioral Science, University of Colorado, 1998.

30. Jones D, Godwin J, Dodge KA, Bierman KL, Coie JD, Greenberg MT, Lochman JE, McMahon RJ, Pinderhughes EE. Impact of the Fast Track prevention program on health services use by conduct-problem youth. *Pediatrics* 2010; 125:e130-e136.

31. Atkeson BM, Forehand R. Home-based reinforcement programs designed to modify classroom behavior: A review and methodological evaluation. *Psychol Bull.* 1979; 86:1298-1308.

32. Barth R. Home-based reinforcement of school behavior: A review and analysis. *Rev Educ Res.* 1979; 49:436-458.

33. Cox DD. Evidence-based interventions using home-school collaboration. *Sch Psychol Q.* 2005; 20:473-497.

34. Bachman JG, O'Malley PM, Johnston J. *Adolescence to Adulthood: Change and Stability in the Lives of Young Men.* Ann Arbor, MI: University of Michigan Institute for Social Research, 1978.

35. Gottfredson DC. *Schools and Delinquency.* New York, NY: Cambridge University Press, 2001.

36. Gottfredson GD. Schooling and delinquency. In: Martin SE, Sechrest LB, Redner R, eds., *New Directions in the Rehabilitation of Criminal Offenders.* Washington, DC: National Academy Press, 1981:424-469.

37. Bry BH, George F. The preventive effects of early intervention on the attendance and grades of urban adolescents. *Prof Psychol.* 1980; 11:252-260.

38. Bry BH. Reducing the incidence of adolescent problems through preventive intervention: One- and five-year follow-up. *Am J Community Psychol.* 1982; 10:265-276.

39. Swanson CB. *Cities in Crisis 2009: Closing the Graduation Gap.* Bethesda, MD: Editorial Projects in Education, Inc., 2009.

40. Of course, this also means that the primary prevention of school dropout by arrangements that promote school success for all students is important.

41. Gottfredson DC, Gottfredson GD, Hybl LG. Managing adolescent behavior: A multi-year, multi-school study. *Am Educ Res J.* 1993; 30:179-215.

42. Gottfredson GD, Gottfredson DC. *Using Organization Development to Improve School Climate* (Report No. 17). Baltimore, MD: Johns Hopkins University, Center for Research on Elementary and Middle Schools, 1987.

43. Farrington DP. Predictors, causes, and correlates of male youth violence. In: Tonry M, Moore MH, eds., *Crime and Justice: A Review of Research, Vol. 24: Youth Violence.* Chicago, IL: University of Chicago Press, 1998:421-475.

44. Centers for Disease Control and Prevention. The effectiveness of universal school-based programs for the prevention of violent and aggressive behavior: A report on recommendations of the Task Force on Community Preventive Services. *MMWR Morb Mortal Wkly Rep.* 2007; 56(RR-7):1-12.

45. For instance, recreational programs, after-school instruction and information campaigns, although often appealing and considered to be good ideas by educators, have generally not been demonstrated to prevent delinquency or gang involvement.

46. Office of Juvenile Justice and Delinquency Prevention. *OJJDP Comprehensive Gang Model: A Guide for Assessing Your Community Youth Gang Problem.* Washington, DC: U.S. Department of Justice, Office of Justice Programs, Office of Juvenile Justice and Delinquency Prevention, 2009.

47. The percentages are higher in urban areas (65 percent in the community, and 9 percent in the school). The data in this paragraph are drawn from a survey of principals and students in a national sample of schools (see reference 1, Gottfredson GD, Gottfredson DC, *Gang Problems and Gang Programs in a National Sample of Schools,* 2001).

48. Gottfredson GD, Gottfredson DC, Gottfredson NC, Jones EM. Community characteristics, staffing difficulty, and school disorder in a national sample of secondary schools. Paper presented at 54th Annual Meeting of the American Society of Criminology, Chicago, IL, November 2002.

49. Gottfredson GD. Schools and delinquency. In: Feld BC, Bishop D, eds., *Handbook of Juvenile Crime and Juvenile Justice.* New York, NY: Oxford University Press, 2011.

50. Gottfredson DC. An evaluation of an organization development approach to reducing school disorder. *Eval Rev.* 1987; 11:739-763.

51. Gottfredson, DC. An empirical test of school-based environmental and individual interventions to reduce the risk of delinquent behavior. *Criminology* 1986; 24:705-731.

52. Gottfredson GD, Hollifield JH. How to diagnose school climate. *Nat Assoc Second Sch Principals Bull.* 1988; 72(506):63-71.

53. The No Child Left Behind legislation required the identification of persistently unsafe schools but left the definition of this to the states. State definitions have generally identified few persistently unsafe schools and, usually, explicit indicators of safety problems — such as rates of student or teacher victimization — are not involved. Instead, such things as suspension rates have been used.

What Should Be Done in the Community to Prevent Gang-Joining?

Jorja Leap

- **There is no need to reinvent the wheel: Communities are rich in resources and strengths that can be inventoried and drawn upon, and existing evidence-based strategies can be used.**

- **Comprehensive approaches that work across disciplines and settings are needed to prevent youth from joining gangs in the first place.**

- **To be successful, community-based gang-membership prevention efforts depend on the collaboration of a wide range of stakeholders; this engagement — reflecting shared involvement and "investment" — builds on a community's strengths and addresses its weaknesses.**

- **Strategies should be designed around core activities such as tutoring, mentoring, life-skills training, case management, parental involvement, connection with schools, supervised recreational activities and community mobilization.**

In Brief

The idea behind a community-based gang-membership prevention strategy is simple: Children and youth safely thrive when the community's members are engaged in their community and invested in the children. This has been well-summarized in the adage, "It takes a village to raise a child." But, needless to say, this is only an adage if there are no clear guidelines for just how the village is supposed to get the job done!

This chapter will look at a handful of comprehensive, community-based prevention efforts. It also explores ways of thinking about community-based gang-membership prevention by drawing on principles that are sound, effective and cost-effective. Because youth violence and delinquency can be risk factors for gang-joining (and vice versa), the discussion is not limited to gang-membership prevention, for which, unfortunately, there is a paucity of research. Therefore, the discussion includes examples of innovative efforts in the arenas of violence and delinquency, including program implementation challenges and what policymakers and practitioners need to know about helping communities plan and carry out gang-membership prevention initiatives.

Although some community-based efforts in the United States and Canada are offered as examples, this discussion primarily "reverse-engineers" these programs to examine core concepts — key principles — by answering the question most often asked by practitioners and policymakers: What do we most need to know? Certainly, what decision-makers should know varies across communities, but this chapter offers some basic concepts that are crucial to build on a community's strengths and avoid reinventing the wheel.

Unfortunately, gangs are often thought of as a separate group from the community in which gang members reside. As a result of this thinking, many programs that address gang problems have tended to be deterrence-heavy attempts to move gangs out of the community. More attention must be paid, however, to strategies that help prevent children from joining gangs in the first place. Such prevention programs are generally implemented in two contexts: In schools, teaching children the dangers of joining gangs and the skills needed to enhance their opportunities and decision-making; and in the community, through prosocial activities and positive role models.

It is critical that these programs take into account the strengths and resources that already exist in a community and that they provide a coordinated approach to addressing youth's needs.

Historically, incorporating community resources and community members in a gang-membership prevention strategy has been overlooked. (Please note that, although the definition of "community" can vary, I use the term to describe a group of people interacting with each other and living in a common, defined location.) Often, gang-membership prevention programs take place outside the community setting and focus on individual children — through education, positive relationships and prosocial activities, for example. But these approaches are often not sufficient to "inoculate" children against the risk factors they face *within* their communities, such as a lack of community activities, cohesion and physical infrastructure; high levels of gang activity or violence; and the availability of drugs and firearms. Children still have to navigate the reality of their communities and may feel that they need to engage in violence or join a gang to survive or to meet their social needs.[1] Attempting to inoculate the individual from his or her environment without addressing the environment itself reduces the likelihood of maintaining emotional and physical health, as even the best treatment cannot succeed if the individual is continually exposed to what is causing the ailment.

Initiatives designed to help prevent youth from joining a gang often do a poor job of building on the strengths of a community, such as positive role models, existing programs and other indigenous resources. To strengthen a community's resilience, it is necessary to look at a range of options, including community mobilization and neighborhood watch groups, media campaigns, graffiti removal, prevention coalitions, and civil remedies such as gang injunctions. Such community-based efforts face significant challenges, however. One of the most significant is

a lack of evaluations, which are necessary for the development of evidence-based models.

Why is there such a lack of evidence? Two primary reasons: a lack of funding for formal evaluations, and the complexity of measuring multiple, simultaneously implemented strategies on a communitywide basis. (For more on evaluation, see chapter 11.) That said, a small body of rigorous evaluation research has examined youth-violence and delinquency prevention, and key elements — or principles — in these areas may also be effective in reducing gang-joining. Here are six principles that practitioners and policymakers should keep in mind when adopting prevention strategies with the goal of preventing gang membership:

1. Build a community's prevention operating system.

2. Develop multidisciplinary collaboration to ensure seamlessness.

3. Start early.

4. Take a comprehensive approach.

5. Address core components.

6. Replace and exceed the attraction of gangs.

Build a Community's Prevention Operating System

There are models for providing coalitions of community stakeholders with the training, tools and technical assistance needed to identify gaps and opportunities, select appropriate prevention strategies based on existing evidence, and implement these strategies to maximize beneficial effects.

For example, the Communities That Care (CTC) operating system uses a public health approach to help coalitions prevent a range of negative youth outcomes, including violence, delinquency, school dropout and substance abuse.

The CTC approach provides a practical guide for planning and implementing community-based prevention efforts in five phases:

1. **Getting started:** Identify stakeholders and define the community to be served.

2. **Organizing, introducing and involving:** Engage stakeholders and develop the vision and organizational structure.

3. **Developing a community profile:** Assess protective and risk factors, strengths, challenges, resources and gaps.

4. **Creating an action plan:** Implement new or previously tested effective programs, policies or practices.

5. **Implementing and evaluating the action plan:** Assess what worked and did not work.

The Social Development Research Group at the University of Washington is currently conducting a longitudinal evaluation that has already reported positive outcomes based on a trial in 24 communities in seven states. The latest results — following CTC youth and a control group of non-CTC youth from the fifth grade on — show significantly lower levels of delinquent and violent behaviors among CTC youth through the 10th grade.[2]

Collaborate to Ensure Seamlessness

Multidisciplinary collaboration is a necessary component of an effective prevention operating system. As we have found in programs that reduce juvenile delinquency and youth violence, community-based gang-membership prevention coalitions should be multidisciplinary, including, for example, education, law enforcement, health and social services. Given the complexity of the factors that contribute to gang-joining, it is important for groups focused on prevention to take advantage of principles from criminology, sociology, psychology and public health. Institutions within the community must collaborate to ensure that

programs address youth's needs both in school and in the community and — this is important — that the connection between them is seamless. One of the most heartbreaking things I saw in my work in gang-membership prevention occurred when I was evaluating a program called Youth Lead at two major high-risk middle schools in Los Angeles. These middle-school kids were at the point, developmentally, where they could join a gang or stay out. Youth Lead had an innovative in-school program that focused on kids only during class hours. After school, I would walk out with the kids — and instead of parents or siblings, gang members would be waiting to pick them up.

Continuous services are critical to successful prevention: What begins in the classroom should be reinforced in the community and even in juvenile justice institutions. Prevention efforts cannot end with the ringing of the school bell. Strategies aimed at keeping kids out of gangs must be provided seamlessly across the community and even in institutional settings.

It is important to note that programs that reduce gang *activity* within a community are also likely to reduce the *attraction* of gang life for youth who have not yet joined. For example, the Broader Urban Involvement and Leadership Development Program (BUILD) employs multiple, targeted prevention strategies to reduce gang violence in some of Chicago's most economically depressed, crime-impacted neighborhoods. As part of its in-school, after-school and out-of-school activities, BUILD has engaged multiple partners, including the Chicago Police Department, Chicago CeaseFire, and Hargrove Hospital as well as the Post-Secondary Partnership Council, After School Matters, the Exelon Stay in School Initiative, and various community-based partnerships and coalitions. These partnerships are dynamic, constantly responding to the changing needs of youth in the BUILD program. To ensure the connection between school and after-school programs in the community, BUILD's strategies include:

• School-based violence-prevention curricula.

• Trained street workers to do outreach and serve as positive role models.

• Violence-prevention curricula at temporary detention centers.

• After-school sports and recreation.

- Career training, college counseling and financial aid.

- Coordination among corporate sponsors, community leaders, parents and activists in local antiviolence initiatives.

An evaluation of BUILD by Loyola University, conducted in 1999, showed that youth who received BUILD services had significantly lower gang-violence recidivism compared with youth who did not receive BUILD services. In fact, recidivism was linked to the amount of time that youth were exposed to the BUILD curriculum in the classroom: Youth who had less exposure were more likely to relapse into gang activity.[3] Community engagement in a multidisciplinary collaboration allows a program to build acceptance and support; it increases a community's strengths and addresses its weaknesses. Developing community collaborations helps target limited resources and reduces duplication of effort.

Start Early

The concept of *primary prevention* is essential to a gang-membership prevention program. Although many programs focus on getting youth out of gangs or stopping gang violence, more work is needed to stop youth from joining gangs in the first place. Early prevention strategies have the potential to change the path that young children are on by enhancing existing protective factors and by helping them overcome risks. One

strategy developed in Canada, the Preventive Treatment Program (PTP), offers a useful example of an early prevention strategy.

Established in Montreal, PTP was designed to reduce antisocial behavior among low-socioeconomic-status boys from 7 to 9 years old. The program uses training — of boys and their parents — aimed at decreasing delinquency, substance use and gang involvement. Parental training focuses on monitoring children's behavior, offering positive reinforcement for prosocial behavior, using punishment effectively and managing family crises. Training for the boys focuses on improving prosocial skills and self-control through coaching, modeling, reinforcement contingency and role-playing.

A 1995 evaluation of PTP demonstrated short- and long-term effects. Boys who participated in PTP when they were 9 years old were — six years later, at age 15 — less likely to report gang involvement or drug use during the previous 12 months than boys who did not participate in PTP. PTP boys were also less likely to report committing delinquent acts or having friends arrested by the police.[4,5]

Take a Comprehensive Approach

The social ecological model highlights the potential for prevention strategies to address risk and protective factors at the individual, relationship, community and societal levels (see figure, "Levels of Social Influence on Youth Violence: The Social Ecological Model"). Unfortunately, most prevention strategies focus only on the risks present in the "individual" youth. Comprehensive strategies that address the factors within families, peer groups, schools and communities have the potential for broader and more sustained effects.

Project Star — a community-based drug-abuse prevention initiative for adolescents, originally called the Midwestern Prevention Program (MPP) — is an example of a well-evaluated program that uses a comprehensive approach to addressing multiples levels of influence. Project Star/MPP has been selected by the University of Colorado's Center for the Study and Prevention of Violence as a Blueprints Model Program (see description below). Although it does not target gang-joining specifically, some of Project Star's principles provide a useful framework for thinking about delinquency and gang-joining prevention programs. The program integrates both demand- and supply-reduction strategies by combining prevention programming with local school and community policy change. These policy changes are implemented by parents, school administrators and community leaders as part of the parent and community organization programs.

Project Star/MPP bridges networks, builds social capital and increases community investment in youth development by focusing on these components:

- **Mass Media:** Introduces the community to components of the program as they are added, seeking especially to inform residents who have influence over youth.

- **School:** In grade 6 or 7 (the transition years), a program works to increase students' skills to resist using drugs and to change the social acceptance of drugs in school.

- **Parent:** Develops family support for a non-drug-use norm within the family and in the community, including parent education when the child is in middle school.

- **Community:** Government and community leaders are trained to form a community organization to strategically plan and implement drug-abuse prevention services and activities.

- **Health policy:** A government subcommittee — including leaders from the community — is formed to implement policy initiatives that reduce demand and limit the supply of cigarettes, alcohol and illicit drugs.

(NOTE: These components are delivered sequentially, six to 12 months apart, over a five-year period; the mass-media component is used during all five years.)

Researchers began tracking Project Star/MPP students in 1985. They randomly assigned sixth- and seventh-graders from eight public middle schools in the Kansas City area to the program or the control group. Results of the evaluation showed long-lasting decreases in tobacco and marijuana use and an increase in parent-to-youth conversations about drug use.[6, 7]

Another example — which is specific to gang involvement — is the Comprehensive Gang Model, implemented and tested by the U.S. Department of Justice's Office of Juvenile Justice and Delinquency Prevention (OJJDP). This model (which researchers sometimes refer to as the "Spergel model") involves a coordinated effort of community mobilization, providing opportunities, social intervention, suppression, and organizational development and change. Based on quasi-experimental evaluations of the Comprehensive Gang Model in five sites (Bloomington, IL; Mesa and Tucson, AZ; Riverside, CA; and San Antonio, TX), researchers found that it was successful when implemented correctly — specifically when the program was implemented in conjunction with integrated agency partnerships.[8]

In Riverside, for example, gang activity and drug-related arrests declined among youth who were in the program. In Mesa, there were lower arrest rates among program youth for specific crimes and fewer reported juvenile-perpetrated crimes. Although gang *membership* was not specifically measured, the reduction in gang activity, drug arrests and juvenile crimes would arguably reduce the influence that gang members have in recruiting new members.

It is important to note, however, that there were no changes in three of the sites (Bloomington, Tucson and San Antonio) that did not implement all of the components of the program. With little room for error, the Comprehensive Gang Model seems to be all-or-nothing in nature; results suggest that only those communities able to accommodate *all* program pieces will see desired results. Also, the model is focused on gang intervention rather than preventing youth from joining gangs. Therefore, it is important for communities to also consider adaptations or other models that include a focus on gang-joining prevention.

Address Core Components of Prevention

Prevention operating systems like CTC can take advantage of what I call a "core menu" of prevention strategies — strategies that can build protective factors within a fragile community and that, in turn, have the potential to help prevent youth from joining a gang. These include a range of positive enhancements such as tutoring, mentoring, life-skills training, case management, increased parental involvement, improving connections with schools, and other opportunities for supervised recreational activities.

These core strategies can work by directly reducing the likelihood of gang involvement or by reinforcing strengths within the family or in the community. Community members and organizations are often more willing to mobilize around prevention efforts, when the focus is on the positive influences that should be enhanced, rather than solely on risks and what is not working. Communities should consider the core activities that are already in place — even if these need improvement or modification — as well as additional activities that are needed to strengthen youth's abilities to avoid gang-joining.

Many existing prevention programs are designed to work by enhancing these types of protective factors. Fortunately, communities can draw from existing evidence-based programs such as those highlighted in the Blueprints review of violence-prevention programs.[9] (For more on Blueprints, see below.) Communities should also think beyond specific programs and consider broader strategies and policies that could be implemented to enhance core protective factors or improve the ability to implement effective programs.

Replacing and Exceeding the Attraction of Gangs

To be effective, a gang-membership prevention strategy should replace — and, indeed, exceed — the attraction that being in a gang has for some youth. An oft-repeated adage in the helping professions is, "Don't take something away without putting something in its place." When urging youth *not* to join gangs, the message should also offer prosocial alternatives. Some of the important but often unrecognized attractions of gangs include the support, sense of belonging, excitement and relationships that youth believe gangs offer. (For more on the attraction of gangs, see chapter 2.)

Relationship-building is a critical component of healthy and prosocial development in youth. The Boys and Girls Clubs Gang Prevention Through Targeted Outreach (GPTTO) program offers one example of this prevention principle. GPTTO reaches at-risk youth ages 6-18 through outreach, referral, relationships with and mentoring by older youth, and exciting activities that increase a sense of belonging. A case-management component assures school attendance and performance and increases participation in the community.

An evaluation of GPTTO has revealed several desired outcomes. In addition to better school performance and attitudes and increased positive peer relationships, youth who attended more GPTTO sessions were less likely to engage in marijuana use and theft in the year after attending the sessions.[10] Looking at whether GPTTO played a role in keeping kids away from gangs, the researchers found that more frequent participation in sessions was associated with:

- Delayed onset of gang-like behavior, such as wearing gang attire.

- Less contact with the juvenile justice system.

- Decrease in delinquent behaviors.

- Improved school performance.

- Better prosocial relationships.

As the GPTTO evaluation showed, positive relationships are a major protective factor for youth who are at risk for gang-joining.

This principle is also integral to Big Brothers Big Sisters of America (BBBSA). The primary prevention strategy of BBBSA is adult support and mentoring through one-to-one relationships with at-risk 6- to 18-year-olds from single-parent homes. The program maintains standards through volunteer orientation and screening, along with youth and family assessment. Volunteers are required to complete training in mentoring, including relationship-building and how to recognize serious problems. Mentors must attend ongoing training in maintaining supportive relationships. Matches between volunteers and youth are based on the youth's needs — including developmental stage — and on parental preferences and volunteers' abilities. BBBSA offers ongoing supervision and quarterly contact between the agency and the family.

An evaluation of BBBSA has shown positive results. Researchers compared youth from eight BBBSA sites (Houston, TX; San Antonio, TX; Columbus, OH; Minneapolis, MN; Rochester, NY; Phoenix, AZ; Philadelphia, PA; and Wichita, KS) with youth in control-group sites over an 18-month period. The youth in the study were 10-16 years old; 60 percent were male and more than half were members of an ethnic minority. Nearly all lived with one parent in a low-income household, reporting family histories of violence or substance abuse. It is important to note that these are risk factors for gang-joining.

The researchers looked at several outcomes — including drug and alcohol use, conduct problems and violent behaviors. They found that youth who participated in BBBSA for 18 months were 46 percent less likely to start using drugs and 27 percent less likely to start using alcohol than youth in the control group. The evaluation also showed that BBBSA youth were less likely to engage in violent behavior, exhibited better classroom behavior and had higher academic performance.[11] (NOTE: BBBSA also has a *school*-based, in addition to this *community*-based, mentoring program that has shown equally positive results.[12])

Community partnership models such as those used by GPTTO and BBBSA use comprehensive strategies that are grounded in prevention principles. They build on strengths in the community and address the attraction of gangs. Chapter 9's sidebar "In the Spotlight: Female Intervention Team" features one program's "lessons learned" as it developed strategies for gang-membership prevention.

Implementation Challenges With Community-Based Prevention Programs

What do we know about the challenges of establishing a gang-membership prevention program in the community? And what do we know about overcoming them?

Substantial research exists regarding the building of program and community collaborations.[13,14,15,16] Based on these key studies — as well as my own ethnographic and evaluation work in the field — here are nine key strategies:

1. Avoid reinventing the wheel: Build from programs that exist.

2. Develop strategic plans.

3. Identify real and imagined boundaries.

4. Make community participation a priority.

5. Maximize partnerships.

6. Involve a balance of community partners.

7. Ensure that efforts are inclusive and draw on diverse talents.

8. Use training and technical assistance to expand organizational capacity.

9. Ensure sustainability.

Avoid Reinventing the Wheel: Build From Programs That Exist

Perhaps the single biggest misconception in trying to implement a gang-membership prevention initiative or program is that the community must start from scratch in developing a new strategy. This is not true. But how can a community draw

IN THE SPOTLIGHT: HOMEBOY INDUSTRIES

▸ *INTERVIEW WITH FATHER GREG BOYLE*

"Nothing stops a bullet like a job." That's the motto of Homeboy Industries (HBI), which began with a grass-roots movement in 1988 in the barrios of East Los Angeles. Faced with a gang-violence epidemic, community members, a handful of probation officers and a young Jesuit, Father Greg Boyle, linked arms and energies to provide youngsters with an alternative to gangs. Twenty-four years later, Father Boyle's beard has whitened and Homeboy Industries has grown into the largest anti-gang program in America, moving from an East L.A. storefront to a large, two-story building in the city center. Serving 12,000 kids from every ZIP code in L.A. County, HBI is an excellent example of a community-based program that helps at-risk youth and those already involved in gang activity and violence. "G" — as Father Boyle is called by politicians and homies alike — talked with me about his work.

How did Homeboy Industries begin?

The mothers in the community came together, insisting we had to do something to stop the violence and save their children from gangs. We began with a school because I noticed — when I was a young priest at Dolores Street — that there was no middle school for kids who had gotten in trouble. There was one school with a huge waiting list and nowhere else for kids to go.

How did establishing the school lead to the recognition that something was needed beyond the classroom

that would help kids leave gang life or see an option other than joining in the first place?

What was needed was jobs, so we started a jobs program. We involved the whole community. We printed pamphlets, and the mothers in the community actually organized a huge march — families, babies, homies, priests, everyone. We went door to door to all the businesses, asking people to just give one job to a homie or to a kid who had obstacles, who couldn't get a job anywhere else. What began with community mobilization led to the development of a training program, "Jobs for a Future."

How did other programs develop?

As needs presented themselves, programs were born. For example, "F*** the World" was tacked onto Frank's forehead … so tattoo removal was born. I was growing weary of constantly going through my Rolodex for an immigration lawyer here, a child-custody lawyer there … so our legal department was born. It was clear that homies and homegirls were both victims and perpetrators of partner violence … so our domestic violence program was born. People came from the community with their special gifts — yoga, guitar, financial literacy, creative writing — so these programs were born, delivered by folks [who were] already part of our family. Everything that is here — both prevention and intervention — it is all organic and born from this population expressing what they need.

What approaches have you used to try to ensure a connection between school and the streets?

This is always a challenge — making sure folks don't fall between the cracks. We have a charter high school here, with dedicated teachers, where kids can get their G.E.D. or earn their diploma. The idea is that if we get them here for school, they can work part-time at headquarters and also get counseling if they need it. [They can] attend any class that is offered here: anger management, yoga, guitar, writing … whatever they might be interested in. We try to make them allergic to the neighborhood, as if they will get sick if they go near their gang.

How, in your opinion, should successes and outcomes be measured?

Outcomes must be measured in ways that accurately reflect the struggles individuals face in deciding not to join a gang or to leave gang life. Our success is that this population comes here — these individuals show up here, day after day. They are utterly unique, unlike any service population. There is a comfort level — everyone feels the therapeutic elixir present in this building. We are a symbolic representation of hope to all 86,000 gang members in the county … whether they are ready to walk in our doors or not. And we represent hope to the kids who may feel they have to join a gang, but don't want to. No other place can claim this. (See the sidebar, "Evaluating Homeboy Industries.")

on its existing strengths and what has been learned elsewhere?

First, existing programs should be inventoried to understand the community's strengths and gaps. In some communities, often identical prevention programs may be operating within a few blocks of each other, duplicating efforts and dividing limited funding. Therefore, a needs assessment — mapping assets and resources — can help prevent program redundancy. This is a core activity in developing a prevention operating system.

It is important that communities take advantage of existing coalitions and partnerships, including those that are not specifically working on the issue of preventing kids from joining gangs. These may start as an informal coalition of community stakeholders that develop organically over time, like Homeboy Industries, or they may already be more formal partnerships with Memorandums of Understanding between programs and public organizations.

Evaluating Homeboy Industries

The University of California at Los Angeles (UCLA) is currently conducting the first formal evaluation of Homeboy Industries (HBI). The five-year longitudinal analysis — which I am conducting along with colleagues Todd Franke and Christine Christie, and which is being funded by the John Randolph Haynes and Dora Haynes Foundation and The California Wellness Foundation — is using quantitative and qualitative measures to assess HBI's impact on reducing violent, gang-related activity and increasing prosocial behaviors.

Conducting a scientific evaluation of any community-based organization can be both rewarding and daunting. Data collection, trust-building and the composition of a comparison group can pose significant challenges. A case study, completed during the first year of the HBI evaluation, looked at factors surrounding exiting gang life and re-entering mainstream society.[17] Preliminary findings suggest that participation in HBI may lead to a significant decrease in recidivism and an increase in prosocial behaviors. Final results of the UCLA evaluation, however, are not expected until 2015.

Best practices and promising models should be reviewed to help community coalitions identify core components — or principles — of evidence-based strategies that may be adapted to meet local conditions and cultural needs. Here are some useful resources:

- Communities That Care (see http://www.sdrg. org/ctcresource/) is a community prevention operating system that systematically builds a coalition of stakeholders and helps them to assess local needs and opportunities and then select and implement effective prevention strategies.

- The Strategic Planning Tool for Community Assessment (see http://www.iir.com/nygc/tool) reviews a range of anti-gang programs and offers a protocol to guide community assessment.

- STRYVE (see http://www.SafeYouth.gov) is an initiative sponsored by the Centers for Disease Control and Prevention (CDC) that provides the latest information, interactive training videos, and customized online workspaces to help communities plan, implement and evaluate an approach to youth-violence prevention that is based on the best available evidence.

- The Urban Networks to Increase Thriving Youth (UNITY) (see http://www.preventioninstitute. org/unity) is funded by CDC as part of the STRYVE initiative to help large urban centers organize their planning and increase their capacity to address youth violence. The UNITY Roadmap uses nine elements, including political support, policies and plans, organizational structure, resources evaluation, community engagement, communication, prevention programming and capacity-building skills.

- Blueprints for Healthy Youth Development (see http://www.blueprintsprograms.com), at the University of Colorado's Center for the Study and Prevention of Violence, provides information on prevention models and promising programs that have been rigorously evaluated and shown to have preventive effects on youth violence or risk factors for violence.

- CrimeSolutions.gov (see http://www. crimesolutions.gov) is sponsored by the Department of Justice's Office of Justice Programs and provides ratings of the evidence for specific criminal justice strategies, including those focused on gang-membership prevention and intervention.

Develop Strategic Plans

Developing short- and long-term strategic plans that are focused and adaptive is critical to community-based prevention efforts. Strategic planning helps programs adjust to shifts in everything from levels of violence to available funding. It ensures that program infrastructure is premeditated, organized, well-implemented and maintained. Needless to say, however, truly effective strategic planning depends on the active collaboration of involved partners.

It is critical that gang-membership prevention initiatives *avoid planning without having a focus.* Often, communities mobilize in the face of a tragedy. When gang violence results in the deaths of innocent bystanders, groups may declare that they will "fight gangs 24/7" and insist that the community "do something." Although such devotion is admirable, it is important that communities try to avoid the risk of falling back into the familiar rather than focusing on what will be effective. One way to ensure long-term change is by using a multipronged, multiagency approach that includes proactive, thoughtful planning and action rather than reactive rhetoric without follow-through.

Identify Real and Imagined Boundaries

Programs often exist in silos, focusing on their geographic area or targeted population, but disconnected from other efforts. For example, school-based gang-membership prevention programs often are not linked to community-based after-school programs. This was a factor in a Los Angeles middle-school leadership program in which there was an anti-gang curriculum during school hours but no after-school activities — so, back in the outside world after school, youth were exposed to gang activity. Professional turf issues and bureaucratic obstacles also added to that program's lack of connection and coordination.

Another example is a community-based gang-membership prevention program that required its program director to have a minimum of four years' experience in county programs, but this requirement foreclosed the potential for innovative thinking that may have been brought by someone with relevant experience from outside the county.

To solve such problems, organizations should seek collaboration opportunities and create mechanisms for providing services through partnerships. School-based and community-based prevention efforts should be coherent and continuous, and every effort should be made to tame bureaucratic obstacles so they do not interfere with program growth and community change.

Make Community Participation a Priority

"Community involvement" must be more than just a sound bite. Networks of individuals, businesses and other organizations can help sustain a gang-membership prevention effort. They can build community strengths and bridge social divisions by integrating those who feel socially or economically marginalized. In this regard, however, it is critical to engage all members of a community, including schools, law enforcement and other local government entities, churches, business groups and associations. Community transformation also depends on using new methods of communication — such as texting, email and social networks — alongside homegrown neighborhood grapevines.

It is critical that everyone involved in a prevention initiative — from foundations, experts and stakeholders to management, staff and participants — understand how specific strategies can lead to positive outcomes. This helps everyone involved to take ownership of the effort.

Maximize Partnerships

Collaborative efforts often ignore important partners. Although law enforcement has learned to work across jurisdictions, the same cannot always be said about gang-membership prevention programs. Such programs must learn to blend the local focus with other programs throughout the geographic region — after all, gangs do not respect city or county lines. Gangs tend to be in focused geographical areas, some for 30 to 40 years. Although maximizing partnerships might mean working across jurisdictions, it may also mean focusing resources in the areas with the greatest need.

Sometimes, even local efforts fail to be inclusive. It is important to consider grass-roots movements, faith-based organizations, and understaffed storefront programs when forming a collaboration for a community-based gang-membership prevention effort.

One of the biggest obstacles to effective gang-membership prevention in the community is the competition for funding. Funding is often awarded to organizations that can mobilize resources to respond to a request for proposals. It may be difficult to ensure that money is given to community-based organizations that actually provide services. Often, a large organization acts as a fiscal agent, providing management but no services. Thus, it is important to link financial support to the ability of groups to collaborate and share resources — including money — appropriately. Private foundations and public funding sources can reinforce this by funding programs and organizations that demonstrate effective collaborations.

Involve a Balance of Community Partners

One of the most critical — and least understood — aspects of effective gang-membership prevention is involving a balance of multidisciplinary community partners. It is important to understand, of course, that "meeting" is *not* "collaborating." Gatherings of organizations and community stakeholders run the risk of being exercises in frustration: long on lip service about "working together" but short on action plans for true partnerships.

There is also a risk that gang-membership prevention activities will end up focusing solely on intervention and be seen primarily as law enforcement activities. Collaborations that become "badge heavy" may run the risk of emphasizing criminal justice approaches and overlooking other models and approaches. This tends to result when primary responsibility for dealing with gangs is assigned to law enforcement. By focusing on early prevention and reducing the likelihood that youth will join gangs in the first place, diverse partners can be engaged and maintained.

Ensure That Efforts Are Inclusive and Draw on Diverse Talents

It is important to draw on the skills of experts — including community leaders and former gang members — when planning and implementing gang-membership prevention programs. Keep in mind, however, that each group poses a challenge to program implementation. Former gang members are frequently met with deep suspicion regarding ongoing gang ties. Practitioners and academics may encounter mistrust over motives and credibility.

To protect the community, there must be both ethical review of and training for diverse types of service providers. For example, former gang members who have completed probation or parole can be required to have drug testing. Professionals can be assessed to ensure sensitivity to community culture, practices and beliefs. Such requirements obviously should be paired with consequences for failing to adhere to expectations. Former gang members who commit crimes and practitioners who demonstrate bias or lack

of sensitivity to community norms must be replaced.

Use Training and Technical Assistance to Expand Organizational Capacity

Because gang-membership prevention involves people with varying backgrounds and levels of expertise, ongoing training must be provided and tailored to their needs. For example, one all-too-familiar scenario involves formerly gang-involved adults who are successful as community organizers or youth mentors. They may establish their own programs but, despite their commitment, find it difficult to do the paperwork and other administrative tasks that are involved. Therefore, it is crucial to the success — and accountability — of a program to provide sufficient training and technical assistance. In fact, it may be valuable to have everyone involved in a joint training: former gang members — now mentors — participating alongside administrators, police officers and social workers.

Technical assistance should be used to develop collaborations as well as build knowledge. For example, universities and community colleges can become partners in providing training. Training and technical assistance should be offered in multiple forms: lectures and both virtual and distance-learning initiatives. And don't forget about social networking!

Social networking tools — such as texting, Facebook and Twitter — can play an important role in mobilizing communities in gang-membership prevention efforts and providing links to training opportunities. In considering how these tools might be used to build community involvement, it is important to be aware of how the specific populations in the community use social networking tools.[18]

Ensure Sustainability

Community programs constantly face the challenge of sustainability, in terms of both funding and staff. Also, because of their grass-roots nature, they may depend heavily on a single visionary, charismatic leader, which can further affect sustainability. Homeboy Industries responded to this challenge, for example, by undertaking long-term strategic and succession planning. The likelihood of sustainability can also be increased by mentoring future leaders and practitioners.

Community-based prevention programs often depend on limited sources, largely public, for financing, using reactive rather than proactive fundraising. Financial sustainability must be pursued with great innovation. Public-private partnerships — combining government, foundation and corporate funding — can offer a good potential for sustaining community-based programs over the long haul. As well-respected gangs researchers Malcolm Klein and Cheryl Maxson say, community-based efforts should have a 10-year plan — "enough to outlast gangs."[19]

Finally, an important factor in sustaining a community-based gang-membership prevention initiative or program is evaluation. Evaluation — measuring outcomes and understanding processes — is essential to short- and long-term planning and funding. (For more on evaluations of programs, see chapter 11.) It is always helpful to present potential funders with evidence that the cost of dealing with gang-involved youth — and their impact on the community — is far greater than the cost of funding programs that prevent kids from joining gangs in the first place.

Policy Issues

What do policymakers and practitioners need to think about when funding and implementing community-based gang-membership prevention strategies? Here are five key principles:

1. Integrate public health and criminal justice approaches.

2. Promote a long-term, comprehensive — rather than "single-solution" — approach.

3. Reinforce prosocial youth-development programs and community strengths.

4. Motivate social involvement.

5. Promote and fund evaluation.

Integrate public health and criminal justice approaches. In the past, many disciplines have led community-based prevention efforts: criminal justice, public health, education and social work. However, particularly in this time of limited fiscal resources, more interdisciplinary collaborations

are required. Part of such collaborations, of course, is ensuring that stakeholders, including the public, agree on vocabulary. (For more on the importance of definitions and vocabulary, see Introduction.)

Policymakers and practitioners should meet — informally and often — to talk about what is working and not working. When this is not convenient, a newsletter or social network may do the trick in terms of sharing ideas and innovations.

Promote a long-term, comprehensive — rather than "single-solution" — approach. It is important to avoid a single-solution mentality to keeping kids from joining gangs; rather, a long-term, comprehensive approach should be promoted. Programs that are focused only on high-risk youth or that work with current gang members have thrived because they may be viewed as more cost-effective than communitywide prevention programs; they have also demonstrated short-term effectiveness. However, it makes no sense to try to prevent gang membership using a short time frame because new youth are continually at risk of joining gangs. It is also important that policymakers and practitioners avoid a "one-size-fits-all" mindset. Indeed, this is one of the primary reasons this book presents "principles" rather than individual, prescriptive programs. Areas dealing with emerging gang problems require community organizing and a more broad-based approach. Areas with chronic gang problems require more opportunities, including jobs.[20,21] The most effective way for a community to figure out what it needs is to inventory its strengths and gaps, and to plan with multiple solutions in mind. Policymakers should consider the benefits of prevention operating systems like CTC for providing long-term, comprehensive prevention activities. Also, programs that address early childhood risks should be a key component. (For more on child development factors that should be considered in gang-joining prevention, see chapter 5.)

Reinforce prosocial youth-development programs and community strengths. Initiatives that emphasize positive youth development have experienced limited but significant success. For example, Geoffrey Canada's much-publicized work in the Harlem Children's Zone exemplifies this approach, as does Los Angeles' "Summer Night Lights" program.[17,22] At-risk youth, families and neighborhoods possess protective factors that should be reinforced. For example, certain communities, despite poverty and limited economic options, have growing neighborhood associations and a strong sense of community identity. This type of community involvement should be expanded by collaboration and financial support.

Motivate social involvement. At the community level, programs and organizations are faced with the challenge of doing more with less. This may be one of the strongest arguments for communities to build coalitions and partnerships. Gang-membership prevention efforts can benefit from involving individuals, families, informal networks, grass-roots programs and community organizations; this includes formalizing ways to include former gang members in helping to increase the community's understanding of gang allure and initiations. Also, youth should be included in program planning and implementation.

Promote and fund evaluation. Too often, policymakers do not understand the role that evaluation should play in program design and implementation, particularly when they are considering the funding of an initiative or program. It is crucial that only programs that work are being funded, and the only way to ensure this is through ongoing monitoring and scientific evaluation.

Conclusion

Community-based prevention of gang-joining remains one of the best ways to reduce gang membership and violence. Such efforts offer the chance to empower the people who are most directly affected by gangs — and by the destruction that gangs cause in individual lives, families, communities and society at large.

Based on research, we know that the core components essential to a successful community-based initiative include mentoring, parental involvement, skill-building, and opportunities for prosocial involvement.

It is important to consider the challenges that community-based gang-membership prevention efforts face. Often, for example, programs in the classroom — and strategies taught to parents — are not connected to "the street." True continuity means that strategies aimed at preventing gang-joining do not end at the school door.

Finally, practitioners and policymakers should be aware that communities may reject solutions imposed on them "from the outside." But leaders can help communities to recognize their strengths and to take ownership in gang-joining prevention efforts.

Perhaps Father Greg Boyle of Homeboy Industries described it best:

> What ultimately works are programs "born from below" — conceived and encouraged from within these underserved communi-ties themselves. If we listen to those most impacted by gangs and understand the lethal absence of hope which undergirds it — then add the expertise [of] what works — the chances are good we will meet this challenge.

About the Author

Jorja Leap

Jorja Leap is an anthropologist with more than 30 years of research experience that has focused on violence, culture and identity. Dr. Leap's work draws on the life histories of current and former gang members, and she is currently conducting a five-year longitudinal evaluation of the Homeboy Industries gang-intervention program. She has authored numerous evaluation studies. Her most recent book is *Jumped In: What Gangs Taught Me About Violence, Drugs, Love, and Redemption*. Dr. Leap received her Ph.D. from the University of California, Los Angeles, where she has been on the faculty for 20 years.

Endnotes

1. Anderson E. *Code of the Street: Decency, Violence and the Moral Life of the Inner City.* New York, NY: Norton, 1999.

2. Hawkins JD, Oesterle S, Brown EC, Brown EC, Monahan KC, Abbott RD, Arthur MW, Catalano RF. Sustained decreases in risk exposure and youth problem behaviors after installation of the Communities That Care prevention system in a randomized trial. *Arch Pediatr Adolesc Med.* 2011: October 3 ePub; doi:10.1001/archpediatrics.2011.183. Available from the American Medical Association, Chicago, IL. Accessed on December 19, 2011. Also in print: *Arch Pediatr Adolesc Med.* 2012(February); 166(2):141-148.

3. Lurigio A, Bensiger G, Thompson SR. *A Process and Outcome Evaluation of Project BUILD: Years 5 and 6.* Chicago, IL: Loyola University, Department of Criminal Justice, 2000.

4. Tremblay RE, Masse L, Pagani L, Vitaro F. From childhood physical aggression to adolescent maladjustment: The Montreal Prevention Experiment. In: Peters RD, McMahon RJ, eds., *Preventing Childhood Disorders, Substance Abuse, and Delinquency.* Thousand Oaks, CA: Sage Publications, 1996.

5. Gatti U, Tremblay RE, Vitaro F, McDuff P. Youth gangs, delinquency and drug use: A test of selection, facilitation and enhancement hypotheses. *J Child Psychol Psychiatry* 2005; 46:1178-1190.

6. Johnson CA, Pentz MA, Weber MD, Dwyer JH, Baer N, MacKinnon DP, Hansen WB, Flay BR. Relative effectiveness of comprehensive community programming for drug abuse prevention with high-risk and low-risk adolescents. *J Consult Clin Psychol.* 1990; 58:447-456.

7. MacKinnon DP, Johnson CA, Pentz MA, Dwyer JH, Hansen WB, Flay BR, Wang EY. Mediating mechanisms in a school-based drug prevention program: First year effects of the Midwestern Prevention Project. *Health Psychol.* 1991; 10:164-172.

8. Spergel IA, Wa KM, Sosa RV. The comprehensive, community-wide, gang program model: Success and failure. In: Short JF, Hughes LA, eds., *Studying Youth Gangs.* Lanham, MD: AltaMira Press, 2006.

9. See http://www.blueprintsprograms.com for more on Blueprints for Healthy Youth Development at the University of Colorado's Center for the Study and Prevention of Violence.

10. Arbreton A, McClanahan W. *Targeted Outreach: Boys & Girls Clubs of America's Approach to Gang Prevention and Intervention.* Philadelphia, PA: Public/Private Ventures, 2002.

11. Tierney JP, Grossman JB, Resch NL. *Making a Difference: An Impact Study of Big Brothers Big Sisters.* Philadelphia, PA: Public/Private Ventures, 1995.

12. Herrera C, Grossman J, Kauh T, Feldman A, McMaken J, Jucovy L. *Making a Difference in Schools: The Big Brothers Big Sisters School-Based Mentoring.* Philadelphia, PA: Public/Private Ventures, 2007.

13. Kubisch AC, Brown P, Chaskin R, Hirota J, Joseph M, Richman H, Roberts M. *Voices From the Field: Learning From the Comprehensive Community Initiatives.* Washington, DC: Aspen Institute, 1997.

14. Putnam RD. *Bowling Alone: The Collapse and Revival of American Community.* New York, NY: Simon & Schuster, 2000.

15. Schorr LB. *Common Purpose: Strengthening Families and Neighborhoods to Rebuild America.* New York, NY: Anchor Books, 1997.

16. Tough P. *Whatever It Takes: Geoffrey Canada's Quest to Change Harlem and America.* New York, NY: Houghton Mifflin Harcourt, 2008.

17. Leap J, Franke T, Christie C, Bonis S. Nothing stops a bullet like a job: Homeboy Industries gang prevention and intervention in Los Angeles. In: Hoffman J, Knox L, eds., *Beyond Suppression: Global Perspectives on Youth Justice.* Santa Barbara, CA: Praeger, 2010.

18. Ellison NB, Steinfield C, Lampe C. The benefits of Facebook "friends": Social capital and college students' use of online social network sites. *J Comput Mediat Commun.* 2007; 12:1143-1168.

19. Klein M, Maxson CL. *Street Gang Patterns and Policies.* New York, NY: Oxford University Press, 2006.

20. Spergel IA, Curry GD. Strategies and perceived agency effectiveness in dealing with the youth gang problem. In: Huff CR, ed., *Gangs in America,* 1st ed. Newbury Park, CA: Sage Publications, 1990.

21. Spergel IA, Curry GD. The National Youth Gang Survey: A research and development process. In: Goldstein A, Huff CR, eds., *The Gang Intervention Handbook.* Champaign, IL: Research Press,1993.

22. Cespedes G, Herz D. The City of Los Angeles Mayor's Office of Gang Reduction and Youth Development (GRYD) Comprehensive Strategy. Unpublished report, 2011.

How Can We Prevent Girls From Joining Gangs?

Meda Chesney-Lind

- **Girls are in gangs, and in fairly large numbers; in the U.S., girls may constitute one-quarter to one-third of all youth gang members.**

- **Although girls join gangs for many of the same reasons boys do, there are a few gender differences; for example, girls — particularly in abusive families — are more likely than boys to regard a gang as a surrogate family.**

- **Most girls join mixed-sex gangs that are run by boys whose attitudes about girls, sexuality and gender roles cause unique risks and harm to girls.**

- **Strategies and programs aimed at preventing youth from gang-joining must address issues that are unique to girls and the contexts that can lead them to join a gang; such strategies and programs include the need to prevent sexual abuse, strengthen family relationships, provide them with safety in their neighborhoods, help them avoid substance abuse and abusive boyfriends, and improve their skills to delay early sexual activity and parenthood.**

In Brief

The United States has seen a sharp increase in gang problems over the past decade. Gang membership is not an exclusively male phenomenon: According to the most recent national data, girls comprise at least one-quarter of the youth in gangs — and one highly respected study found the percentage among youth in a sample from Denver, for example, to be as high as 46 percent. Unfortunately, these facts are often obscured because those watching the gang problem — particularly law enforcement — typically pay more attention to the behavior of boys than of girls. Another reason for the relative "invisibility" of girls in gangs is that girls enter gangs — and exit from gang activity — at earlier ages than boys.

Gangs can offer both boys and girls a sense of belonging and a perceived sense of fun, excitement and protection. There are some gender differences, however. For boys, more than for girls, a gang may be seen as a place to make money. Girls, by contrast, are more likely to join a gang because of a perceived sense of safety and security that they cannot find at home. Although a gang may provide girls — particularly those from abusive or troubled families — with a sense of a surrogate family, girls in gangs actually face a greater risk of serious delinquency than their nongang counterparts, including gang-fighting, drug use and sales, and weapon-carrying. Gangs also expose girls to greater risk of sexual victimization and violence from other gang members in their own or other rival gangs.

"Gender-informed" prevention efforts are critical to helping prevent girls from joining a gang. Such efforts should focus on:

- Preventing sexual abuse.
- Improving family and peer relationships.

- Helping girls avoid substance abuse and abusive boyfriends.

- Improving skills to delay early sexual activity and parenthood.

Of course, other efforts are likely to decrease the risk of gang-joining for both boys and girls, such as improving the quality of public education, helping them stay in school, and providing youth in economically marginalized communities with safety in their schools and in their neighborhoods. Without effective, gender-responsive prevention efforts, however, there is reason to believe that we will continue to see significant numbers of girls as well as boys joining gangs.

After years of decline, the gang problem in the United States has re-emerged as a challenge, with the number of jurisdictions reporting gang problems increasing in the early 2000s and remaining elevated (see chapter 1).[1] Despite the image of gangs as stereotypically male, studies consistently show that girls are in gangs, and they are there in substantial numbers.

Studies that ask youth themselves about their gang membership tend to find that girls represent between 20 percent and 46 percent of youth in gangs.[2, 3] For example, a national self-report study conducted in 1997 found that girls comprised one-third of youth who reported "belonging to a gang."[4] On the other hand, police estimates of the proportion of female members tend to be low — often considerably less than 10 percent.[1,5] As Buddy Howell describes in chapter 1 of this book, although boys tend to outnumber girls two to one in gangs nationwide, these figures can vary, depending on the method used to estimate gang members. For example, researchers who study gangs in the field tend to find larger numbers of girls than are revealed through surveys of youth, which are often administered in school.[6, 7] Variations in survey results are best explained by the age of the sample being surveyed: Girls tend to join gangs at a younger age and leave gangs earlier than boys.[8,9] One study of youth ages 11-15 found that nearly half of the gang members were girls; however, another survey of an older group (ages 13-19) found that only one-fifth were girls.[3] In the sample of young people drawn to evaluate the Gang Resistance Education and Training (G.R.E.A.T.) program, girls represented 38 percent of those reporting gang membership in the eighth grade (13- to 15-year-olds).[10, 11] This means that, in addition to focusing on girls when seeking to prevent youth from joining gangs, we especially need to focus on the "tweens."

Why Do Girls Join Gangs?

Girls join gangs for many of the same reasons as boys: a perceived sense of fun, respect, protection and affirmation (see chapter 2).[10, 11, 12] In a multistate study of gang youth, many gang-involved girls (and boys) reported having friends in gangs (41 percent of boys and 46 percent of girls) or having a brother or sister in a gang (26 percent of boys and 32 percent of girls). About half of both girls and boys reported joining gangs for "protection." However, boys in the study were significantly more likely to join a gang for money: 47 percent of boys compared with 38 percent of girls.[10, 11] In another study, girls who were gang members reported greater neighborhood disorder and crime, more family disadvantages and peer fighting, less parental attachment, and more concerns about school safety than girls who were not gang members.[12]

Researchers who have looked more closely at the reasons youth give for gang-joining found that girls tended to "tap an emotional or affective aspect of gang membership" more than boys did.[11] This basically means that girls were more likely than boys to agree that "my gang is like family to me." Gang girls were also more likely than gang boys to report that they were lonely in school and with friends, and that they felt isolated from their families. Finally, girls in gangs had lower self-esteem than did boys in gangs, who, the researchers found, "actually appear to have quite positive self-assessments."[10, 11] Girls who are in gangs also have significantly lower self-esteem than girls who are not in gangs.[13]

Researchers, particularly those who have performed ethnographic studies, also note that girls are often around gangs in other roles — such as girlfriend, sister or daughter — that might put them at risk, even if they are not full-fledged gang members. In a Texas study, for example, researchers found that, "regardless of their relationship to the gang, all the females were prone to some degree of substance use, crime and high-risk sexual behavior."[14]

Although some youth have the *perception* that being in a gang offers fun, excitement and protection, the *reality* is otherwise. For girls as well as boys, gang membership increases delinquent behavior. Here are some self-reported risk behaviors comparing young women who are not in a gang to young women who are in a gang.[2,3,13]

	Girls in a gang	Girls not in a gang
Carried concealed weapon	79%	30%
Been in a gang fight	90%	9%
Attacked with a weapon to cause serious injury	69%	28%

Gang-Joining: Risk Factors for Girls

To prevent girls from joining a gang, we need to understand and address the particular risks that girls confront in their families, schools and neighborhoods. Compared with their non-gang-joining peers, girls who join gangs are more likely to:

• Have a history of sexual abuse and trauma.

• Live in a destructive or distraught family.

• Have problematic peer relationships.

• Abuse drugs.

• Live in dangerous neighborhoods and attend unsafe schools.

Abuse and Trauma

To prevent girls from joining gangs, we need to effectively address child maltreatment, particularly child sexual abuse. Girls join gangs, at least in part, because they are suffering abuse at home, their families are deeply troubled, and they are searching for a "surrogate family."[15] Therefore,

early gang-membership prevention efforts should focus on families most at risk of physical or sexual child abuse or neglect.

Girls in gangs are far more likely than nongang girls from the same neighborhoods to have been sexually assaulted — 52 percent compared with 22 percent — with "most of the sexual victimization occur[ring] in the context of the family."[2,3] Seventy-one percent of child sexual abuse victims are girls, and most of this is family-related.[16] Researchers have found that 60 percent of the gang girls were victims of physical or sexual abuse within the family.[17]

Girls in gangs have serious histories of sexual and physical abuse. In one study, researchers found that 62 percent of the girl gang members had been sexually abused or assaulted in their lifetime; three-fourths of the girls (and more than half of the boys) reported suffering lifetime physical abuse.[18] Gangs also continue to put their female members at risk for sexual assault and abuse.[14,17]

Three-quarters of girls in a 1999 study of gang youth in Los Angeles reported that they had run away from home, more than twice the proportion of male gang members.[19] Running away from home — which has long been correlated with sexual and physical abuse — leads to further criminal involvements (like drug use and sales), affiliating with other deviant peers, and further victimization.[20,21]

Because child abuse plays such a major role in placing girls at risk for gang membership, programs that prevent this abuse have the potential to reduce gang-joining by girls. There is strong evidence, for example, that early childhood home-visitation programs reduce child maltreatment. In these programs, parents and children (generally, younger than age 2) are visited in their home by nurses, social workers, paraprofessionals or community peers. The parents are given guidance on parenting (such as how to care for and have constructive interactions with young children) and how to strengthen social supports, including linking families with social services. One such program in particular, Nurse-Family Partnerships, has been shown to prevent sexual and physical abuse of girls and to be effective in preventing delinquency in youth born to high-risk mothers.[22]

In 2005, the Task Force on Community Preventative Services — an independent volunteer body of public health and prevention experts appointed by the Director of the Centers for Disease Control and Prevention — recommended early childhood home-visitation programs for reducing child maltreatment among high-risk families:

> Early childhood home visitation programs are recommended to prevent child maltreatment on the basis of strong evidence that these programs are effective in reducing violence against visited children. Programs delivered by professional visitors (nurses or mental health workers) seem more effective than programs delivered by paraprofessionals, although programs delivered by paraprofessionals for ≥2 years also appear to be effective in reducing child maltreatment. Home visitation programs in our review were offered to teenage parents; single mothers; families of low socioeconomic status (SES); families with very low birth-weight infants; parents previously investigated for child maltreatment; and parents with alcohol, drug, or mental health problems."[23]

For more information on The Community Guide, a resource that contains recommendations by the Task Force, see http://www.thecommunityguide.org/violence/home/homevisitation.html.

Destructive or Distraught Families

To prevent girls from joining a gang, it is important to strengthen family and peer relationships and, when appropriate, enhance connections with other adults who can serve as parent figures. This is particularly true in communities with high rates of crime and violence, where pressure to join a gang can be intense.

Some girls in gangs feel isolated from their families and they regard the gang as an alternative family. Also, some girls who join gangs report highly problematic relationships with their families, with both mothers and fathers. In fact, girls in gangs are significantly more likely than nongang girls to say they have less attachment to their mothers, less interest in talking with their mothers, and less parental monitoring.[24] In one California study of girls in the juvenile justice system who reported more than six types of emotional abuse, all but one were in a gang.[25]

Thirty-two percent of girls (26 percent of boys) say that one of the reasons they joined a gang is because they had a brother or a sister in the gang. This suggests that the families themselves can contribute, for many girls, to the risk of gang-joining.[10,11]

When developing strategies and programs to help prevent girls from joining a gang, it is crucial to consider important cultural contexts. Some girls experience the strain of immigration in addition to the pressures produced by poverty. (See the sidebar "Girls, Gangs, and Cultural Context.")

We also must address the need of some girls to be protected *from* their families. A study conducted in Hawaii showed that some girls turned to gangs in response to family violence, saying that the gang provided instruction and experience in fighting back physically and emotionally.[18] Other researchers have found that gangs can provide girls with an escape from duties that are assigned by their families, such as taking care of siblings and housework.[17,26]

Problematic Peer Relationships

Many girls join a gang because they have friends in the gang. One study found that 46 percent of girls (41 percent of boys) gave this as one of the reasons they joined a gang.[10,11] However, most girls who are in gangs are in mixed-sex gangs; one researcher estimated that 88 percent of the gang girls she studied were in gangs with boys and young men.[2,3] Because mixed-sex gangs tend to be male-dominated in both structure and activities, girls may be at considerable risk not only for greater delinquent behavior but also for further sexual assault and domestic violence.[6,27,28]

Despite the fact that some girls look to a gang as a surrogate family, the reality is that gangs rarely offer the "protection" girls may be seeking. Not only does gang life increase the risk of delinquency, some girls are "trained" into the gang, meaning they are raped by multiple male gang members as a form of "initiation."[14,17] Male gang members may also seriously endanger girls by including them in very violent crimes, such as drive-by shootings, or asking girls to serve as "mules," decoys or couriers in drug- or weapon-carrying; they are also used as bait in "setting up" rival gang members.[14,28]

Girls, Gangs and Cultural Context

Cultural context is an important factor in understanding why some girls join a gang. For example, Latina and Hispanic girls must negotiate the traditional gender-role ideologies of machismo and marianismo. Machismo dictates that Latino boys and men should be tough, sexually assertive, and dominating; marianismo stresses that girls and women should be submissive and passive in their relationships with boys and men.[29]

Young Latinas often resent such constraints. In one study of Latina and Portuguese mothers and daughters in the late 1990s, researchers found that some Latina girls chafed at controls imposed on them, saying that their parents were "too concerned" about their safety. They also reported feeling constrained and frustrated as they saw their mothers being bound by a culture that expected them to "do everything for everybody." The girls said that, if they complained about people taking advantage of their mothers, their mothers got angry.[30]

Many African-American girls must learn to cope with both sexism and racism, to say nothing of dangerous communities. Research has shown that some African-American mothers teach their daughters "race-related resistance strategies," like how not to fall prey to corrosive effects of the white standard of American beauty.[31] Black mothers may also ensure that their daughters learn two cultural scripts: one for living in the white world and another for living as an African-American.[32] Other research has found that because many African-American girls grow up in very violent neighborhoods, their women may also teach their daughters to "physically defend themselves"

because they do not want them to become "a statistic."[36]

In fact, conflicts between African-American mothers and their daughters might well escalate precisely *because* the girls learn resistance strategies from their mothers. As Dr. Nikki Jones, from the University of California at Santa Barbara, has noted in her book, *Between Good and Ghetto: African American Girls and Inner City Violence,* published in 2010, African-American mothers defended their attempts to curtail their daughters' "freedom" by pointing to the "often hostile and dangerous environments" that their teens lived in as well as the fact that "they were also less likely to be given a break when they err than white teens."[36]

Female African-American gang members differ from Latina and Hispanic gang members in one very interesting way: how they feel about their futures, especially heterosexual marriage. Seventy-five percent of African-American girls — and only 43 percent of the Latinas — agreed with the statement, "The way men are today, I'd rather raise my kids myself." Similarly, when asked about the statement, "All a woman needs to straighten out her life is to find a good man," 29 percent of Latinas — and none of the African-American girls — agreed.[37]

Prevention efforts must be shaped by the cultures in which they operate; they must be cognizant of the dynamics between girls and their mothers, in particular, because research shows that, although these relationships are important, they are likely to be strained with respect to girls who are at the greatest risk.[24]

Some girls in gangs also have problematic relationships with other girls. Girls in mixed-sex gangs often fight with other girls because of jealousy over boys.[26,33] And, because girls in gangs generally identify more with males than with females, they may:

• Tend to ignore male violence toward girls.[34]

• Blame other girls for male infidelity.[35]

• Use their sex appeal to "set up" rival gang members.[14,17]

• Set up other girls for sexual assault.[14,34]

All this can lead to a system of sexual inequality that encourages male violence and contributes to girls seeing themselves through the eyes of males. Because relationships are so important to girls — and because girls say that they are drawn to gangs for a sense of belonging — it is important that prevention programs focus on promoting a girl's access to positive peer groups — like culturally appropriate, school-based empowerment programs — while giving them the skills to critically challenge destructive cultural themes.[38] Prevention strategies that work with potential bystanders or witnesses to sexual violence or dating violence also have the potential to change norms and behaviors by addressing bystander behavior before, during and after violence occurs.[39]

Substance Abuse

One of the top reasons that both girls and boys give for joining gangs is "for fun," and ethnographic research suggests that this "fun" often includes drug use and abuse. To prevent girls from joining gangs, we need to prevent substance abuse. Gang membership is clearly associated with increased substance abuse and the sale of drugs. Comparing girls in gangs with their nongang peers in the same community:[2,3]

	Girls in a gang	Girls not in a gang
Smoked marijuana	98%	52%
Sold marijuana	58%	11%
Sold crack cocaine	56%	7%

A study of risks associated with gang involvement among Mexican-American girls found that a cultural view of them as "hoodrats" — girls who are regarded as sexually available to gang members — put girls at unique risk.[14] Male gang members reported two kinds of parties: those with family members and "good girls" (girlfriends and relatives), where drugs and alcohol were present but use was moderate; and those attended by gang members and hoodrats at which there was heavy alcohol and drug use, and the primary purpose was to get loaded and high.[14] For girls, such a "party" can sometimes include gang rape, which is often justified by the fact that the girls were high or because no one "knew her" and she was drunk.[14,17] One study found that, in some mixed-sex gangs with older men, girls are given drugs, which produces the odd anomaly that more girls than boys were exposed to more expensive drugs like methamphetamines.[40]

It is important to keep in mind that substance abuse can also be a response to trauma, including abuse at home, and, for some runaway girls, this can be magnified by the trauma of street life — all of which can be a risk for gang-joining. Prevention efforts should also focus on helping youth avoid or cope with depression and trauma so that girls are not joining gangs for protection and using drugs to self-medicate. One study found that female juvenile offenders were three times more likely than girls who were not in the system to show clinical symptoms of anxiety and depression.[41] The links between post-traumatic stress disorder (PTSD) and drug use are certainly more pronounced in girls than in boys. In another study, 40 percent of substance-abusing girls were experiencing PTSD compared with 12 percent of boys.[42]

Urban Women Against Substance Abuse is an example of an effective program that uses many of the girl-oriented gang-membership prevention elements discussed above. Initially focused on reducing substance abuse among African-American girls, the program explores attitudes and consequences of substance abuse and teaches alternative stress-reduction techniques. It also strengthens mother-daughter communication and relationships through interventions for the girls, parallel curricula for mothers and monthly mother-daughter sharing sessions. The program also includes home visits, recreation and cultural activities. Short-term effects showed increased school attendance, healthy substance-use attitudes, increased control over sexual expression (sexual self-efficacy) and improved mother-daughter communication. Longer-term follow-up study revealed that the girls in the program maintained the same level of healthy substance-use attitudes, while girls in the control group experienced increased substance use and deterioration in substance-use attitudes.[43]

Dangerous Neighborhoods and Unsafe Schools

To prevent girls from joining gangs, we must take very seriously the deteriorated state of neighborhoods and communities. We know, for example, that in some communities, the ability to fight, even for girls, is considered desirable and, at a minimum, youth are encouraged to know how to negotiate neighborhoods saturated with gang members and gang activity.[36] Remember that the reason mostly frequently cited by girls for why they join gangs is to seek protection in these conditions.[10,11] A key to effective prevention, then, is to address the contexts that give rise to gang membership among girls and impede the success prevention strategies.

In a hostile San Francisco Bay street environment, girl gang members explained that they were violent with each other in an attempt to look tough and protect themselves. As low-income girls of color and given the constraints of their location — on the streets dominated by powerful males — fighting brought these girls status and honor and made it possible for them to confirm they were "decent" and "nobody's fool."[44]

In fact, from Maine to inner-city Philadelphia to a Michigan deindustrialized town, some families tacitly support violence as means for girls' self-protection and so that people will not disrespect them and they can "hold their own."[45,46,47,48] For girls who are violent in response to their environment, it is critical that strategies and programs for gang-membership prevention address the environment. It simply is not enough only to teach girls to "cope" or "control their anger" without providing them a safe place.

Preventing truancy and school dropout is key to addressing gang-joining for both girls and boys. In fact, attending inadequate and dangerous schools is a common theme among girls who are involved (or suspected of being involved) in a gang.[49] Girls in gangs are far more likely than nongang girls to say that they feel unsafe at school, to report gang fights and racial conflict at school, and to be less committed to their academic work.[13]

Many young African-American girls report that their teachers routinely ethnically stereotype them, punishing them for being "loud" and "insufficiently feminine." Latinas report that they are ignored and assumed to be headed for dropping out and early motherhood.[49,50]

Ethnographies of public schools that serve impoverished communities powerfully document precisely how these issues arise in the schooling of girls at risk for gang membership.[50,51] During elementary school, young African-American girls are often praised by their teachers for their "social maturity," while their white counterparts are encouraged to work on academic skills. By high school, however, the assertiveness of African-American girls is often seen as something that must be "squelched" for the sake of order in the classroom. For example, in her seminal work, *School Girls: Young Women, Self-Esteem, and of the Confidence Gap*, Peggy Orenstein argues that, while African-American girls reach out to their teachers more than white girls (or boys of any race), they are "most frequently rebuffed, they actually receive far less attention," and end up "pressed into disengaged silence."[51]

Orenstein also argues that sexual harassment of girls "has an accepted, codified venue in gangs" and that teachers routinely ignore boys' sexual and physical bullying of girls (regardless of their ethnicity), leaving girls to have to fend for themselves, which creates an atmosphere in these marginalized schools of "equal opportunity abusiveness."[51]

Finally, the links between educational failure and gang membership are clear: Low-achieving students reported greater awareness of gangs, were more often asked to join gangs, reported more friends in gangs and, most importantly, were more likely to say they are in a gang.[52] Therefore, to prevent girls from joining gangs, we must address the failure of public schools to pay attention to girls and address girls' problems. Schools tend to shortchange girls compared with boys: For example, girls are less frequently called on by teachers, they are encouraged to be dependent, their assertiveness is punished, and they are shunted into subjects and majors that are less financially remunerative.[53,54] For many girls at risk of gang-joining, however, such failure is amplified by racism. Some schools ignore or discriminate against girls — particularly girls of color — and focus on obedience, order and control instead of on creativity and developing challenging intellectual and social environments.[50,51,52]

In totality, research on the quality of schooling available to girls in gang-saturated neighborhoods argues for school-based initiatives that support girls' resilience and promote their attachment to school. For example, the increase of girls' participation in sports over the past few decades as a result of Title IX — and the growing body of research suggesting good outcomes for girls engaged in sports — is an important example of how such programming empowers girls.[55,56]

▶ *INTERVIEW WITH MARIAN DANIEL*

Marian Daniel is the founder of the Female Intervention Team (FIT), which operates within the traditional probation structure of the Maryland Department of Juvenile Justice. FIT offers a good example of how to go beyond the superficial adaption of an existing program when truly trying to address the unique needs of girls.

Ms. Daniel recently retired as Maryland's Director of Girls Services for Maryland's Department of Juvenile Services; however, she still works with FIT, which, in addition to providing services for girls in Baltimore, offers training on gender-responsive programming in other Maryland jurisdictions. Although FIT might be considered more of an "intervention" than a classic gang-membership prevention program, it is highlighted here to illustrate some of the core principles of gender-responsive programming. FIT focuses on girls' unique challenges (including family trauma) and it builds on their need for positive relationships. The program also uses "natural" girl allies and resources, and does so with a clever use of existing resources. In this interview, Ms. Daniel reflects on the two decades that FIT has been in existence.

I know you have some strong opinions about how we, as a nation, have historically worked with girls.

For years, people assumed that all you had to do to make a program designed for boys work for girls was to paint the walls pink and take out the urinals. Even in my facility, they painted the girls' walls pink in a boys' institution and said, "So, okay, now we have a girls program."

Can you describe some of the FIT programs?

We have family counseling for teens, their parents and, in some groups, grandparents. Most groups are designed for 8- to 15-year-old girls. Counselors strive to provide a nurturing but firm environment. We also offer tutoring. We recruit guest speakers from the community to share their stories, showing clients that females like them can overcome abuse and other difficult life circumstances. Our Rite of Passage program gives older teens a positive introduction to womanhood and opportunities for community service.

Tell me about the girls in FIT.

The typical girl in FIT is a 16-year-old African-American from a single-parent family. A large percentage have a sexually transmitted infection and other chronic problems. Nearly one in five is pregnant. Their most typical offense was simple assault. Some were in a gang, and that presented a special challenge, since the gang mentality is a challenge. Virtually all came from impoverished neighborhoods, and they were in danger of going further into the juvenile justice system. But I knew, drawing on my experience as a probation officer, that the girls needed someone to listen, really listen to them.

Is it true that FIT began with no money?

Yes — and I think it's important to understand that sometimes it's not all about money or saying, "We can't afford to do it." It's about changing the way that we do business. We had so many girls and so many different probation officers — and nobody really understood the complexity of the few girls they had in their caseloads. I believed that if we had just one group of workers, we could train them to identify issues early. I hoped that, by working intensely with the girls, they wouldn't go so deeply into the system. I knew we could do this with the probation officers we had — but how? How could we clear our probation officers of the boys in their caseloads? Being a probation officer myself, I knew many probation officers felt that working with girls was far more difficult than working with boys. Girls were often seen as a burden within the typical caseload.

Policy Implications

Girls who are at risk for gang involvement have histories of abuse, strained family relationships (particularly with their mothers), and troubled relationships with their peers (particularly boys); they attend unsafe schools and live in dangerous neighborhoods. Despite this reality, media portrayals of girls in gangs often show a glowering girl, peering over the barrel of a gun and looking very much like her male counterpart.[57] This tends to fuel a climate where the victims of poverty, racism and sexism can be blamed for their own problems — and this, in turn, can be used to "justify" society's inattention to the genuine underlying problems of marginalized girls.

Such inattention to girls' needs comes at a cost. The trends we are currently seeing — of girls' increasing involvement in the criminal justice system — suggest that we are failing to prevent girls from joining gangs. In recent years, the rates of arrest, detention and incarceration of girls — particularly for violent offenses — have skyrocketed. For example:

- In the mid-1970s, only 15 percent of juveniles arrested were female; four decades later, it is nearly one-third.[58,59]

- Between 1996 and 2005, there was an 18 percent increase in court-ordered residential placement of girls for assault.[60]

How did you approach that challenge?

Girls were seen as so much of a burden that the FIT program director offered staff not working in the FIT unit the "opportunity" to transfer one girl's case for every 10 boys' cases they accepted. We put up an ad, almost as a joke: 'Wanted, 10 boys for 1 girl.' We didn't think they would be willing to take that many — and we thought we'd need to bargain — but, instead, within three weeks, the caseloads were shifted, and I had created a female-only caseload for my band of volunteers.

How did you address the lack of services for girls?

We didn't have a lot of money for training, but I knew that there were a lot of girl-serving organizations in Baltimore, so I reached out to them. Everybody was willing to lend a hand. One of my first successes was to get training from the Maryland Infant and Toddlers Program, which helped the staff understand the unique needs of pregnant and parenting teens. I also reached out to African-American organizations in the city. FIT and the Urban League staff conducted a series of information sessions covering choices, resolving conflicts, and getting along in the home and community for girls who came to the office for weekly group meetings at no cost to the state. These proved to be so popular that girls started bringing along their friends. I also knew that folks at Johns Hopkins [University] might be interested in working with my girls, so I reached out to them and got family planning services for a year at no cost to the girls or their families.

How has FIT evolved over the years?

After receiving a technical assistance grant from the U.S. Department of Justice's Office of Juvenile Justice and Delinquency Prevention, FIT added specific components to address the girls' educational challenges. We assessed whether girls were being properly supported by the educational system and also provided tutoring assistance. The program continued to address the girls' health problems but also strengthened its treatment resources. We did a lot of the counseling, but, as probation officers, we did not take on issues outside of our expertise. We brought in trauma specialists or sent the girls to those services. Finally, we reached out to the Girl Scouts, and the troop that was started is among the most popular groups at FIT.

You talk about breaking the cycle that often "pits a girl against a judge" — what do you mean by that?

As probation officers for the girls, FIT's case managers make formal recommendations to the judge regarding the girl's dispositions.

FIT workers have helped to break the cycle that often pits a girl against the judge and results in her detention for failure to abide by the judge's disposition — which, in turn, often lands girls in detention. As a result of this shift in the way of doing probation, in the two years following its establishment, FIT saw a 50-percent reduction in the number of girls committed to the state's secure facility. The following year, the decline was 95 percent, according to an in-house evaluation of the program.

What changes have you noticed over the years with respect to the girls FIT works with?

The girls we now see are bringing new challenges. There is the terrible problem of urban poverty, and these girls have been exposed to high levels of violence and abuse. I think all we have to do is look at the environments they come from — it's what they see. Our children, our young people, have seen more than I've seen in my 68 years of life. At the heart of their problems, though, is family dysfunction, so the real work is to help that family system heal, if possible. We also need broader societal concern about the high levels of violence in low-income communities.

- Between 1997 and 2006, there was a 12.8 percent decrease in boys' incarcerations (in both detention and residential facilities) compared with only a 3.7 percent decrease in girls' incarcerations.[61]

One study showed that, overall, girls were incarcerated for less serious offenses than boys. About half (46 percent) of girls who were committed for a "person" offense were committed for simple assault — compared with 22 percent of boys.[4] Many of these are arguments between girls and their parents or are minor schoolyard arguments.[62, 63] Marian Daniel, the founder of FIT (see the sidebar "In The Spotlight: Female Intervention Team"), says that these can be situations where the girl gets into a "push/pull" and is arrested for assault. "That's not to simplify things," Daniel said, "but some of these fights have no business coming into juvenile court."

All of this suggests that early and comprehensive gang-membership prevention efforts are needed to address the underlying gang-joining risks for girls — and we need such efforts to be part of a broader strategy to prevent girls' delinquency. Such work will be challenging, however, given years of inattention to girls' programming and the consequent lack of robust, gender-informed program models.[43] We urgently need strategies to help the girls who are at the greatest risk for gang-joining, particularly those who may turn to a gang for "protection" or a sense of belonging. The success of programs like Urban Women Against Substance Abuse and FIT demonstrate that we can take preventive action that is gender-responsive and culturally appropriate. Frankly, without such programs, there is no reason to believe that the trends regarding the involvement of girls in the criminal justice system will abate.

Certainly, such work will be challenging, particularly in the current economic climate, where proposals to spend money are very carefully scrutinized. This is precisely why Marian Daniel's words are so relevant: Sometimes, it's not all about adding new money. As Daniel's experience showed, targeting girls in efforts to prevent gang-joining does not have to mean spending more money — it *can* just mean that we change the way we do business.

Conclusion

Despite the image of gangs as overwhelmingly male, between one-quarter and one-third of gang members are female. Therefore, gang-membership prevention efforts must focus on girls as well as boys.

Despite the fact that girls join gangs for many of the same reasons boys do (fun, respect, protection), there are crucial gender differences in terms of gang-joining and of the consequences of gang membership. Most girls end up in gangs that are male-focused and male-dominated, and there is scant evidence that they provide girls with either the physical or emotional safety they seek. Rather, these girls are more likely to be involved in criminal activities than are girls from their neighborhoods who are not in gangs, and they are also at substantial risk for further victimization.

Strategies and programs for gang-membership prevention must be gender-informed. This can be done by preventing child abuse through working with high-risk parents. Strategies and programs should also seek to reknit frayed connections between girls and their families. We must implement effective, culturally informed, school-based prevention programs, particularly those that assist girls in achieving academic success, especially in schools in gang-infested neighborhoods. Combined with programming that works on issues that girls share with boys, these additional gender-informed prevention efforts can offer powerful tools to help girls avoid gang membership and overcome the many challenges in their environments.

About the Author

Meda Chesney-Lind
Meda Chesney-Lind teaches Women's Studies at the University of Hawaii. Dr. Chesney-Lind is nationally recognized for her work on women and crime, and her testimony before Congress was crucial in building national support of gender-responsive programming for girls in the juvenile justice system. Her most recent book on girls' use of violence, *Fighting for Girls* (co-edited with Nikki Jones), won an award from the National Council on Crime and Delinquency for "focusing America's attention on the complex problems of the criminal and juvenile justice systems."

Endnotes

1. National Gang Center. National Gang Survey Analysis. Available at http://www.nationalgangcenter.gov/Survey-Analysis/Defining-Gangs. Accessed on May 15, 2012.

2. Miller J. Young women in street gangs: Risk factors, delinquency, and victimization risk. In: Reed W, Decker SH, eds., *Responding to Gangs: Evaluation and Research.* Washington, DC: U.S. Department of Justice, Office of Justice Programs, National Institute of Justice, 2002:68-105.

3. Esbensen F-A, Huizinga D. Gangs, drugs, and delinquency in a survey of youth. *Criminology* 1993; 31:565-589.

4. Snyder H, Sickmund M. *Juvenile Offenders and Victims: 2006 National Report.* Washington, DC: U.S. Department of Justice, Office of Juvenile Justice and Delinquency Prevention, National Center for Juvenile Justice, 2006.

5. Curry GD, Ball RA, Fox RJ. *Gang Crime and Law Enforcement Recordkeeping.* Washington, DC: U.S. Department of Justice, National Institute of Justice, 1994.

6. Moore J. *Going Down to the Barrio: Homeboys and Homegirls in Change.* Philadelphia, PA: Temple University Press, 1991.

7. Chesney-Lind M, Hagedorn JM, eds. *Female Gangs in America: Essays on Girls, Gangs and Gender.* Chicago, IL: Lakeview Press, 1999.

8. Peterson D, Miller J, Esbensen F-A. The impact of sex composition on gang member attitudes and behavior. *Criminology* 2001; 39:411-440.

9. Williams K, Curry GD, Cohen MI. Gang prevention programs for female adolescents: An evaluation. In: Reed W, Decker SH, eds., *Responding to Gangs: Evaluation and Research.* Washington, DC: U.S. Department of Justice, National Institute of Justice, 2002:225-263.

10. Esbensen F-A, Winfree LT. Race and gender differences between gang and non-gang youth: Results from a multi-site survey. *Justice Q.* 1998; 15:505-525.

11. Esbensen F-A, Deschenes EP, Winfree LT. Differences between gang girls and gang boys: Results from a multi-site survey. *Youth Soc.* 1999; 31:27-53.

12. Bell KE. Gender and gangs: A quantitative comparison. *Crime Delinq.* 2009; 55(3):363-387.

13. Deschenes EP, Esbensen F-A. Violence among girls: Does gang membership make a difference? In: Chesney-Lind M, Hagedorn J, eds., *Female Gangs in America.* Chicago, IL: Lake View Press, 1999.

14. Cepeda A, Valdez A. Risk behaviors among young Mexican-American gang-associated females: Sexual relations, partying, substance use, and crime. *J Adolesc Res.* 2003; 18:90-106.

15. Joe-Laidler K, Hunt G. Violence and social organization in female gangs. *Soc Justice* 1997; 24(4):148-169.

16. Finkelhor D, Baron L. Risk factors for child sexual abuse. *J Interpers Violence* 1986; 1:43-71.

17. Portillos EL. The social construction of gender in the barrio. In: Chesney-Lind M, Hagedorn J, eds., *Female Gangs in America: Essays on Girls, Gangs and Gender.* Chicago, IL: Lake View Press, 1999:232-244.

18. Joe K, Chesney-Lind M. Just every mother's angel: An analysis of gender and ethnic variations in youth gang membership. *Gend Soc.* 1995; 9(4):408-430.

19. Moore J. Gang members' families. In: Chesney-Lind M, Hagedorn J, eds., *Female Gangs in America: Essays on Girls, Gangs and Gender.* Chicago, IL: Lake View Press, 1999.

20. Chen X, Tyler KA, Whitbeck LB, Hoyt DR. Early sex abuse, street adversity, and drug use among female homeless and runaway adolescents in the Midwest. *J Drug Issues* 2004; 34:1-21.

21. Tyler KA, Hoyt DR, Whitbeck LB, Cauce AM. The impact of childhood sexual abuse on later sexual victimization among runaway youth. *J Res Adolesc.* 2001; 1:151-176.

22. Olds D, Henderson CR, Cole R, et al. Long-term effects of nurse home visitation on children's criminal and antisocial behavior. *JAMA* 1998; 280(14):1238-1244.

23. Task Force on Community Preventive Services. Recommendations to reduce violence through early childhood home visitation, therapeutic foster care, and firearms laws. *Am J Prev Med.* 2005; 28(2S1):6-10.

24. Deschenes EP, Esbensen F-A.Violence and gangs: Gender differences in perceptions and behavior. *J Quant Criminol.* 1999; 15:63-96.

25. Acoca L, Dedel K. *No Place to Hide: Understanding and Meeting the Needs of Girls in the California Juvenile Justice System.* San Francisco, CA: National Council on Crime and Delinquency, 1998.

26. Hagedorn JM, Devitt ML. Fighting females: The social construction of the female gang. In: Chesney-Lind M, Hagedorn JM, eds., *Female Gangs in America: Essays on Girls, Gangs and Gender.* Chicago, IL: Lake View Press, 1999.

27. Campbell A. *The Girls in the Gang.* Oxford, England: Basil Blackwell, 1984.

28. Miller J. *One of the Guys: Girls, Gangs and Gender.* New York, NY: Oxford University Press, 2001.

29. Marin BV. HIV prevention in the Hispanic community: Sex, culture, and empowerment. *J Transcult Nurs.* 2003; 14:186-192.

30. Taylor, J. Cultural stories: Latina and Portuguese daughters and mothers. In: Leadbeater B, Way N, eds., *Urban Girls: Resisting Stereotypes, Creating Identities.* New York, NY: New York University Press, 1996:117-131.

31. Ward J. Raising resisters: The role of truth telling in the psychological development of African American girls. In: Leadbeater B, Way N, eds., *Urban Girls: Resisting Stereotypes, Creating Identities.* New York, NY: New York University Press, 1996:85-99.

32. Cauce A, Hiraga Y, Graves D, Gonzales N, Ryan-Finn K, Grove K. African American mothers and their adolescent daughters: Closeness, conflict, and control. In: Leadbeater B, Way N, eds., *Urban Girls: Resisting Stereotypes, Creating Identities.* New York, NY: New York University Press, 1996:100-116.

33. Campbell A. 1999. Self definition by rejection: The case of gang girls. In: Chesney-Lind M, Hagedorn JM, eds., *Female Gangs in America: Essays on Girls, Gangs, and Gender.* Chicago, IL: Lake View Press, 1999:100-117.

34. Dennehy G, Newbold G. *The Girls in the Gang.* Auckland, New Zealand: Reed Publishing, 2001.

35. Artz S. *Sex, Power and the Violent School Girl.* Toronto, Canada: Trifolium Books, 1998.

36. Jones N. *Between Good and Ghetto: African American Girls and Inner City Violence.* New Brunswick, NJ: Rutgers University Press, 2010.

37. Moore J, Hagedorn J. What happens to the girls in the gang? In: Huff RC, ed., *Gangs in America.* 2nd ed. Thousand Oaks, CA: Sage Publications, 1996.

38. Brown LM. *Girlfighting: Betrayal and Rejection Among Girls.* New York, NY: New York University Press, 2003.

39. Coker AL, Cook-Craig PG, Williams CM, Fisher BS, Clear ER, Garcia LS, Hegge LM. Evaluation of Green Dot: An active bystander intervention to reduce sexual violence on college campuses. *Violence Against Women* 2011; 17:777-796.

40. Pasko LJ. *The Female Juvenile Offender in Hawaii: Understanding Gender Differences in Arrests, Adjudications, and Social Characteristics of Juvenile Offenders.* Honolulu, HI: State of Hawaii: Department of the Attorney General, 2006.

41. Kataoka S, Zima B, Dupre D, Moreno K, Yang X, McCracken J. Mental health problems and service use among female juvenile offenders. *J Am Acad Child Adolesc Psychiatry* 2001; 40(5):549-555.

42. Deyken EY, Buka SL. Prevalence and risk factors for posttraumatic stress disorder among chemically dependent adolescents. *Am J Psychiatry* 1997; 154:752-757.

43. Chesney-Lind M, Morash M, Stevens T. Girls' troubles, girls' delinquency, and gender responsive programming: A review. *Aust NZ J Criminol.* 2008; 41(1):162-189.

44. Hunt G, Joe-Laidler K. Situations of violence in the lives of girl gang members. *Health Care Women Int.* 2001; 22:363-384.

45. Brown LM. *Raising Their Voices: The Politics of Girls' Anger.* Cambridge, MA: Harvard University Press, 1998.

46. Ness CD. Why girls fight: Female youth violence in the inner city. *Ann Am Acad Pol Soc Sci.* 2004; 595:32-48.

47. Leitz L. Girl fights: Exploring females' resistance to educational structures. *Int J Sociol Soc Policy* 2003; 23(11):15-43.

48. Tapper K, Boulton M. Social representations physical, verbal and indirect aggression in chil-Sex and age differences. *Aggress Behav.* 26:442-454.

49. Morris EW. "Tuck in that shirt!": Race, class, gender, and discipline in an urban school. *Sociol Perspect.* 2005; 48:25-48.

50. Kelly D. *Last Chance High: How Girls and Boys Drop In and Out of Alternative Schools.* New Haven, CT: Yale University Press, 1993.

51. Orenstein P. *School Girls: Young Women, Self-Esteem, and the Confidence Gap.* New York, NY: Doubleday, 1994.

52. Lopez EM, Wishard A, Gallimore R, Rivera W. Latino high school students' perceptions of gangs and crews. *J Adolesc Res.* 2006; 21(3):299-318.

53. Sadker M, Sadker D. *Failing at Fairness: How Our Schools Cheat Girls.* New York, NY: Touchstone, 1995.

54. Reay D. "Spice girls," "nice girls," "girlies," and "tomboys": General discourses, girls' cultures and feminities in the primary classroom. *Gender Educ.* 2001; 1(2):153-167.

55. Miller KE, Sabo DF, Farrell M, Barnes G. Sports, sexual behavior, contraceptive use, and pregnancy among female and male high school students: Testing cultural resource theory. *Sociol Sport J.* 1999; 16:366-387.

56. Stevenson B. Beyond the classroom: Using Title IX to measure the return to high school sports. National Bureau of Economic Research Working Paper 15728, February 2010. Available at http:// www.nber.org/papers/w15728.pdf. Accessed on September 7, 2011.

57. Leslie C, Biddle N, Rosenberg D, Wayne J. Girls will be girls. *Newsweek,* August 2, 1993:44.

58. Federal Bureau of Investigation. *Crime in the United States, 2007.* Washington, DC: U.S. Department of Justice, Federal Bureau of Investigation, September 2008. Available at http://www2.fbi.gov/ucr/cius2007/index.html. Accessed on September 7, 2011.

59. Federal Bureau of Investigation. *Crime in the United States, 2009.* Washington, DC: U.S. of Department of Justice, Federal Bureau of In-dren: vestigation, September 2010. Available at http:// 2000; www2.fbi.gov/ucr/cius2009/data/table_33.html. Accessed on September 7, 2011.

60. Sickmund M, Sladky A, Kang W. *Easy Access to Juvenile Court Statistics: 1985-2005.* Available at http://www.ojjdp.ncjrs.gov/ojstatbb/ezajcs/. Accessed on September 7, 2011.

61. Sickmund M, Sladky TJ, Kang W, Puzzanchera C. *Easy Access to the Census of Juveniles in Residential Placement.* Available at http://www.ojjdp.gov/ojstatbb/ezacjrp/. Accessed on September 7, 2011.

62. Buzawa ES, Hotaling GT. The impact of relationship status, gender, and minor status in the police response to domestic assaults. *Vict Offender* 2006; 1(4):323-360.

63. Wallace JM, Goodkind S, Wallace CM, Bachman JG. Racial, ethnic, and gender differences in school discipline among U.S. high school students: 1991-2005. *Negro Educ Rev.* 2008; 59(1-2):47-62.

Race and Ethnicity: What Are Their Roles in Gang Membership?

Adrienne Freng and Terrance J. Taylor

- The roles of race and ethnicity in gang membership are becoming increasingly complicated, and it is important to understand that the term *gang membership* is not "code" for race or ethnicity; the truth is that more and more gangs include white gang members and are becoming multiracial.

- Different risk factors exist — and young people give different reasons — for gang-joining; however, most risk factors cut across racial and ethnic lines, including the negative consequences associated with poverty, immigration, discrimination and social isolation, such as limited educational opportunities, low parental monitoring and drug use.

- To prevent gang-joining, resources should be used to revitalize deteriorating, poverty-stricken, racially/ethnically isolated communities.

- We can act now on what we know about shared risk factors — such as poverty, immigration, discrimination and social isolation — to implement general prevention strategies and programs that are racially, ethnically and culturally sensitive while continuing to explore whether additional racially and ethnically specific gang-membership prevention programming is needed.

In Brief

The connection between race/ethnicity and gang membership has long existed. Early gang members traditionally came from white ethnic immigrant groups such as the Irish and Polish, whereas starting in the 1950s, we have seen gang membership increasingly concentrated among racial minorities such as African-Americans, Hispanics, Asians, and American Indians.[1,2,3,4,5,6] Current data indicate that there are a considerable number of white gang members as well.[7,8,9] Additionally, emerging gangs have be-come much more multiracial, impacting the role that race/ethnicity plays, especially with respect to issues such as gang conflict.[10] Although a number of theories and a fair amount of research have exam-ined the connection between race/ethnicity and gang membership, surprisingly little information exists regarding whether racially or ethnically *specific* programming is needed. For example, do we need more targeted programs that focus on specific factors for different racial and ethnic groups? Or is general gang-membership prevention programming — which includes some racially and ethnically *sensitive* elements — sufficient?

Early gang research focused on investigating the development of gangs among newly arrived ethnic groups, emphasizing the connection to immigration, urbanization, poverty and social isolation. In fact, these factors seem to represent the common denominator when considering gang-joining — regardless of racial/ethnic group membership — and they remain at the center of many recent works explaining gang membership among racial/ethnic minorities. Furthermore, general risk factors for gang membership often are more prevalent in racial/ethnic minority populations, which results in higher rates of gang membership for these populations. However, there does seem to be some question regarding which risk factors matter the most in understanding gang membership among the various racial and ethnic groups.[11,12]

> Communities cannot address gang-joining among minority populations without fully understanding the factors that influence risk. There is some recent evidence — including a study by the authors — that racially and ethnically specific gang-membership prevention programming may not be necessary but rather, that general prevention programming, which includes racially and ethnically sensitive elements, may be sufficient.[13] To date, however, most research has focused on gangs in specific locations without fully considering race or ethnicity as a factor. Therefore, to know whether racially or ethnically *specific* programming would be more successful than general gang-membership prevention programming, it is important that current prevention programs be better evaluated to determine whether race or ethnicity has an impact on prevention efforts and outcomes.

The roles of race and ethnicity in gang membership are becoming increasingly complicated. Several factors contribute to this complexity:

- Gang members are not only minorities; whites are involved at higher levels than previously thought.[14]

- Gangs are becoming increasingly racially or ethnically mixed.[10] The changing ethnic composition of gangs may be increasing the likelihood of intra- (rather than inter-) racial/ethnic conflict; instead of conflict between African-Americans and whites, for example, we are seeing more and more conflict between opposing Hispanic groups such as MS-13 and 18th Street.[15] Thus, race/ethnicity may not be the chief reason for gang conflict.

- Gang membership is often portrayed, especially by the media, as a minority issue affecting the barrios and inner cities of the United States.[16] Although a disproportionate share of gang members are in fact minority youth, this image ignores the significant number of white (non-Hispanic Caucasian) individuals involved in gangs, and creates inaccurate representations of the large number of minority youth who do *not* join gangs.[7,17] Further confusing the issue is that, although racial and ethnic minorities constitute the majority of gang members, according to both official and self-report data, these sources do not agree on the level of involvement of racial/ethnic minorities.[9]

The National Gang Center,[9] for example, reports law enforcement data that indicate 84 percent of gang members are racial or ethnic minorities: 49 percent Hispanic, 35 percent African-American,

4.6 percent Asian or Pacific Islander, and 1.4 American Indian or Alaska Native. Additionally, findings from ethnographic studies — most of which tend to focus on African-American or Latino gangs — further contribute to the perception that gang membership is only a problem among racial or ethnic minority youth.[2,4,5,6] On the other hand, self-report studies — such as the one conducted to evaluate the G.R.E.A.T. (Gang Resistance Education and Training) program — indicate that about 25 percent of gang members are white.[7] Other self-report studies that describe the percentage of youth who report gang membership by race or ethnicity suggest approximately equal percentages of gang members among white (7 percent), African-American (8 percent) and Hispanic (9 percent) youth; multiracial individuals are involved in gangs at higher rates than those identifying as one race or ethnicity (13 percent).[18]

Some of the discrepancy in estimates of gang involvement of racial or ethnic minorities could be due to the fact that the racial/ethnic makeup of a gang tends to reflect the racial/ethnic composition of the community; that is, gang members tend to be white in areas with large concentrations of white residents, tend to be primarily Latino in predominantly Latino areas, and predominantly African-American in areas with a large African-American population.[19] For example, although the National Gang Center reports that, overall, 9 percent of gang members are white, this percentage increases to 17 percent in rural counties and 14 percent in smaller cities where populations, as a whole, tend to consist of larger percentages of whites.[9] Likewise, African-American and Hispanic gang members are the most prevalent in larger cities.[9] Thus, because most of the information on gang membership is often generated from large urban areas, these are the populations represented, once again fueling the impression that gang membership is solely a minority issue.

There is also a tendency, based on the available data, to separate gangs into groups, such as African-American gangs, Hispanic gangs, Asian gangs and American Indian gangs. However, doing so ignores the dynamics within groups (such as the differences between Chinese and Vietnamese gangs) as well as the fact that, increasingly, gangs are taking on the characteristics of hybrid gangs, which include being multiracial/ multiethnic.[10] By 1998, it was estimated that as many as one-third of gangs were racially/ ethnically mixed.[10] This mixed nature remains more prominent in jurisdictions that experienced a later onset of gang formation. For example, agencies that reported gang onset as recently as 1991-1992 indicated that 55 percent of gangs consisted of racially and ethnically mixed membership — compared with 38 percent for those with the onset of gang problems in 1981-1985, and 18 percent for those with the onset of gang problems before 1981.[20]

Multiracial gangs have created a new dynamic, especially in terms of conflict between gangs. Historically, many gangs developed in response to the threat from other racial/ethnic groups, thus creating conflict.[21] Movies such as "West Side Story" and "Gangs of New York" presented the image of racial/ethnic groups fighting with each other, often with deadly consequences. Evidence does exist, for example, that African-American gangs in New York developed in response to threats from white gangs.[21] However, intraethnic conflict also appears to have played a role in the development of gangs such as MS-13 (a Salvadoran gang) as they tried to protect themselves from other Hispanic gangs such as the 18th Street gang.[15] Thus, as gang membership becomes more diverse in terms of race/ethnicity, it can potentially impact the group conflict dynamic as gangs might be less likely to conflict with each other based primarily on race/ethnicity.

Targeting Concentrated Disadvantage

Community and environmental factors play a critical role in the creation of youth gangs. In

current American society, members of racial/ ethnic minority groups are much more likely than whites to live in disadvantaged communities with characteristics that exacerbate risk for gang-joining, including the following:[2,22,23,24,25]

- Concentrated poverty.

- Social and geographic isolation.

- Resource-deprived social institutions, such as schools and hospitals.

- Fewer meaningful employment opportunities because of industrial and manufacturing jobs moving out of the cities during the 1970s and 1980s, coupled with a deteriorating public education system that struggles to prepare students for new high-technology jobs.

- Rundown and decaying housing.

- Relatively high rates of crime and violence.

- A criminal justice system that removes a disproportionate share of residents — particularly young men — from the area.

Although there is no doubt that the community in which an individual develops has important implications for youth's likelihood of joining gangs, the reality is that few programs have the means to change these larger societal factors. Consequently, most evidence-based practices have focused on individual-level characteristics that are assumed to be more easily addressed. To truly reduce racial/ethnic disparities in youth gang-joining and violence, however, we must address the conditions that create the types of communities where gangs thrive.

Programs that focus on changing the structure of communities — by reducing prodelinquent opportunities and promoting prosocial opportunities — will most likely provide the greatest return on investment in terms of effectively addressing the root causes of gang membership and violence. This is no small order, as it would require policymakers to make a concerted effort to address factors such as the concentrations of high unemployment, the increase in households where the father is absent, the disruption these areas experience as a result of higher levels of mental and physical illness and other disabling conditions, and the overburdened health care system and community services.[26]

Concentrated disadvantage, exacerbated by demographic and economic flight from the cities since the 1960s, has resulted in increasingly racially/ethnically segregated communities.[22, 24, 27] Furthermore, this flight and its consequences impact communities and transcend racial/ethnic lines.[2, 24] As a result, gangs provide a setting in which nonconforming norms, values and behaviors are developed, shared, sustained and become deeply engrained.[28,29,30] In communities with the greatest isolation and disruption, risks — including those for gang-joining — developed. This occurred:

- In settings that are socially isolated from "mainstream" society.

- In response to an absence of legitimate opportunities to achieve "the American Dream."

- As a mechanism of social support among marginalized members of society.

- As a way to defend against groups with competing values.

For example, particularly for African-Americans, the accumulating concentrated-disadvantage processes of the 1970s and 1980s may have ushered in a "new era" of gangs.[2, 24] During the 1980s and 1990s, blue-collar jobs, which have traditionally increased social mobility, became scarce. As these jobs required more skills and became less available, minority individuals living in disadvantaged urban areas had a harder time finding employment. When jobs and educational preparation are limited, young males especially have fewer legitimate opportunities as they become young adults. Historically, as meaningful employment became unavailable, many minority youth stayed in gangs longer, further embedding gangs in the community. In fact, research indicates that many young men would choose the opportunity for legitimate employment over illegitimate activities such as drug dealing for several reasons, including that most do not make a substantial amount of money through illicit activities.[2,31] In the presence of limited opportunities for employment, gangs provide an alternative way to "make it" in inner-city environments.[2, 24] However, although the gang may fulfill the immediate need for financial resources, gang involvement alienates youth from society and decreases their ability to interact with conventional society in the long run.[32,33] As a result, gang members are often

not prepared to enter mainstream society and are not able to prepare their children to enter it either, creating a cycle of violence and gang involvement in these disadvantaged neighborhoods.[32]

Additionally, when considering gang expansion and activities, it is important to consider the different historical experiences of racial/ethnic groups.[6] For example, the experiences of African-Americans in the crack cocaine trade during the late 1980s through mid-1990s have been documented as one element fostering violence and gang activities in inner-city neighborhoods during that era.[34] However, self-reporting by gang members indicates no significant differences between racial/ethnic groups when it comes to selling illegal drugs — and a greater percentage of white gang members actually report more individual participation in drug selling.[8] Thus, although it is important to consider the historical context and any residual effect of race or ethnicity when trying to understand gang-membership prevention, there is generally insufficient or conflicting information for a thorough comparison of the activities of white, African-American and Hispanic gangs. Additionally, recent evidence — that gangs may be becoming more multiracial — renders some of the traditional typologies less relevant than they were in the past.

The isolation created by concentrated disadvantage often results in the spread of violence. Citizens in these environments can feel left behind and forgotten, including by local law enforcement. Feeling under attack by members of their own communities, coupled with a lack of trust in the formal justice system, residents may feel the need to be always ready — and, when necessary, willing — to use violence to solve disputes.[22,35] When the threat of violence becomes a part of residents' daily existence, it creates an environment favorable to gangs, which can be further exacerbated by the sense of isolation people feel from mainstream institutions, such as schools and law enforcement, and from legitimate employment opportunities. Of course, participation in violence results in even more isolation from the community and conventional society.[35]

These feelings of isolation may be further increased when the marginalization occurs in multiple contexts, such as due to racism, discrimination, or the unique pressures faced by recent immigrants. The fact that immigration — legal or illegal — can put individuals in a position to be discriminated against and impact their economic situation ties it to risks for involvement in criminal behavior and gang membership.

MS-13, a Salvadoran gang receiving consider-able publicity recently, provides one example of the relationship between immigration and gangs. Many individuals left El Salvador in the 1980s to escape a civil war. They settled in the United States, and some youth formed a violent gang as a way to protect themselves from other groups. Policy efforts, such as deportation, resulted in the establishment of this gang within post-civil war El Salvador and created a pipeline through which many either enter or return illegally, representing a continual problem for many of the communities where these gangs exist.[36] (See the sidebar "One Child's Journey.")

Despite the risks associated with concentrated disadvantage, even in the most disadvantaged communities, involvement of youth (white and minority) in gangs is the exception.[37] Thus, we must examine other risk and protective factors to gain a more complete understanding of who joins gangs.

Are Risk and Protective Factors for Gang-Joining "Race/Ethnic-Specific"?

The risk and protective factors approach has become more popular in terms of looking at the predictors of gang membership. However, there is limited information on the differences and similarities of risk and protective factors for gang-joining across different racial/ethnic groups. The evidence that we do have, however, shows that although some differences exist across groups, many risk factors often impact youth regardless of race and ethnicity.

In fact, the reason that more minority youth are involved in gangs might not be because the risk and protective factors are different but, rather, because they are exposed to greater risk levels based on the communities in which they typi-cally live. That said, reliable data is scarce. We need more research on whether different risk and protective factors predict differences in gang membership between the racial/ethnic groups and whether this warrants racially and ethnically specific programming.

Some of the more promising research that examines the relationship between racial/ethnic membership and gang involvement includes in-vestigating the various risk and protective factors for gang membership. This perspective, devel-oped from the public health model (see chapter 3), identifies factors that put an individual more at risk for (or protect against) a number of outcomes, including gang membership.[38,39,40] Although the literature on risk factors for gang membership has become more extensive over the last decade, it is important to note the scarcity of literature that explores the similarities and differences in risk and protective factors for the various racial/ethnic groups.[11,12,13,39,40,41,42,43] Research that examines group-specific factors that predict gang member-ship for whites, African-Americans, Hispanics and other groups remains relatively rare.[8,11,12,13,14]

Much of the research on risk factors for youth violence more generally, and gang membership specifically, indicates that most risk factors for gang-joining operate similarly across groups. Most of what we know about risk factors for gang-joining generally applies for white, African-American, American Indian and Asian youth. Additionally, research examining risk factors for gang membership among middle-school-aged youth has found that the effects of risk factors in the individual (for example, lack of self-control, low levels of guilt for negative behavior), family (such as poor parental monitoring), school (such as perceived vulnerability to violence), and peer (for example, commitment to delinquent peers, unstructured time spent where adults were not present, and time spent where drugs or alcohol are available) domains operate similarly for youth of different racial/ethnic backgrounds.[13] Also, regardless of racial/ethnic background, youth who experienced a greater accumulation of risk factors and those who reported risk factors from multiple domains were more likely than other youth to report being gang members.

Although studies show that many key risk factors influencing gang membership are similar across races and ethnicities, evidence also indicates that some gang-joining risk factors may influence cer-tain groups more than others. For example, when compared with Hispanics, more African-American gang members are influenced by social vari-ables such as having family members in a gang, gang members in their classes, and friends who

One Child's Journey

Imagine this scenario: A family consisting of a mother, father and preadolescent son move from a distant land to the United States. The family settles into a community with immigrants of similar heritage. As new arrivals, they face a number of hardships. First, the father needs to find a way to support the family, but his employment opportunities are limited because of the lack of meaningful jobs in the area, few social connections to rely on for assistance, language barriers, and the existence of stereotypes that his "kind" is uneducated, undermotivated, and possibly here on fake registration papers.

In the home country, women are expected to focus on family rearing; however, it quickly becomes clear that the mother will need to get a job if the family is to pay its bills. Both the husband and the wife take on new jobs in the secondary labor market — father works seasonal labor, mother works at a fast-food establishment. The family is constantly bombarded by messages encouraging materialism and financial success. Both parents work as many hours as possible, but their financial means do not allow for the lifestyle they desire. In fact, a recent change in the public transportation route has compromised the mother's means of getting to work, and the father, on his way home from work, was recently robbed of his paycheck, which was entirely in cash because of his distrust of social institutions like banks. He does not report the crime because he knows the man who stole his money is a neighbor, although not a good one.

The couple's son, who immigrated with the family at age 5, has now become a teenager. He observes all of this and experiences strains of his own. He attends a school with outdated resources and a leaky ceiling. To and from school each day,

he passes groups of young men and women making quick (if meager) money by selling drugs. Over time, more and more of his friends are dropping out of school, selling and using drugs, and hanging out with the older kids who show them how. As he has aged, the desire for more material wealth has been ingrained in his psyche, and now that he is a teenager, it is more important than ever to fit in and impress his friends. Several of his friends encourage him to just hang out with them for a while and "give the game a try." He rarely sees his parents because they work so much, but he realizes that they do not seem to be successfully moving up the social ladder. Based on his poor school experience, with its resource-depleted environment failing to provide useful education or job training, the difficulty of learning in English while primarily speaking in his native tongue at home, and the physical and social disorder he faces just traveling to school and back, the teenager decides to give it a try. Keeping it secret from his parents, of course, the teen quickly begins to enjoy the camaraderie, networking, partying, and money associated with the group affiliation. The appearance of solidarity and the illusion of protection the gang offers also provide peace of mind that he will not be robbed like his father or, if he is, he will have a group to back him up when he retaliates.

Can you tell the race of the person in this example? Can you tell what country that he emigrated from? No. This is why it is important to understand that the issue of preventing kids from joining gangs is so much broader than race. It's not that race/ethnicity does not matter. It's just very important to understand the larger social context in which race — and ethnicity and immigration — are but factors.

use drugs.[11] On the other hand, risk factors for Hispanic gang members tend to be more related to educational frustration and lower school self-esteem.[11] For white gang members, risk factors included having parents with lower educational levels and increased levels of social isolation. African-Americans and Hispanics, on the other hand, were more likely to join gangs when they were less committed to school, had poor opinions of or interactions with the police, and were socialized on the street.[12]

These group differences in the relative influence of some risk factors suggest the potential benefit of some tailoring of prevention strategies that address cross-cutting risks to be sensitive to the motivations and concerns of specific groups.

Other research highlights the *differential exposure* to risk factors for members of different racial/ethnic groups. The results from these studies have led researchers to propose that the reason we see more minority youth involvement in gangs is not because of differences in the types of risk factors. Rather, they argue, gang-joining is related to the fact that minority youth are often more exposed to risk factors based on the environments in which they live. So, for example, living in a deteriorating community without jobs and quality schools and with high crime rates represent risk factors for gang membership — and youth from *any* racial/ethnic group exposed to this type of environment would be more likely to join a gang. The difference is that minority youth are more likely than whites to grow up in communities with these characteristics, thus increasing their chances of gang involvement. So, the risk factors are not necessarily different for minority individuals, but the rate at which they are exposed to risk factors does differ.

As with all aspects of youth violence, important racial and ethnic differences in the social contexts in which youth develop can be neither ignored nor overstated when examining gang-joining (see chapter 5). Thus, prevention strategies focused on youth and families in racial and ethnic minority communities with high degrees of concentrated disadvantage should be considered. Ideally, integrative, macro-level strategies aimed at reducing concentrated disadvantage and the problems that result should be implemented. Although comprehensive programs are expensive, take time to develop, and can be difficult to implement and assess, these realities should not deter us.

As discussed throughout this book, very few "gang-specific" prevention programs exist, and even fewer have been found to be effective. We have found no established evidence-based programs that are directly focused on addressing racial/ethnic differences in risk factors for gang membership. Unfortunately, research on gang-joining and related programming has not evolved as quickly as other areas of youth-violence prevention.[44] However, there is some evidence that general prevention programming is equally effective for whites and minorities. For example, looking at numerous programs, researchers found that mainstream delinquency-prevention programs do, in fact, work equally well for minority and white youth.[45] These findings mirror those found in evaluations of other culturally specific juvenile justice programs.[46] Similarly, the Community Guide review of universal, school-based violence-prevention programs found significant preventive effects on violent behavior, regardless of the predominant race/ethnicity of students.[47] Furthermore, some general prevention programs — such as the school-based G.R.E.A.T. program — have been found to reduce gang membership among racially/ethnically diverse groups of youth[48] (see chapter 11).

In short, there is no consensus on whether programs should be racially or ethnically specific or whether they should be more general — that is, simply addressing underlying risk and protective factors that are likely to be relevant across racial/ethnic subgroups and communities, including risk factors for gang membership that are also related to substance abuse, risky sexual behavior, and aggression and violence.[13] With that in mind, we recommend funding and rigorously evaluating programs that focus on general risk and protective factors for overlapping problems — such as gang membership, delinquency and drug use — while carefully tailoring programs to meet the needs of racial and ethnic groups. This could be done by gathering and acting on feedback regarding examples of culturally appropriate programs. Pending future research results, the current evidence based on the risk factors for violence and victimization (both of which are related to gang involvement) suggests that making existing evidence-based programs racially and ethnically sensitive may be preferred over the development of new racially and ethnically specific programs.[13] For example, the elements of successful evidence-based programs should be administered to diverse groups, but it may be necessary to modify programs so they are relevant to the specific experiences of clients being served.[49] For example, in many minority communities, gang participation may indicate the need for protection and may not necessarily be a consequence of community values that support violence. Understanding these differences is important in terms of programmatic focus.[49]

IN THE SPOTLIGHT: THE STRENGTHENING FAMILIES PROGRAM

To highlight how race and ethnicity can be taken into account when modifying standardized prevention programs, we focus on an evidence-based drug prevention program: the Strengthening Families Program (SFP). It is important to note that although this program does not focus on reducing gang-joining *per se*, we believe it is relevant to gang-joining prevention because it addresses a number of overlapping risk factors related to youth problem behaviors — such as drug use, aggression and violence — and focuses on entire families (see chapter 6). SFP also addresses factors that are likely to reduce the risk for gang-joining, such as increasing social competency skills, improving attitudes inconsistent with drug use, aggression and delinquency and increasing prosocial peer connections.

In fact, the evolution of SFP also serves as a model for tailoring general evidence-based prevention programs to the culture. Through its expansion, SFP has become adapted to different groups (diverse racial and ethnic backgrounds) and settings (urban and rural), thus providing a roadmap for other prevention programs.

Beginning in 1987, the U.S. Department of Justice's Office of Juvenile Justice and Delinquency Prevention (OJJDP) began working with researchers at the University of Utah to assess the state of research on families.[50] The work highlighted that family-skills training is an effective method for improving family functioning and reducing problem behavior. Family-skills training programs are more comprehensive because they address entire family units rather than focusing only on the youth or the parents. Such efforts may be particularly relevant for African-American families, as research has illustrated a preference among African-Americans for incorporating the entire family unit in prevention programs.[51]

This OJJDP review was unique in focusing on important family-related *protective* and *resiliency* factors associated with a number of youth problem behaviors, including substance abuse, aggression and violence. That is, rather than focusing only on risk factors — those that increase the likelihood that problem behavior will result — it also focused on increasing a young person's resiliency in countering problem behaviors. When protective and resiliency factors are enhanced, they can reduce the likelihood of problem behavior even in the presence of risk factors. The OJJDP review highlighted five major protective factors in the family domain:

- Supportive parent-child relationships.

- Positive disciplining methods.

- Parental monitoring and supervision of youth.

- Family advocacy for their children.

- Parental information and help-seeking.

For more on family-specific risk and protective factors and how they relate to program effectiveness, see chapter 6. The bottom line is that programs teaching these protective and resiliency factors are expected to reduce youth problem behaviors even when risk factors are present.

In addition to being recognized as a program of distinction by OJJDP, the SFP has also been classified as *"promising"* by the Blueprints series, meaning that there was evidence of a preventive effect using a rigorous research design.[52]

History and Evolution of SFP

SFP was developed by Karol Kumpfer and her colleagues at the University of Utah in the late 1980s. The original program focused on increasing resiliency skills to prevent substance abuse, and targeted families with drug-abusing parents and elementary school-age youth who were racially and ethnically diverse. The program consisted of a highly structured approach, delivered through 14 lessons, each lasting 2½-3 hours, with separate 1-hour sessions for the parents and the children, and the entire family together for the second hour. Additional time was devoted to logistical issues such as meals, rewards or additional family activities.[53]

Children are taught communication skills to:

- Improve peer refusal and recognition of feelings.

- Cope with anger and criticism.

- Increase compliance with parents' demands.

- Increase self-esteem.

- Increase knowledge about alcohol and other drugs.

- Reduce aggression, behavior problems and substance use.

Parents learn to increase positive attention and praise by learning to empathize with the child, reduce physical punishments, increase effective discipline, and reduce the use of drugs. As a whole, families learn to reduce family conflict by improving communication among family members, increasing the time parents and children spend together, and increasing family planning and coordination.[54]

Parent-training sessions are focused on group building, teaching parents to use attention and reinforcements to increase the desired behaviors in their children, goal setting, communication, problem solving, and skills related to effective child management strategies. Child-training sessions are focused on social skills associated with problem solving, communication, emotional recognition and control, peer resistance and good behavior. The joint family training provides a setting in which the learned skills are practiced; trainers also provide feedback to the parents and children.[53]

The original SFP received recognition from the National Institute on Drug Abuse (NIDA) and OJJDP on the basis of early evaluation results. Generally, these programs have been found to reduce a host of youth problem behaviors in both the short and the long term. Research has shown that the program improves family relationships and parenting practices[55] and reduces substance abuse[56, 57, 58, 59, 60] and aggressive behavior.[61]

The current Strengthening Families Program exists in two forms: one focuses on elementary school youth (SFP) and the second focuses on middle school youth (SFP 10-14).[53]

Although there is considerable overlap in program components, SFP 10-14 was developed to prevent misbehavior of middle school youth (rather than elementary school youth). Additionally, the elementary school program consists of 14 lessons, whereas the middle school program consists of seven lessons. A series of boosters is also recommended after the conclusion of each program.

SFP 10-14, which targets the age group at which most youth join a gang, focuses on seven key resiliency factors — optimism, empathy, insight, intellectual competence, self-esteem, direction or purpose in life, and determinism/perseverance — that are associated with seven main coping or life skills — emotional management skills, interpersonal social skills, reflective skills, academic and job skills, the ability to restore self-esteem, planning skills, life skills, and problem-solving ability.[13, 53] Recently, SFP 10-14 has been deemed *promising* by the Blueprints series at the University of Colorado's Center for the Study of Violence Prevention, indicating that SFP 10-14 has illustrated a significant preventive effect using a strong research design.[52] SFP 10-14 has demonstrated success on a variety of targeted outcomes, including preventing drug use, aggression, and several mediating (risk and protective) factors related to problem behavior.

Evolving to Address Diverse Cultures

Given the success of the original SFP, it has been disseminated to other contexts and has evolved to meet the needs of diverse groups by making several cultural adaptations to the program. These range from minor modifications — such as using more culturally relevant examples and graphics — to more extensive content revisions. Most of these cultural modifications were "surface level" efforts to improve communication with and retain the racial and ethnic minority families in the program.[62] These modifications were driven by input from community stakeholders[63] and positive results from the program outcome evaluations.[64] Of particular importance are the modifications that tailor the program content to the culture and diversity of the audiences. This blueprint provides a model for developing culturally relevant exercises and examples with each program modification.[55] For example:

• The SFP for African-Americans includes the same substantive content as the original SFP, but the manuals include pictures and wording more relevant to African-American clients. Additionally, the program manuals include more information about African-American families and communities.[65]

• The SFP for Hispanic families includes a Spanish-language version and additional content on respecting family traditions.[55]

• The SFP for Hawaiian families received the most revisions; an additional 10 sessions were added on respect for family values.[55]

Some evidence suggests that the program received more support from African-American participants when it was tailored to reflect African-Americans' historical experiences and culture.[56] However, more research is needed to determine how tailoring programs to the culture affects program effectiveness.

Policy Issues

It is important for policymakers to understand the relationship between gang membership and race and ethnicity because what we know — or think we know — can significantly impact resource allocation, policy decisions, and a community's level of fear of crime.[66] The perception that gang membership is a minority issue has long influenced our decisions about policies regarding the gang problem. For example, during the 1990s, one of the consequences of increasing gang problems was a massive influx of resources, primarily to law enforcement agencies, to try to address the problem, especially in those minority communities that were most affected. However, those policies were mainly focused on suppression and apprehension of gang members and concentrated less on specifically addressing those risk factors that result in gang membership among minority youth. For many communities, this meant losing generations of young males, which further contributed to the deterioration of these areas and put the next generation at more risk, continuing the cycle of gang involvement.

To be effective in preventing gang-joining, we need to understand why it happens. This includes more than just the reasons that youth in specific neighborhoods give for joining; it also includes the broader set of individual, family, school, peer and community factors that influence the risk for gang-joining. (For more on the attraction of gang-joining, see chapter 2.) When considering preventing gang membership among racial and ethnic minorities, the defining question is: Is racially or ethnically *specific* programming needed? The question asks us to consider whether general prevention programming that targets individuals regardless of their racial or ethnic group status is sufficient, or if we need more targeted programs that focus on specific factors related to gang membership for the various racial/ethnic groups.

The answer to this question is not insignificant, as the research regarding *the relationship between race/ethnicity and gang membership* has typically highlighted the importance of larger, socialstructural factors — poverty, immigration, discrimination and social isolation, for example — that differentially impact the lives of individuals of different races and ethnicities. Enhancing existing strategies and developing new programs that focus on social-structural differences to provide greater equality to all racial and ethnic groups should be a priority. Clearly, however, such programs require a significant restructuring of current efforts. Primarily, they would involve a move from focusing on individual-level risks (such as risk-seeking and hanging out with peers without adults present) to community and societal influences (such as poverty, disorganized communities and poor schools). These influences are infinitely more complex and, as a result, more challenging to address.

Refocusing would also require a reallocation of resources from enforcement and suppression to prevention efforts. Obviously, this represents a huge undertaking that would involve many different stakeholders, agencies and jurisdictions as well as political support — no easy task!

Fortunately, much of the existing research suggests that general prevention programming — with some additional racially or ethnically sensitive elements — provides benefits across groups. Research to date shows that there may be some differences across races and ethnicities regarding factors that influence gang-joining, but most of the risk factors for gang membership are shared by youth of all racial and ethnic backgrounds. Thus, programs that address social isolation or school commitment would help prevent gang membership for all youth. For this reason, we suggest that, as a starting point, existing empirically supported general prevention programs should be used for youth of *all* racial and ethnic groups.

That said, efforts should be undertaken to make programs culturally relevant for participants. For example, one domain that is often highlighted as being important — but structurally different based on race or ethnicity — is the family unit. Clearly, different patterns of family composition are seen across racial and ethnic groups in modern American society; these units often face issues related to poverty, immigration, discrimination and social isolation. Additionally, there is evidence that — particularly for African-Americans — there is a desire to have the entire family unit involved in programs aimed at preventing youth problem behaviors.[55] For these reasons, programs that focus on entire family units may be particularly important in reducing youth gang involvement.

What is clear from the Strengthening Families Program (SFP) is that programs can be modified to improve program recruitment, completion and satisfaction of specific audiences. This should be done through a process of "scaling up,"[64] where promising programs are developed and delivered to a diverse group of clients. The programs are evaluated as they are delivered, particularly in terms of how clients view the suitability of the program components; modifications are made on the basis of evidence of program effectiveness, including feedback from the program clients. Drawing from the examples of SFP, it is clear that standardized programs can be effectively used to prevent problem behavior among youth of different racial and ethnic groups, but efforts to tailor programs to the culture should be devised in ways that ensure program fidelity and effectiveness. (For more on the importance of program evaluation, see chapter 11.)

Conclusion

Although there are a number of theories and a fair amount of research examining the connection between race and ethnicity and gang membership, there is little information regarding how — or if — race and ethnicity affect gang-membership prevention policies, strategies and programs. Even though additional research examining the relationship between race and ethnicity and gang membership is certainly needed to examine whether racially or ethnically specific gang-membership prevention programming is effective, we do not have to wait. We can act now on what we know about shared risk factors — poverty, immigration, discrimination and social isolation — and their consequences in terms of substance abuse, limited educational and job opportunities, family stress, neighborhood crime and the influence of gangs — by implementing prevention programs that are racially, ethnically and culturally sensitive and are known to reduce relevant risks. The fact that similar risk factors are tied to gang membership regardless of race or ethnicity supports the contention that general prevention programming should work. We should implement prevention strategies that have been shown to be effective at reducing established risks for gang-joining and that are likely to apply across groups while taking advantage of what is known about group differences to tailor our prevention efforts.[8,11,12] For example, targeting factors such as having family members in the gang — a factor tied to gang membership for African-Americans — should also have an impact on gang membership for individuals regardless of their racial or ethnic background. Thus, until more is known about how race and ethnicity specifically relate to gang membership, it seems realistic to consider general prevention programming or expand upon existing promising programs to ensure that they are culturally appropriate and relevant.

About the Authors

Adrienne Freng

Adrienne Freng is an associate professor in the Department of Criminal Justice at the University of Wyoming. Dr. Freng's work has focused on program evaluation, juvenile delinquency, gangs, and race and crime issues, specifically how they relate to American Indian populations. A former managing editor for *Justice Quarterly,* Dr. Freng received her Ph.D. from the University of Nebraska–Lincoln.

Terrance J. Taylor

Terrance J. Taylor is an assistant professor at the University of Missouri–St. Louis. His focus is on youth violence, specializing in the prevention of juvenile victimization and offending and in police/citizen relations. The role of race and ethnicity has been a key issue throughout his research. He has published extensively and was a co-investigator on an in-depth evaluation of the Gang Resistance Education and Training (G.R.E.A.T.) program. Dr. Taylor received his Ph.D. in Criminal Justice from the University of Nebraska.

Endnotes

1. Chin K-L. Gang violence in Chinatown. In: Huff CR, ed., *Gangs in America.* 2nd ed. Thousand Oaks, CA: Sage Publications, 1996:157-181.

2. Hagedorn JM. *People and Folks: Gangs, Crime, and the Underclass in a Rustbelt City.* Chicago, IL: Lake View Press, 1988.

3. Major AK, Egley Jr A, Howell JC, Mendenhall B, Armstrong T. *Youth Gangs in Indian Country.* Washington, DC: U.S. Department of Justice, Office of Justice Programs, Office of Juvenile Justice and Delinquency Prevention, 2004.

4. Moore J. *Going Down to the Barrio: Homeboys and Homegirls in Change.* Philadelphia, PA: Temple University Press, 1991.

5. Vigil JD. *Barrio Gangs: Street Life and Identity in Southern California.* Austin, TX: University of Texas Press, 1988.

6. Vigil JD. *A Rainbow of Gangs: Street Cultures in the Mega-City.* Austin, TX: University of Texas Press, 2002.

7. Esbensen F-A, Osgood DW. Gang Resistance Education and Training (G.R.E.A.T.): Results from the national evaluation. *J Res Crime Delinq.* 1999; 36:194-225.

8. Freng AL, Winfree Jr LT. 2004. Exploring race and ethnic differences in a sample of middle school gang members. In: Esbensen F-A, Tibbetts SG, Gaines L, eds., *American Youth Gangs at the Millennium.* Long Grove, IL: Waveland Press, 2004:142-162.

9. National Gang Center. National Youth Gang Survey Analysis, 2009 [online]. Available at http://www.nationalgangcenter.gov/Survey-Analysis. Accessed on February 15, 2013.

10. Starbuck D, Howell JC, Linquist DJ. *Hybrid and Other Modern Gangs.* Washington, DC: U.S. Department of Justice, Office of Justice Programs, Office of Juvenile Justice and Delinquency Prevention, 2001.

11. Curry GD, Spergel IA. Gang involvement and delinquency among Hispanic and African-American adolescent males. *J Res Crime Delinq.* 1992; 29:273-291.

12. Freng A, Esbensen F-A. Race and gang affiliation: An examination of multiple marginality. *Justice Q.* 2007; 24:600-628.

13. Esbensen F-A, Peterson D, Taylor TJ, Freng A. *Youth Violence: Understanding the Role of Sex, Race/Ethnicity, and Gang Membership.* Philadelphia, PA: Temple University Press, 2010.

14. Esbensen F-A, Winfree Jr LT. Race and gender differences between gang and nongang youth: Results from a multisite survey. *Justice Q.* 1998; 15:505-526.

15. Corbiscello GV. Border crossings: A look at the very real threat of cross border gangs to the U.S. *J Gang Res.* 2008; 15:33-52.

16. Esbensen F-A, Tusinski K. Youth gangs in the print media. *Crim Just Pop Culture* 2007; 14:21-38.

17. Curry GD, Ball RA, Fox RJ. *Gang Crime and Law Enforcement Recordkeeping.* Washington, DC: U.S. Department of Justice, Office of Justice Programs, National Institute of Justice, 1994.

18. Esbensen F-A, Brick TB, Melde C, Tusinski K, Taylor TJ. The role of race and ethnicity in gang membership. In: Genert FV, Peterson D, Lien I. *Street Gangs, Migration, and Ethnicity.* Portland, OR: Willan, 2008:117-139.

19. Esbensen F-A, Peterson D. Youth gang members in a school survey. In: Klein M, Kerner H-J, Maxson C, Weitekamp E, eds., *The Eurogang Paradox: Street Gangs and Youth Groups in the U.S. and Europe.* Amsterdam, The Netherlands: Kluwer Press, 2001.

20. Howell JC, Egley A, Gleason DK. *Modern Day Youth Gangs.* Washington, DC: U.S. Department of Justice, Office of Justice Programs, Office of Juvenile Justice and Delinquency Prevention, 2002.

21. Howell JC, Moore JP. *History of Street Gangs in the United States.* National Gang Center Bulletin No. 4. Tallahassee, FL: Institute for Intergovernmental Research, National Gang Center, 2010.

22. Anderson E. *Code of the Street: Decency, Violence, and the Moral Life of the Inner City.* New York, NY: W.W. Norton, 1999.

23. Bursik RJ, Grasmick HG. *Neighborhoods and Crime: The Dimensions of Effective Community Control.* Lanham, MD: Lexington Books, 1993.

24. Wilson WJ. *The Truly Disadvantaged: The Inner City, the Underclass, and Public Policy.* Chicago, IL: University of Chicago Press, 1987.

25. Roberts DE. The social and moral costs of mass incarceration in African American communities. *Stanford Law Review* 2004; 56:1271-1306.

26. Viner RM, Ozer EM, Denny S, et al. Adolescence and the social determinants of health. *Lancet* 2012; 379:1641-1652.

27. Massey DS, Denton NA. *American Apartheid: Segregation and the Making of the Underclass.* Cambridge, MA: President and Fellows of Harvard College, 1993.

28. Akers RL. *Deviant Behavior: A Social Learning Approach.* 1st ed. Belmont, CA: Wadsworth, 1973.

29. Akers RL. *Criminological Theories: Introduction and Evaluation.* 2nd ed. Los Angeles, CA: Roxbury Publishing, 1997.

30. Sutherland EH. *Principles of Criminology.* 3rd ed. Philadelphia, PA: J.B. Lippincott, 1939.

31. Padilla F. The working gang. In: Egley Jr A, Maxson CL, Miller J, Klein MW, eds., *The Modern Gang Reader.* Los Angeles, CA: Roxbury Publishing, 2006.

32. Fleisher M. *Dead End Kids.* Madison, WI: University of Wisconsin Press, 1998.

33. Melde C, Esbensen F-A. Gang membership as a turning point in the life course. *Criminology* 2011; 49:513-552.

34. Blumstein A, Rosenfeld R. Explaining recent trends in U.S. homicide rates. *J Crim Law Criminology* 1998; 88:1175-1216.

35. Decker SH, Van Winkle B. *Life in the Gang: Family, Friends, and Violence.* New York, NY: Cambridge University Press, 1996.

36. Adams JJ, Pizarro JM. MS-13: A gang profile. *J Gang Res.* 2009; 16:1-14.

37. Fagan J. Social processes of delinquency and drug use among urban gangs. In: Huff CR, ed., *Gangs in America,* 1st ed. Newbury Park, CA: Sage Publications, 1990:183-222.

38. Farrington DP. Explaining and preventing crime: The globalization of knowledge. American Society of Criminology 1999 Presidential Address. *Criminology* 2000; 38:1-24.

39. Thornberry T. 1998. Membership in youth gangs and involvement in serious and violent offending. In: Loeber R, Farrington DP, eds., *Serious and Violent Juvenile Offenders: Risk Factors and Successful Interventions.* Thousand Oaks, CA: Sage Publications, 1998:147-166.

40. Thornberry TP, Krohn MD, Lizotte AJ, Smith CA, Tobin K. *Gangs and Delinquency in Developmental Perspective.* New York, NY: Cambridge University Press, 2003.

41. Hill K, Howell JC, Hawkins JD, Battin-Pearson S. Childhood risk factors for adolescent gang membership: Results from the Seattle Social Development Project. *J Res Crime Delinq.* 1999; 36:300-322.

42. Howell JC. *Youth Gangs: An Overview.* Washington, DC: U.S. Department of Justice, Office of Justice Programs, Office of Juvenile Justice and Delinquency Prevention, 1998.

43. Howell JC, Egley Jr A. Moving risk factors into developmental theories of gang membership. *Youth Viol Juv Just.* 2005; 3:334-354.

44. National Institutes of Health, U.S. Department of Health and Human Services. Final Statement: "Preventing Violence and Related Health-Risking Social Behaviors in Adolescents: An NIH State-of-the-Science Conference" [online], October 13-15, 2004, Washington, DC. Available at http://consensus.nih.gov/2004/2004YouthViolence PreventionSOS023html.htm.

45. Wilson SJ, Lipsey, MW, Soydan H. Are mainstream programs for juvenile delinquency less effective with minority youth than majority youth? A meta-analysis of outcomes research. *Res Soc Work Practice* 2003; 13:3-26.

46. Wooldrege J, Hartman J, Latessa E, Holmes S. Effectiveness of culturally specific community treatment for African American juvenile felons. *Crime Delinq.* 1994; 40:589-598.

47. Guide to Community Preventive Services. The Community Guide: School-based programs to reduce violence. Available at http://www.thecommunityguide.org/violence/schoolbasedprograms.html. Accessed on February 15, 2013.

48. Esbensen F-A, Peterson D, Taylor TJ, Osgood DW. Results from a multi-site evaluation of the G.R.E.A.T. Program. *Justice Q.* 2012; 29:125-151.

49. Reese LE, Vera, EM. Culturally relevant prevention: The scientific and practical considerations of community based programs. *Couns Psychol.* 2007; 35:763-778.

50. Kumpfer KL, Alvarado R. *Effective Family Strengthening Interventions.* Washington, DC: U.S. Department of Justice, Office of Justice Programs, Office of Juvenile Justice and Delinquency Prevention, 1998.

51. Kumpfer KL, Alvarado R, Smith P, Bellamy N. Cultural sensitivity and adaptation in family-based prevention interventions. *Prevention Sci.* 2002; 3:241-246.

52. Center for the Study and Prevention of Violence, Institute of Behavioral Science, University of Colorado at Boulder. *Blueprints for Healthy Youth Development.* Available at http://www.blueprintsprograms.com.

53. Kumpfer KL, Molgaard VK, Spoth RL. The Strengthening Families Program for the prevention of delinquency and drug use. In: Peters RD, McMahon RJ, eds., *Preventing Childhood Disorders, Substance Abuse, and Delinquency.* Banff International Behavioral Science Series. Thousand Oaks, CA: Sage Publications, 1996:241-267.

54. Kumpfer KL. Selective prevention interventions: The Strengthening Families Program. In: Ashery RS, Robertson EB, Kumpfer KL, eds., *Drug Abuse Prevention Through Family Interventions.* Rockville, MD: National Institute on Drug Abuse, 1998:160-207.

55. Kumpfer KL, Alvarado R, Tait C, Turner C. Effectiveness of school-based family and children's skills training for substance abuse prevention among 6- to 8-year-old rural children. *Psyc Addict Behav.* 2002; 16:S65-S71.

56. Atkan G. A cultural consistency evaluation of a substance abuse prevention program with inner city African-American families. *J Prim Prevention* 1999; 19:227-239.

57. Spoth R, Randall GK, Shin C, Redmond C. Randomized study of combined universal family and school preventative interventions: Patterns of long-term effects on initiation, regular use, and weekly drunkenness. *Psychol Addict Behav.* 2005; 19:372-381.

58. Spoth RL, Redmond C, Shin C. Randomized trial of brief family interventions for general populations: Adolescent substance use outcomes 4 years following baseline. *J Consult Clin Psych.* 2001; 69:627-642.

59. Spoth R, Redmond C, Shin C, Azevedo K. Brief family intervention effects on adolescent substance initiation: School-level growth curve analyses 6 years following baseline. *J Consult Clin Psych.* 2004; 72:535-542.

60. Trudeau L, Spoth R, Lillehoj C, Redmond C, Wickrama KAS. Effects of a preventive intervention on adolescent substance use initiation, expectancies, and refusal intentions. *Prevention Sci.* 2003; 4:109-122.

61. Spoth RL, Redmond C, Shin C. Reducing adolescents' aggressive and hostile behavior: Randomized trial effects of a brief family intervention 4 years past baseline. *Archives of Pediatr Adoles Med.* 2000; 154:1248-1257.

62. Kumpfer, KL, Whiteside, HO, Greene, JA, Allen, KC. Effectiveness outcomes of four age versions of the Strengthening Families Program in statewide field sites. *Group Dynamics: Theory Res Practice* 2010; 14:211-219.

63. Spoth R, Randall GK, Shin C. Increasing school success through partnership-based family competency training: Experimental study of long-term outcomes. *School Psych Q.* 2008; 23:70-89.

64. Spoth RL, Redmond C. Project Family prevention trials in community-university partnerships: Toward scaled-up preventive interventions. *Prevention Sci.* 2002; 3:203-221.

65. Kumpfer, KL, Tait, CM. *Family Skills Training for Parents and Children.* Washington, DC: U.S. Department of Justice, Office of Justice Programs, Office of Juvenile Justice and Delinquency Prevention, 2000.

66. Decker SH, Kempf-Leonard K. Constructing gangs: The social definitions of youth activities. *Crim Just Policy Rev.* 1991; 5:271-291.

Program Evaluation: How Do We Know If We Are Preventing Gang Membership?

Finn-Aage Esbensen and Kristy N. Matsuda

- A well-designed program evaluation can determine the effectiveness of a program; the purpose of an evaluation is to determine whether a program (and not some other factor) caused the intended outcomes.

- Because the veracity of statements regarding a program's effectiveness depends on the quality of the program evaluation, practitioners and policymakers should understand basic research design concepts (such as *comparison group* and *pretest*) and sampling concepts (such as *representativeness* and *bias*).

- An *outcome evaluation* assesses whether a program or strategy achieved the desired outcome or result.

- A *process evaluation* assesses the extent to which a program or strategy was implemented as designed; confidence in the success of a program is diminished if implementation is flawed, and a process evaluation can help identify why and where program improvements should be made.

- Cost-effectiveness or cost-benefit analyses (conducted during or after a program evaluation) can help policymakers, practitioners and communities determine the most economically efficient gang-joining prevention strategies to implement.

In Brief

Program evaluations are essential to determining if a prevention program is effective, whether the program is focused on gangs or on other issues. Although evaluations require time and money, they are central to making well-informed decisions about resource allocation and support of prevention programs. This chapter reviews key components of program evaluations and highlights the importance of adhering to these components. Because rigorously designed process and outcome evaluations are the best way to determine program effectiveness — and calls for "evidence-based" programs and policies have become more frequent — the components of the term *rigorous* are also discussed. In addition, the value of cost-effectiveness and cost-benefit analyses in program assessment is introduced. To use the knowledge produced by program evaluations effectively, policymakers and practitioners must be able to interpret the quality of the research.

Most strategies and programs with the potential to prevent kids from joining gangs have not been adequately evaluated to assess their impact on gang membership. This is unfortunate. Significant human and financial resources are allocated to solving social problems, such as gangs, but not enough attention is paid to whether or not these efforts are successful. Because resources are finite, there is a need to determine which policies and programs actually achieve the intended results and which do not.

One often hears stories, anecdotes or testimonials that are presented as "evidence" of a program's or policy's effectiveness. Many policymakers and practitioners are motivated by the most salient or unique "success stories." But, although they may be inspirational — and even capture some of a program's impact — such stories, absent other data, are not sufficient measures of effectiveness. Judgments about a program's effectiveness should not be based on the salient or the unique; they should be based on science. The primary goal of evaluation research is to assess whether a program *causes* a desired outcome to everyone — or at least to a substantial proportion of those who have been exposed to the program — and not just the few exceptional cases. How do we know that certain prevention programs, policies or initiatives "work" and others do not? First, we must understand the evidence that exists or why it is important to "know what we know." Would it not be easier to support all programs and policies intending to reduce gangs (or anything else, for that matter)? Isn't something always better than nothing? There are three primary reasons the answer to both of these questions is "no."

First, resources are limited. It is a matter of necessity to prioritize programs when allocating financial and other support. There are a number of ways to accomplish this — for example, by looking at measures of cost-effectiveness or the number of people affected. One excellent way to determine which program to fund is to determine whether the program achieves its goals or, as this book discusses, whether it actually prevents gang membership.

Second, it is often impractical to implement multiple programs with the same intended outcome in the same population or community. This is simply the way the "real world" works: Loyalty to an ineffective or less effective program can make it impossible for a more effective program to be implemented. For example, the D.A.R.E. (Drug Abuse Resistance Education) program is one of the most widely implemented programs aimed at reducing drug use among adolescents. It has been in operation for more than 25 years and has been implemented in 43 countries.[1] D.A.R.E. is taught in 75 percent of school districts in the United States.[2] Evaluations of the program, however, have consistently failed to conclude that D.A.R.E. reduces drug use among youth.[3] The wide implementation of the program — and continued allocations of scarce resources to support it — decreases the likelihood that another drug-prevention program will be implemented in D.A.R.E. districts.

Finally, it is misguided to believe that, even if a program is not effective, it at least does no harm. An evaluation of a gang-intervention program in Los Angeles showed that participation in the program actually *increased* delinquency, solidarity and resistance among the gang members who participated.[4] In short, we need to know what works and why, and this chapter provides the groundwork for how this should be done.

To date, the Gang Resistance Education and Training (G.R.E.A.T.) program is the only program specifically focused on reducing gang membership that has been rigorously evaluated. The evaluation of the original G.R.E.A.T. program showed modest positive results with respect to several risk factors that are associated with delinquency and gang membership: peer group association, attitudes about gangs and law enforcement, and risk-seeking behaviors. However, the original evaluation showed no significant effects on delinquency or gang membership itself.

In response to those results — revealed through a rigorous evaluation — G.R.E.A.T. underwent a thorough review that resulted in a revised curriculum that emphasizes a skills-building approach. This revised program is currently being evaluated; the results after one year are promising: for example, there was a 39-percent reduction in the odds of gang-joining among the G.R.E.A.T. students compared with students in the control group.[5]

Although other gang-membership prevention programs exist, they either have not been evaluated or have not been evaluated using a research design that was rigorous enough to assess program effectiveness. For example, one common evaluation approach is to simply collect data on participants before and after participating in a program and then attribute any change in the post-test to the program. Such a conclusion, however, is not supported by evidence from a simple "pre-post" design because any number of factors could actually have caused the observed change — if, for example, another prevention strategy had been implemented in the community at the same time. Increasing the number of rigorous program evaluations is certainly the first step in determining what programs are effective. But spending resources on poorly designed program evaluations is almost as problematic as conducting no evaluation at all. This is particularly salient with a topic such as gang-membership prevention, where the will to implement programs is high but the knowledge of what works is limited. It is tempting to implement programs without, or with limited, evaluations; but a poor evaluation can lead to erroneous conclusions in either direction: that a truly effective program did not work or that an ineffective program had a benefit. Erroneous conclusions can lead to wasted resources if an ineffective program is continued; erroneous conclusions can also lead to missed opportunities if an effective program is stopped.

A well-designed program evaluation is critical to making the most strategically sound policy decisions. In the following discussion, we explain the characteristics of a well-designed evaluation, including factors that commonly impact the quality of a program evaluation.

The Basics of a Well-Designed Evaluation

There are three primary steps in evaluating a program or policy. First, program evaluators must identify the program's goals or intended outcome. This may seem basic, but it is fundamental. Although it is tempting — and often appropriate — to look for other outcomes, programs should be judged on the outcome that practitioners are *intending* to achieve.

Second, one must determine if the program was implemented as intended and designed; researchers call this program fidelity. Programs can have considerable variety in terms of content, duration, frequency and general delivery style. For a program to be deemed effective, however, it must bring about the intended changes as designed. For instance, the G.R.E.A.T. program is designed as 13 lessons to be taught by a law enforcement officer to middle-school students; if, however, the G.R.E.A.T. program were taught by current gang members (instead of police officers) and an evaluation found that it *increased* gang-joining, it would be inaccurate to say that the program does not work. Effectiveness — or ineffectiveness — cannot be assessed if a program has not been implemented with sufficient fidelity to its design.

Once a program's intended outcome is identified and it is determined that the program was implemented as designed, it can be evaluated to determine whether it had the intended result. A determination of effectiveness must also be based on (1) valid and reliable measures, and (2) appropriate sampling and research design.[6] Without appropriate measures and research design, it is possible, at best, to establish only an *association* between the program and its effect; but a determination that the program *caused* the change cannot be established.

An association between a program and its outcome (that youth in the program are less likely to join a gang, for example) is only the first element necessary to establish causality. Does the fact that gang membership is found to be lower after the introduction of a gang-membership prevention program mean that the program caused the reduction? Maybe yes, but possibly no. It could be that a decline in gang membership was part of a trend that started well before the program was implemented. It could be that a police crack-down on gangs occurred during the same period the program was implemented. It could be that people who participated in the program were the type of people who were less likely to join a gang. To conclude that participation in a program actually *caused* the decline in gang membership, researchers must use a strong evaluation design.

Only after an appropriate and well-designed program evaluation is in place can issues related to cost-effectiveness of the program be assessed. From a policymaker perspective, cost-effectiveness is paramount. Can an initial investment in a prevention program lead to a reduction in costs associated with youth joining gangs? The answer depends on the effectiveness of the program. It must first be determined how much of a reduction in the outcome — in this case, fewer kids joining gangs — can be attributed to the program.

Program Design: Identifying Goals

Identifying a program's goals or intended outcomes may seem straightforward but, in reality, it is the foundation of an evaluation and should not be taken lightly. It is a task that must come early in the process because a strong evaluation hinges on this determination. Program administrators need to work with evaluators and make explicit what the programmatic goals are. Program administrators also need to clearly inform evaluators about the program components and the goals they are expected or designed to achieve. Absent a clear statement of program goals in the program design and a specific statement about how the program components are intended to achieve the desired outcomes, it is virtually impossible to assess a program's effectiveness.

In a recent evaluation, for example, my (Finn-Aage Esbensen) colleagues and I sifted through countless descriptions of a delinquency-prevention program to identify its goals — and found more than a dozen different stated goals.[7,8] Through a review of the program design materials and discussions with program staff, we were able to specify three main program goals, including the reduction of victimization. Only after we had a clear understanding of the program's intended goals were we able to determine which program components were designed to achieve which goals. From this information, we were able to develop an evaluation (including the research design and instruments) that would measure the program goals.

Process Evaluation: Assessing Implementation Fidelity

It is important that policymakers and practitioners understand the importance of conducting a process evaluation of a program, policy or initiative in conjunction with an outcome evaluation.[6,9,10,11,12] A process evaluation assesses the quality of program implementation, or what

researchers call program fidelity. A process evaluation determines if what is actually being delivered is consistent with what was intended. As Peter Rossi and his colleagues state in their work on the importance of evaluations, "A precondition for impact on the social conditions a program addresses is that the program actually be implemented in a manner that could plausibly affect those conditions."[13]

One of the key predictors of a program's effectiveness is the quality of its implementation.[14] Unfortunately, program implementation failure is common. Gary Gottfredson and his colleagues concluded, in the *National Study of Delinquency Prevention in Schools,* that "about half of school-based prevention activities are of such poor quality that they cannot reasonably be expected to make a difference in levels of problem behavior."[10] Process evaluations are necessary to determine which programs fail because of poor design as opposed to poor implementation. One of the reasons researchers often cannot tell policymakers and practitioners precisely which programs do — and do not — "work" is that programs fail to provide services consistent with the program's design, reducing their chances of effectiveness or success. Too often, there are fundamental changes in who delivers the program, content is skipped, or the program is modified in ways that were not part of the original program design.

There are a number of ways to determine whether a program was implemented with fidelity. It is important for policymakers and practitioners to be aware that there are pros and cons associated with each method. One of the simpler strategies is to ask program providers to indicate the extent to which they comply with the program design. This method can be a cheap and easy way to obtain useful information, but the disadvantage is that self-reported representations of fidelity to a program's design would not be independently verified.

In an evaluation of a school-based delinquency program, self-reports from program staff revealed that most were not engaged in one core feature of the program — using outside experts to supplement the program content.[7,8] This was a major indicator of the lack of program fidelity. A downside to this approach is that individuals involved in program delivery may have a vested interest in showing their own compliance or effectiveness or in concealing other variations from the design that should have been exposed. Given these sources of potential bias, results from the self-reported process evaluations should be interpreted with caution.

Having a third-party evaluator observe program delivery is a more objective approach than self-evaluation in assessing program fidelity. With the cooperation of program personnel, many types of prevention programs can be observed for consistency in implementation. Observations are well-suited for lesson-based programs like those common in schools. In the G.R.E.A.T. program evaluation, for example, my (Finn-Age Esbensen) fellow researchers and I developed a detailed

instrument for each lesson taught by officers in the classroom.[15] A trained observer provided an overall assessment of the fidelity (quality, dosage and adherence) of the officer's program delivery. Each classroom included in the study was observed multiple times to assess whether problems with program delivery were a one-time occurrence or a common event. This observational process evaluation strategy is far more costly and time-intensive than the self-evaluation approach, but it offers much more reliable information about the quality of program implementation.

In our "In the Spotlight" interview (below), Lieutenant Raj Ramnarace, with the LaCrosse (WI) Police Department, describes his experience with

IN THE SPOTLIGHT: THE G.R.E.A.T. PROGRAM

▸ *INTERVIEW WITH RAJ RAMNARACE*

The Gang Resistance Education and Training (G.R.E.A.T.) program is a national, school-based gang and violence prevention program taught by trained law enforcement officers. The program has three primary goals:

1. Teach youth to avoid gang membership.

2. Prevent violence and criminal activity.

3. Assist youth to develop positive relationships with law enforcement.

We interviewed Lieutenant Raj Ramnarace, M.Ed., the former regional administrator of G.R.E.A.T.'s Midwest Atlantic Region. Ramnarace currently serves with the LaCrosse (WI) Police Department.

How did you become involved in G.R.E.A.T.?

I became a certified G.R.E.A.T. instructor in 1993. A year later, I joined the National Training Team and began training other officers to become G.R.E.A.T. officers.

How did your work influence the actual development of G.R.E.A.T.?

For 10 years (1998–2008), I was the Midwest Regional Administrator and, as a member of the National Training Team, I served on the

committee that produced the new curriculum. Because we knew that program implementation fidelity was the best way to ensure success, we supported the use of monitoring program implementation and effectiveness.

How was this actually manifested?

The U.S. Department of Justice's Bureau of Justice Assistance, the agency responsible for operational control of G.R.E.A.T., trained a select group of senior G.R.E.A.T. officers to conduct program audits during site visits to observe program delivery. As another way of enhancing program fidelity, a number of cities began pre- and post-testing of students.

What other approaches does G.R.E.A.T. use to improve the program's effectiveness?

We use evaluation forms to survey teachers, and we conduct periodic reviews with school districts to assess how their G.R.E.A.T. program fits into other curricula the school district is providing.

What challenges have you faced in ensuring implementation fidelity?

Once officers are in the classroom, they are on their own. Many teachers are not familiar enough with G.R.E.A.T. curricula to know whether the curriculum is being delivered

appropriately. We have to rely on G.R.E.A.T. instructors and their agencies to provide information on the curriculum to the classroom instructors.

How do you address this?

Over the years, I've seen officers who represent two different points on the fidelity-effectiveness continuum. The first are those who lack either the experience or the motivation to deliver the curricula in a way that engages students, regardless of whether they are following the curriculum outlines. The second are those who are really experienced and are able to add examples from their own experiences to the program's curriculum when they see a teachable moment. The key, of course, is knowing how much an instructor can add without violating program fidelity. For that reason, we stress program fidelity and interpersonal skills to our instructors in training. We consistently stress the benefits of adherence to the curriculum, while also trying to impress upon our instructors that building positive relationships with students will improve the curriculum's effectiveness. Nationally, G.R.E.A.T. has offered training for G.R.E.A.T. supervisors in local agencies so that they know what is expected of the G.R.E.A.T. instructors they supervise. And, as I mentioned before, we do conduct classroom audits, which are very valuable.

strategies for determining whether a program is being implemented with fidelity to its original design and goals.

Outcome Evaluation: Assessing Program Effectiveness

A program's effectiveness cannot be determined without a rigorous research design that is able to causally link its components to outcomes and excludes other potential explanations for the outcomes. A rigorous outcome evaluation can establish that a change in behavior — for example, preventing youth from joining gangs — is due to the program and not to other external factors such as maturation (aging of the participants), selection of program participants who were not at high risk of becoming gang-involved (what researchers call *sample selection bias,* or "creaming the sample"), or some other shared experiences by program participants. It is important that policymakers and practitioners understand the components of the most rigorous evaluations and, most important, be able to articulate to their constituents the real-world occurrences that sometimes make an outcome evaluation difficult to execute.

The research community has been proactive in determining what kind of evaluation leads to the determination of an effective program. Although there are different criteria that can define program effectiveness, the most rigorous classification is the one used by the University of Colorado's Blueprints program.[16] To be classified as a "promising" Blueprints program, the program evaluation must have used an experimental design (which involves random assignment to the treatment or to the control group, along with pre- and post-test measures) or a quasi-experimental design (with treatment and control groups matched on key variables) and have found evidence of significant effects.

To earn the "Blueprints model" label, the program must meet two additional criteria: The significant effect must be sustained for at least one year post-treatment, and the program must have at least one high-quality replication that also shows effectiveness.[11]

As we know, youth gangs are found all over the U.S., yet a gang-membership prevention program that is effective in Minot, ND, may not be as effective in an urban area with greater population diversity. To have confidence that a program works, it must be replicated in multiple locales with different characteristics.

When all is said and done, program evaluators may make definitive statements regarding the effectiveness or ineffectiveness of a program, but informed policymakers and program administrators are responsible for deciding what such findings mean for the future of the program. For example, policymakers and practitioners are likely to face the situation where a program may be found to be effective in one group of individuals but not another. Should the program be eliminated or refocused on a narrower client base? Perhaps additional resources should be allocated to evaluate the program in a different area, with a different population or with a commitment to better methods. Perhaps the program could be revised? Practitioners and policymakers are best equipped to determine the most appropriate course of action only if the quality of the program implementation was high and a rigorous outcome evaluation design was used.

Control or comparison groups, and pretests. To determine whether a program reduces gang membership, two things must occur:

- Treatment and control or comparison groups must be employed.

- Answers to gang affiliation questions after program completion must be compared with answers before implementation of the program.

Without both the comparison group and pretests, the important questions, "Compared with what?" and "Compared with whom?" cannot be answered. The following example illustrates the importance of these comparisons.

Gang-joining starts relatively early, around 12 or 13 years old, and escalates through the mid-teen years. A prevention program that targets 12-year-olds may seem ineffective when gang involvement has increased from the pre- to the post-test.

Such a conclusion, however, may not be the entire story; such an increase could be due to aging or maturation of the students. If, however, one also compared the rate of gang membership of the treatment group with a group of students not exposed to the program, the results may show that the increase in gang membership for program participants is less than that observed among nonprogram participants — that is, the program does have a preventive effect.

Realities of random assignment. To ensure that no other factor is the actual cause of a change the outcome, the comparison group needs be as similar as possible to the treated group before exposure to the program. The surest way for an evaluation to accomplish equality between treatment and control groups is to follow the true experimental method and randomly assign individuals to each group. Of course, it is important that policymakers and practitioners understand that this is not always practical. For example, with school-based prevention programs, it would be impractical (from the school's perspective) for researchers or program administrators to randomly assign students to receive, or not receive, the intervention because this would disrupt intact classrooms. Does this mean that equitable groups cannot be created? No. It is possible to randomly assign *classrooms* to receive or not receive the program. In this way, treatment and control groups are still available, educators can deliver the program with ease, and the school is minimally disrupted.

It is important that policymakers and practitioners understand the ethical considerations of random assignment. A common concern is the ethics of withholding services from individuals (those in the control group) who might benefit from the program. For example, assigning individuals who qualify for treatment as part of standard practice to the "no treatment" control group would be unethical despite the use of the evaluation "gold standard" of a randomized control trial (RCT). There are a number of ways to address this issue. At a minimum, control subjects should receive whatever intervention or treatment they would otherwise receive. This can be considered the "usual care" condition. When there is no usual intervention, it is often still desirable to provide

a minimal version or different form of intervention, or the control subjects could be put on a "wait list," going without treatment only until a spot in the treatment group becomes available. However, when assessing a program evaluation, it is important to keep the treatment and control groups distinct. Undermining the randomized assignment, for any reason, can jeopardize the validity of study results and lead to over- or under-estimating the true effect of the program.

Attrition. The Blueprints standard requires that the outcome show at least some sign of stability: evidence of a program effect one year after participants complete the program. This requires that study participants be tracked across time. Whenever such follow-up is required, evaluators must deal with the issue of sample loss or attrition. People move, die or otherwise disappear — and, therefore, it is important that policymakers and practitioners understand the potential consequences of attrition.

First, attrition can lead to a loss of statistical power, which means that if too many subjects are lost, it might not be possible to detect meaningful differences across groups. Second, individuals "lost" over time may represent higher-risk youth, and this may bias the results. Especially in gang-related research, gang members may be more likely to leave a study, and the loss of the most extreme members may compromise the findings. Evaluators need to make every effort to retain study participants, but attrition is a reality in longitudinal research — and it is important that policymakers and practitioners understand the challenges that attrition may pose for interpreting evaluation results.

Bias due to attrition may be indicated when the final treatment and control samples are notably different from the original samples. Assume, for example, that there were 50 high-risk kids in both the original treatment group and the control group but, at the end of the study, there were 45 high-risk kids in the control group and only 20 in the treatment group. In this case, if the final treatment group is at low risk for gang membership, it would be difficult to know whether this was because the program worked or because many high-risk kids could not be assessed.

Generalizability and selection bias. In addition to being essential in assessing the effectiveness of a program, proper sampling can also increase what researchers call the *generalizability* of the outcome results. A robust sample size drawn from a diverse study population is crucial to making well-informed inferences about the potential effectiveness of a program or policy in a variety of settings. Subsequent replication with other populations should also be conducted. As researchers, practitioners and policymakers know, however, program evaluations are time-consuming and costly. In addition, local evaluations can tell us things that a national evaluation cannot — and vice versa. That is why it is important that everyone understands this reality: an evaluation concluding that a program is effective for 14 participants in town X in year Y with counselor P is certainly informative, but it is not as informative as being able to conclude that a program is effective in a diverse population in several cities over multiple years and across many program administrators. Evaluations can get "more value for their dollar" with careful planning and effort in the design phase.

Generalizability is possible only if the sample that is included for treatment, and therefore evaluation, is not biased. Bias can occur in a number of ways during the recruitment of study participants. This is particularly important to keep in mind when considering research on gangs and gang-membership prevention programs. Sometimes clients can be selected or deselected based on certain criteria. A *gang-membership prevention* program may be reluctant to accept *current gang members,* which would limit the generalizability of the findings only to individuals with no prior history of gang membership.

Another type of selection bias may occur if, for example, youth at greatest risk for gang-joining are excluded due to staff concerns about meeting program goals or expectations. This type of selection bias, restricting a program to youth at low risk of gang membership, is referred to as "creaming the sample" and it could increase the probability of finding benefits, such as might occur if these youth are inherently easier to work with or more likely to participate fully in the program.

Selection Bias: What Is the Role of Informed Consent?

Another issue related to selection bias is informed consent. When governmental agencies and research institutions (universities and private research firms) conduct research involving human subjects, they must detail plans and strategies to guarantee the protection of the participants' rights.

When this research involves minors — as it inevitably will with programs or strategies to prevent gang-joining — this protection generally requires obtaining parental consent for the child's participation.

Two types of parental consent exist — *passive* and *active:*

- Passive parental consent requires a form to be returned only if the parents *do not* want their child to participate.

- Active parental consent mandates that the researcher obtain permission for every child to be included in the study.

Active consent is more difficult to obtain and increases the risk of the selective loss of higher risk subjects.[17, 18] If the parents of only the high-risk youth were to refuse to sign the form, for example, this would reduce the generalizability of the results.

Under certain circumstances — if, for example, the study involves a sample for which parental consent is not a reasonable requirement to protect a child — an organization's Internal Review Board (IRB) can grant a waiver of parental consent.

For example, imagine a program in which gang members *volunteer* to participate in an evaluation. The evaluation design randomly assigns some to the program and others to the control group. The program is eventually shown to reduce gang involvement. Is the program an effective gang-reduction program? Yes and no. Yes, it is effective in reducing the involvement of the participants, but who are the participants? As two highly respected researchers, Malcolm Klein and Cheryl Maxson, have observed, it is important to understand this potential bias in gang research: Gang members who are willing or interested in participating in research "are likely to be atypical of the general gang membership."[19] Gang members who volunteer to participate in gang programs may be looking for a way out of the gang or may be less serious gang members to start with and, therefore, would not likely be representative of the gang members who did not volunteer.

Without due attention, selection bias can confound program evaluations and lead to results that only apply to specific subgroups. Practitioners and policymakers using program evaluations to inform their decisions should pay particular attention to possible selection bias in any program and evaluation — and be prepared to question inflated claims. If, for example, representations are made that a program "works" for *all* gang members, but it was administered to and evaluated only for male gang members, the veracity of the claim should be questioned. (See sidebar, "Selection Bias: What Is the Role of Informed Consent?")

Cost-Effectiveness

One important, but often overlooked, aspect of program evaluation is assessing the relative cost associated with achieving a desired outcome. Once evaluators have determined that a program reduces gang membership, the question then becomes one of cost. Two strategies for addressing this issue are cost-benefit and cost-effectiveness analyses. Cost-benefit analyses are more difficult to implement because program benefits must be expressed in some form of monetary terms. For instance, in reducing gang membership, a cost could be placed on the savings of crimes not committed, arrests not having to be made, and savings associated with lower incarceration rates.

A cost-benefit analysis of a variety of crime and delinquency prevention programs, including the Blueprints programs, has been conducted.[20,21] The cost-benefit analysis of Multisystemic Therapy, for example, revealed a benefit of $4.36 for every $1.00 of program costs. The cost-benefit analysis of Functional Family Therapy revealed a savings of $10.42 for every $1.00 of program costs.[20,21] Most of the savings are from reduced crime. Although neither of these programs has gang-membership prevention or gang-crime reduction as a primary programmatic outcome, both include principles that may help keep kids from joining a gang.

On the other hand, a cost-effectiveness analysis calculates only the cost to run a particular program — such as personnel, supplies, space, transportation — but assesses program *effectiveness* in terms of behavioral or performance outcomes. For gang-membership prevention, for example, we could examine the percentage reduction in gang membership relative to the actual cost of delivering the program. Of importance is determining the extent to which a given program, relative to other programs or to program costs, is cost-effective and therefore worthy of implementation or continuation.

Policy Issues

Policymakers are key players in ensuring accountability in gang-membership prevention programs and policies. The first step is to understand that program evaluations are crucial. Unfortunately, many policymakers fail to require program evaluations when they award funding to new prevention programs or when a program has been substantially modified or is being used with a new population. This practice should change. Evaluation of both the implementation (delivery process) of the program and the outcome (effectiveness) should become the norm. Policymakers should encourage evaluators to conduct the most rigorous evaluations, based on the criteria described above, if possible. This will help ensure that evaluations are both fruitful and economical. Policymakers should also encourage practitioners to develop partnerships with researchers (from local universities, for example) to facilitate objective, rigorous evaluation of their programs.

A solid, scientifically dependable "evidence-based" gang-membership prevention program demands the collaboration of practitioners, policymakers and researchers. To achieve the best results, it is critical that a program evaluation be funded and designed *prior* to implementation of the program. Program personnel must cooperate with evaluators to reduce problems of selection bias and sample attrition. If program goals are not clearly articulated to allow evaluators to develop appropriate measures of key outcomes, the evaluators are forced to design their evaluation based on previous decisions made by the program's practitioners, which may lead to sacrifices in the rigor of the evaluation that could have been avoided. For example, if a program is designed to be administered to every child in a state prior to "pretesting," program evaluators will have no comparison group within that state. They will be forced to select a control group from a different, but hopefully similar, state. Or — if a program is delivered with minimal design detail — it could be implemented without consistency (fidelity) across all sites, rendering a determination of effectiveness impossible or unreliable.

To really be confident about what works to prevent gang-joining, we must have rigorous evaluations. Funding, commitment and a shared belief in the importance of evaluations are what it takes to get the job done. To improve the prospects for accurately concluding that a program works, there must be sufficient funds allocated to conduct a rigorous evaluation. Without rigorous process and outcome evaluations, it is unlikely that scarce community resources — both monetary and personnel — will be used as effectively as possible.

About the Authors

Finn-Aage Esbensen

Finn-Aage Esbensen has conducted research in the areas of youth violence and gangs for more than three decades. For the past 18 years, Dr. Esbensen has focused on the evaluation of school-based prevention strategies, most notably the multisite evaluations of the Gang Resistance Education and Training (G.R.E.A.T.) program. He received his Ph.D. from the University of Colorado and is currently a professor in the Department of Criminology and Criminal Justice at the University of Missouri-St. Louis.

Kristy N. Matsuda

Kristy N. Matsuda studies the causes of and responses to juvenile delinquency and gang membership. In addition to evaluating a national gang-membership prevention program, Dr. Matsuda has extensive experience in evaluating programs, policies and the causes of violence for the California Department of Corrections and Rehabilitation. She received her Ph.D. from the University of California, Irvine, and is currently an Assistant Research Professor at the University of Missouri-St. Louis.

Endnotes

1. D.A.R.E. America. *25 years D.A.R.E. America.* Los Angeles, CA: D.A.R.E. America, 2008.

2. Berman G, Fox A. *Lessons From the Battle Over D.A.R.E.: The Complicated Relationship Between Research and Practice.* Washington, DC: U.S. Department of Justice, Bureau of Justice Assistance, 2009.

3. Ennett ST, Tobler NS, Ringwalt CL, Flewelling RL. How effective is drug abuse resistance education? A meta-analysis of project D.A.R.E. outcome evaluations. *Am J Public Health* 1994; 84:1394-1401.

4. Klein M. *The American Street Gang.* New York, NY: Oxford University Press, 1995.

5. Esbensen F-A, Peterson D, Taylor TJ, Osgood DW. Results from a multi-site evaluation of the G.R.E.A.T. program. *Justice Q.* 2012; 29:125-151.

6. Summerfelt WT. Program strength and fidelity in evaluation. *Appl Dev Sci.* 2003; 7:55-61.

7. Esbensen F-A. *Evaluation of the Teens, Crime, and the Community and Community Works Program.* Washington, DC: U.S. Department of Justice, Office of Justice Programs, National Institute of Justice, 2005.

8. Melde C, Esbensen F-A, Tusinki K. Addressing program fidelity using onsite observations and program provider descriptions of program delivery. *Eval Rev.* 2006; 30:1-27.

9. Fagan AA, Mihalic S. Strategies for enhancing the adoption of school-based prevention programs: Lessons learned from the Blueprints for Violence Prevention replications of the Life Skills Training program. *J Community Psychol.* 2003; 31:235-253.

10. Gottfredson GD, Gottfredson DC, Czeh ER. *National Study of Delinquency Prevention in Schools, Final Report.* Ellicott City, MD: Gottfredson Associates, Inc., 2000.

11. Mihalic S, Fagan A, Irwin K, Ballard D, Elliott D. *Blueprints for Violence Prevention Replications: Factors for Implementation Success.* Boulder, CO: University of Colorado, Center for the Study and Prevention of Violence, 2002.

12. Mihalic SF, Irwin K. Blueprints for violence prevention: From research to real-world settings — factors influencing the successful replication of model programs. *Youth Violence and Juv Justice* 2003; 1:307-329.

13. Rossi PH, Freeman HE, Lipsey MW. *Evaluation: A Systematic Approach.* 6th ed. Thousand Oaks, CA: Sage Publications. 2004.

14. Lipsey MW. The primary factors that characterize effective interventions with juvenile offenders: A meta-analytic overview. *Vict Offender* 2009; 4:127-149.

15. Esbensen F-A, Peterson D, Taylor TJ. *2009 Report to Schools and Communities: Program Implementation Quality and Preliminary Outcome Results.* St. Louis, MO: University of Missouri-St. Louis, 2009.

16. Center for the Study and Prevention of Violence. Blueprints for Healthy Youth Development. Boulder, CO: University of Colorado at Boulder, 2010. Available at http://www.blueprintsprograms.com. Accessed on May 30, 2012.

17. Esbensen F-A, Miller MH, Taylor TJ, He N, Freng A. Differential attrition rates and active parental consent. *Eval Rev.* 1999; 23:316-335.

18. Esbensen F-A, Melde C, Taylor TJ, Peterson D. Active parental consent in school-based research: How much is enough and how do we get it? *Eval Rev.* 2008; 32:335-362.

19. Klein M, Maxson CL. *Street Gang Patterns and Policies.* New York, NY: Oxford University Press, 2006:164.

20. Aos S, Lieb R, Mayfield J, Miller M, Pennucci A. *Benefits and Costs of Prevention and Early Intervention Programs for Youth.* Olympia, WA: Washington State Institute for Public Policy, 2004.

21. Lee S, Aos S, Drake E, Pennucci A, Miller M, Anderson L. Return on investment: Evidence-based options to improve statewide outcomes (Document No. 12-04-1201). Olympia, WA: Washington State Institute for Public Policy, April 2012.

Conclusion: An Invitation to Contribute to Gang-Joining Prevention

The National Institute of Justice (NIJ) and the Centers for Disease Control and Prevention (CDC) intend this book to serve as a foundation for the development and implementation of coordinated strategies, programs and policies that prevent youth from joining gangs. We call this concluding chapter an "invitation" because — by providing key definitions, conceptual models, core principles, implications for policy, and examples of programs — we invite action.

As Dr. Buddy Howell (chapter 1) and many of the authors of the chapters in this book describe, the U.S. faces a persistent and serious problem with youth gangs. The consequences of the problem are clear. The risks for delinquency and violence (as both perpetrator and victim) dramatically increase after a young person joins a gang. Young gang members are also at higher risk for substance abuse, high-risk sexual behavior, dropping out of school, criminal behavior, and numerous other negative consequences.

However, there is reason for optimism: By preventing youth from joining gangs in the first place, we significantly improve their chances for a safe and productive life. That's why we call this book *CHANGING COURSE: Preventing Gang Membership.*

Although there has been little scientific study of gang-joining in particular, research regarding youth delinquency and youth violence offers substantial insights for preventing youth from joining gangs. Like delinquency and violence, gang-joining can be prevented. This has the potential for enormous savings for communities in terms of medical, law enforcement, incarceration, and lost productivity costs — not to mention reductions in personal tragedy and fear, increases in school security, enhancements of property values, and greater community cohesion.

Although decision-makers and practitioners should work together to reduce the risks for gang-joining, we must go beyond simply reducing risk. We must understand and enhance the "protective factors" within youth, families, schools and communities that reduce the likelihood of gang-joining. By building on existing strengths, rather than focusing solely on risk reduction, prevention strategies will be more helpful to youth and more welcomed within communities.

As Dr. Carl Taylor and Ms. Pamela Smith describe in chapter 2, youth can be attracted to gangs because their needs are not being met — needs for safety, positive relationships, and fun and excitement — and because they do not see educational and job opportunities that can help them become healthy, productive adults. These needs cannot be filled by working on a single aspect of a child's life. The success of strategies that enhance youth's skills, ease the struggle of families, improve connections between families and schools, enhance positive social activities in communities, and train youth for jobs are all limited if these activities occur in isolation.

Law enforcement and public health have important roles to play in preventing gang-joining. Dr. Tamara Haegerich and her co-authors (chapter 3) and Dr. Scott Decker (chapter 4) highlight the complementary aspects of the public health and law enforcement approaches to prevention. Law enforcement officers have an important perspective on the nature of the gang problem and the particular consequences within their communities; they know where activities are occurring and which youth are at risk. They offer valuable insights about prevention needs and opportunities, and they can provide youth and their families with referrals to preventive services. But it is clear that gang membership is not just a criminal justice problem. It is also a public health problem — and public health professionals have experience in building, evaluating and disseminating strategies that help prevent health problems before they start. Therefore, public health has a role to play in ensuring that gang-joining prevention strategies are comprehensive, are based on the best available evidence, and include the necessary partners. Indeed, preventing gang-joining demands the collaboration of multiple sectors of our society — and comprehensive programs and policies must move beyond the law enforcement and public health sectors to include education, social services, labor, urban planning, the business community, and other groups that are concerned with the health and well-being of youth.

Spanning the chapters in this book, the following six themes offer broad, strategic actions that can help reduce gang-joining, and the violence and crime that often result:

1. Build partnerships.

2. Use data.

3. Frame the issue.

4. Create a plan.

5. Implement the plan.

6. Evaluate the effectiveness.

Build Partnerships

The complex problem of gang-joining has multiple contributing factors. Therefore, *preventing* gang-joining requires more than simple, individual solutions. It requires that diverse sectors work together. As evidenced by the partnership between NIJ and CDC that produced this book, we believe that collaborations must be forged and actions must be coordinated to plan and implement a comprehensive approach.

To do this, groups or individuals interested in gang-joining prevention should:

• Join an existing partnership that is addressing gang-joining or youth-violence prevention, or form a new partnership if one does not exist.

• Ensure that partners include key sectors, such as law enforcement, public health, education, the business community, social service agencies, parents and other adults, as well as young people who are concerned about gang-joining and interested in promoting healthy youth and communities.

• Address the ambiguity about what constitutes a "gang" and "gang-joining" by developing a shared understanding of what these terms mean for your group. Consider using a straightforward definition such as the one offered in the Introduction. In some communities, for example, it might be more productive to focus on preventing youth involvement with negative peer groups and avoiding a "gang/nongang" determination altogether. Given the strong influence of peers on youth behaviors, community partnerships aimed at stopping the development and growth of negative peer groups more broadly could be critical to addressing the underlying risks for gang-joining and other health risks or criminal behaviors.

• Affirm a shared commitment to gang-joining *prevention* to complement gang and violence intervention and suppression strategies.

Use Data

A true understanding of the nature of a gang problem and opportunities for prevention demands that data from multiple sources are used. As Gary Gottfredson discusses in the chapter on schools (chapter 7), it is also important to consider issues that can affect the accuracy and completeness of data; for example, school administrators may be unable or unwilling to fully describe the gang challenges they face. Indeed, when feasible, systematic data collection from youth themselves can provide the most useful source of information, not just about their own gang affiliation but also about local gang activities, the attractions to gangs, opportunities for prevention and emerging problems.

Gang-joining prevention partnerships should use data:

- From multiple sources — hospitals, law enforcement agencies, schools, local surveys, and interviews with youth and parents — rather than a single source.

- To develop a common understanding of the problem, including rates of gang activity and the hot spots, as well as contributing factors and variations across social context such as gender, race and ethnicity, and socioeconomic class.

- To promote knowledge and action within the community along with the development and implementation of prevention activities.

Frame the Issue

The framing of any issue — including gang-membership prevention — is crucial. How a message is framed impacts how it is understood and addressed. It can be helpful for practitioners and policymakers to frame gang-joining as part of the *larger* constellation of youth problems, including violence, substance abuse and criminal behavior. Framing prevention strategies and programs in this way can increase buy-in from the community. It also can help decision-makers prioritize prevention programming, policies and resources aimed at reducing risks or enhancing protective influences that impact multiple problem behaviors.

In framing strategies and programs that address gang-joining, practitioners and policymakers should emphasize that *prevention* is key to raising healthy, productive youth. Because the most common age for gang-joining is 13-15 years old, early prevention is crucial. In fact, early prevention is often highly cost-effective, resulting in significant savings to the health and criminal justice systems — and, ultimately, to taxpayers.

It is important to use your data to guide the framing process and work with partners to:

- Describe the local problem — and proposed solutions — in ways that compel key stakeholders to engage in the discussion.

- Consider how the benefits of gang-joining prevention can be communicated to motivate action within the community and across specific target audiences.

- Anticipate concerns and barriers to prevention and address them proactively. For example, some groups might resist sharing responsibility for prevention because they do not see the consequences of gang-joining for their groups or do not understand their role in prevention. Practitioners and policymakers must be prepared to explain the connections and how specific stakeholder groups are impacted.

Create a Plan

Once the collaboration has the right partners who are committed to working together with a shared understanding of goals and the use of data, the next step is to develop a strategic plan. The principles in this book should be considered when planning prevention strategies. We encourage readers to look across all the "levels of influence" to consider what can be done for the individual youth and within families, schools and communities to prevent gang-joining. The chapters by Drs. Nancy Guerra, Deborah Gorman-Smith, Gary Gottfredson, Jorja Leap, and their co-authors (chapters 5, 6, 7 and 8) discuss each of these levels of influence in more depth.

When planning a prevention strategy, it is important to consider:

- The risks that the plan is being designed and implemented to prevent (such as hypervigilance to threat, cognitive impairments, insecure attachment, negative peer relationships, delinquent behavior, a highly visible presence of gangs in the school and community, or high concentrations of poverty or social disorganization); and the protective factors that the plan is being designed to enhance (such as academic success and connectedness to school, and appropriate, consistent parental discipline, monitoring and attachment).

- What is already being done to reduce risks and enhance protection, what evidence exists to support those strategies, and what else is needed. Your plan should incorporate the best available evidence about strategies that have been evaluated and shown to impact the factors you want to address. Although most existing strategies have not been evaluated to determine their specific effects on gang-joining, consider successes in changing related behaviors (substance use, delinquency, family functioning and school success, for example) rather than starting from scratch.

- Strategies that enhance what Dr. Leap (chapter 8) refers to as "core activities" such as tutoring, mentoring, life-skills training, case management, parental involvement, connection with schools, supervised recreational activities, and community mobilization; improvements in these areas are likely to result in a range of benefits for youth that, in turn, should reduce the risk for gang-joining.

- Whether prevention strategies adequately address the needs of specific subgroups of youth. For example, as Dr. Meda Chesney-Lind points out in chapter 9, living in an abusive family is an important risk factor for girls. With respect to race and ethnicity, Drs. Adrienne Freng and T.J. Taylor (chapter 10) argue that — even when information is lacking about possible differences in risk and protective factors among specific subgroups — it is important to act on the basis of the best available evidence. They conclude, for example, that prevention efforts that address risks such as low parental monitoring or limited educational opportunities are likely to be beneficial regardless of race or ethnicity.

Implement the Plan

Partners must work together to secure or align the resources necessary to implement new prevention activities or, if activities are already in place, to ensure that they are sustained over time. This may require working as a group to move resources from an ineffective or less directly relevant activity to one that has more evidence of effectiveness in preventing gang-joining. Implementation might also require working with partners to obtain new resources, such as grants from foundations or businesses.

When considering implementation, it is important to remember that:

- There is often a tendency to focus only on the most urgent needs and strategies for addressing youth who are at immediate risk for gang-joining. However, it is important to balance this goal with the need to start working with children at a young age. Dr. Guerra and her co-authors emphasize how gang-joining should be understood as part of a life course that begins from the time a child is born (chapter 5).

- The reach of programs and strategies must be broad. Because resources are limited, prevention efforts often start with a small segment of the population. As Dr. Gorman-Smith and her co-authors describe (chapter 6), it is important that communities work toward scaling up prevention efforts so that everyone who can benefit is eventually given the opportunity to participate. This approach is consistent with the public health focus on population-level reductions in risk.

- Look for immediate and lasting ways to make youth feel safer in their communities and at school. Dr. Taylor and Ms. Smith (chapter 2) highlight the importance of perceived safety as a reason for gang-joining, and Dr. Gottfredson (chapter 7) emphasizes that the ability to provide a safe environment within schools is vital to reducing gang-joining.

Evaluate the Effectiveness

Careful evaluation is critical to ensuring that gang-joining prevention activities are being implemented as intended and are having the expected effects. Drs. Finn-Age Esbensen and Kristy Matsuda describe types of evaluations and their key design elements (chapter 11). Data based on a solid evaluation can be used to secure new partners and resources or to sustain or expand prevention activities. Evaluation data are also important in refining prevention plans and implementation strategies.

A rigorous evaluation is an investment that can pay off substantially over the long run. To maximize the impact of an evaluation, it is important to:

- Incorporate evaluation planning in the overall prevention plan. Consider the best data sources and ways to compare what is happening after the prevention program or strategy to what happened before to individuals or groups that did and did not participate in the prevention activity. Gathering baseline data (before implementation of a prevention program) is a crucial part of evaluation planning.

- Use as rigorous a design as possible. If your collaboration includes or has access to a researcher, engage her or him in planning the evaluation. If not, seek assistance from a local university that could have a research team looking for new projects.

- Conduct multiple types of evaluation to determine how well a program was implemented (process evaluation), what outcomes were found relative to what would have been expected without the strategy or program (outcome evaluation) and, ideally, how much money was saved (cost-effectiveness or cost-benefit evaluation).

- Remember that even negative results are important. Learning that something is not working gives you the opportunity to refine it or to invest resources elsewhere. It is important that the evaluation is done well, however, because negative results from a poorly designed evaluation do not tell you if the results are because the program or strategy did not work or because the data are limited.

- Disseminate what you are learning. This is important not only to further local prevention efforts but also to assist other communities that are struggling with the same issues.

We hope that this book — with its emphasis on prevention — is a first step in broadening the thinking on how to deal with gang crime and violence. By bringing together the criminal justice and public health perspectives and by drawing lessons from what is known about other youth problem behaviors, we offer principles that practitioners and policymakers can use in gang-membership prevention.

Finally, we hope that this book inspires readers to embrace NIJ's and CDC's shared commitment to the principles that will help prevent our nation's young people from joining gangs. The impacts of gang membership — and the burden it places on our health, law enforcement, corrections and educational systems — are significant. We believe that, faced with the current economic realities, prevention is the best way to halt the cascading impact of gangs on our kids, families, neighborhoods and society at large. If we work together to focus on the prevention of gang membership — rather than solely caring for victims of gang violence and arresting gang-involved youth — we can change the course of the future for our young people. We hope you accept our invitation to use these prevention principles in your work.

www.ingramcontent.com/pod-product-compliance
Lightning Source LLC
Chambersburg PA
CBHW081350280526
45788CB00009B/2836